Cebes' Tablet

+

Prodicus'

"Choice of Heracles"

AN INTERMEDIATE

ANCIENT GREEK READER

C. T. Hadavas

Cebes' Tablet + Prodicus' "Choice of Heracles"

An Intermediate Ancient Greek Reader
Ancient Greek text with vocabulary and notes

First Edition

© 2018 by C. T. Hadavas

ISBN-13: 978-1985703780
ISBN-10: 1985703785

Published by C. T. Hadavas

Cover Design: C. T. Hadavas

Cover Image: Batoni, *Study of Hercules* (1740-1742); the image is used by permission of The Philadelphia Museum of Art (Bequest of Anthony Morris Clark, 1978). For more on Batoni's *Study of Hercules*, and the painting for which it was a prefatory drawing, see **Appendix G:** Batoni, *Ercole al Bivio* and *Study of Hercules* (pp. 186-9).

Fonts: (English) Times New Roman, Book Antiqua; (Greek) GFS Porson

TABLE OF CONTENTS

PREFACE

This text contains two works, *Cebes' Tablet* and Xenophon's paraphrase of Prodicus' "Choice of Heracles," that are particulary suitable to students of Ancient Greek who are making the transition from first-year grammar and morphology to reading narratives of unadapted prose. These works are also thematically related, for both describe through an allegorical lens what effects the choices one makes in life might have on achieving philosophical wisdom and happiness.

In addition to providing introductions, extensive vocabulary assistance, and grammatical, historical, cultural, and literary notes for each work, this edition also includes several appendices that contain: (1) textual and visual materials for understanding better certain aspects of these two narratives within their cultural and historical contexts; (2) a facsimile of Kenneth Sylvan Guthrie's 1910 English translation of *Cebes' Tablet*; (3) four works (Jacob Matham and Hendrick Goltzius' 1592 engraving *TABVLA CEBETIS*, Benjamin West's 1814 holograph "Allegorical Sketch," Albrecht Dürer's *c.* 1498 engraving *Der Hercules*, and Pompeo Girolamo Batoni's 1742 painting *Ercole al Bivio* together with his 1740-1742 *Study of Hercules*, a prefatory drawing for one of the three figures that appear in *Ercole al Bivio*) that engage the moral and ethical propositions of the two ancient texts in a visual medium; (4) William Dunkin's eighteenth-century poem "The Judgment of Hercules," an innovative translation-cum-adaptation of Xenophon's paraphrase of Prodicus' "Choice of Heracles."

ACKNOWLEDGMENTS

To Charles S. Jerram, who after nearly a century of comparative neglect, resurrected *Cebes' Tablet* as a "bridge-text" for students with his fine 1878 edition.

To Richard Parsons, whose 1887 edition of *Cebes' Tablet* features a section of questions that challenge students to think carefully about grammar, syntax, accents, and the idiomatic differences between Ancient Greek and English.

To Robert J. Schork, who advocated for an updated version of Parsons' commentary in a wittily written 1995 article ("*Cebes' Tablet* as a Bridge-Text in the Greek Program," *The Classical Journal*, Vol. 91, No. 1 [1995], 65-69).

To Cynthia King, whose 1996 edition of selections from *Cebes' Tablet* innovatively included facing vocabularies and notes (which were later incorporated into *Athenaze: An Introduction to Ancient Greek: Workbook II*).

To Kenneth Sylvan Guthrie, whose self-published 1910 translation of *Cebes' Tablet* is an idiosyncratic gem of a book "ornamented" with elements of graphic design both archaizing and of its time. (For a complete facsimile of Guthrie's translation, see **Appendix B**.)

To Tanya Paul, Isabel and Alfred Bader Curator of European Art at the Milwaukee Art Museum, for her assistance with Matham and Goltzius' print of *Cebes' Tablet*.

To Stephanie Schliesmann, for her word-processing assistance (she had to learn how to type Ancient Greek!) with many of the notes to *Cebes' Tablet*.

****

To Albrecht Dürer, whose art captivated me as a child and stimulated my interest in becoming a graphic designer before I chose instead (with some regret) to follow the path of the more sober-minded figure of Academia.

To Malcolm Davies, David Sansone, and Robert Mayhew, whose work on Prodicus' "Choice of Heracles" has extended my understanding of its possible meanings.

To Tom McBride, emeritus professor of English, Beloit College, for his assistance with understanding certain lexical aspects of eighteenth-century English verse.

LIST OF ILLUSTRATIONS

Kenneth Sylvan Guthrie, *The Greek Pilgrim's Progress, Generally Known as the Picture of Kebes, a Disciple of Socrates?* (pp. 116-71). Facsimile of the original London: Luzac and Company / Philadelphia: Monsalvat Press 1910 edition. This text is in the Public Domain.

Matham and Goltzius, *TABVLA CEBETIS* (pp. 173-9). The image is courtesy of the Rijksmuseum, and is in the Public Domain.

West, "Allegorical Sketch" (p. 181). The image is courtesy of the Walters Art Museum (acquired by Henry Walters), and is in the Public Domain.

"The Three Goddesses" (east pediment, Parthenon; figures K, L, and M) (p. 182). The image is courtesy of © Marie-Lan Nguyen (Wikimedia Commons), and is licensed under the Creative Commons Attribution 2.5 Generic license.

"Nike Adjusting Her Sandal" (parapet, Temple of Athena Nike) (p. 183). The image is courtesy of Marsyas (Wikimedia Commons) and is licensed under the Creative Commons Attribution-ShareAlike 2.5 Generic license.

Dürer, *Der Hercules* (p. 186). The image is courtesy of the Metropolitan Museum of Art (Fletcher Fund, 1919), and is in the Public Domain.

Batoni, *Ercole al Bivio* (p. 191). The image is courtesy of the Fondazione Federico Zeri at the University of Bologna, and is used with their permission.

Batoni, *Study of Hercules* (cover; p. 194). The image is courtesy of the Philadelphia Museum of Art (Bequest of Anthony Morris Clark, 1978), and is used with their permission.

HOW TO USE THIS BOOK

The reader is assumed to have a basic acquaintance with Ancient Greek grammar. All vocabulary found in the passage of *Cebes' Tablet* and Prodicus' "Choice of Heracles" at the top of the page, with the exception of the verb εἰμί, personal pronouns, and the most common conjunctions (e.g., ἀλλά, καί), adverbs (e.g., οὐ, μή), and particles (e.g., μέν, δέ), is given in the vocabulary list in the middle of the page directly below the text. For many verbs only the first person singular present active indicative form is provided. For verbs with unusual forms (e.g., those with deponent futures, second aorists, or with futures and aorists from unrelated stems) the first person singular active forms of the present, future, and aorist are, where warranted, given. For -μι verbs the second aorist active and/or the perfect active, where warranted, are also provided. After a word appears for the fifth time in the vocabulary lists, it will not occur again in such lists, though it will be found in the **GLOSSARY** at the end of this book.

On the understanding that the majority of readers who will use this text have either just finished the first or second year of college Ancient Greek, or are returning after a hiatus of some time from their study of the language, I have provided grammatical and syntactical notes immediately below the vocabulary list on each page. These notes are not exhaustive. They do, however, identify – and sometimes explicate – certain aspects of Ancient Greek (e.g., idioms, non-indicative verb usages, genitive absolutes, etc.) that many students in their second and third year of study still have questions about. For many grammatical and morphological explanations, references to Smyth's *Greek Grammar*, the standard text on the subject in English, occur throughout the notes.[1] In addition to such linguistic assistance, this section contains brief notes on the few literary/rhetorical tropes employed by these authors as well as a small number of explanations for particular people, places, and things that will probably be unfamiliar to most readers. Finally, this section also contains some of the thoughts of previous commentators on these texts.

The sequence I have chosen for the two texts of this edition, in which the chronologically later *Tablet* precedes Prodicus' "Choice of Heracles," might

---

[1] Smyth's *Greek Grammar*, in its 1920 original edition, is available at the Perseus website (http://www.perseus.tufts.edu/hopper/text?doc=Perseus:text:1999.04.0007). Although the online edition is not the later one revised by Gordon Messing in 1956, it is essentially the same since Messing's revisions were generally very minor.

seem peculiar to certain readers. After all, the latter probably antedates the former by four or five centuries. In addition, in terms of comparative analysis, the earlier text clearly contributed to the latter (if only, perhaps, indirectly as part of an allegorical tradition connected to Socrates' and moral education). The reason I have chosen this order is that the *Tablet*, though of greater length, is, at least from a syntactical standpoint, somewhat easier for students to read than Prodicus' tale (which even in Xenophon's paraphrase, still displays more than a hint of rhetorical sophistication that is largely lacking from the more straightforward prose of the *Tablet*).

ABBREVIATIONS

= is equivalent to

< derived from

[ ] (in vocabulary) (1) hypothetical reconstruction of non-extant form (in boldface); (2) etymological origin of select compound words, sometimes including the literal meaning of the word; (in text) material within the brackets has been inserted by various scholars to complete the sense in the readings contained in the manuscripts of *Cebes' Tablet*

acc.(usative)

act.(ive voice)

adj.(ective)

adv.(erb)

aor.(ist)

c. circa

C-to-F = Contrary to Fact

cf. (*confer*, Latin "bring together") compare

cl.(ause)

Cl. Gk. = Classical Greek (i.e., Greek in use in the 5th-4th centuries BCE)

comp.(arative)

cond.(ition)

conj.(unction)

contr.(acted)

d.(ied)

dat.(ive)

dep.(opent)

dim.(inutive)

dir.(ect)

esp.(ecially)

fem.(inine)

fl. (*floruit*, Latin "he/she flourished") the period in which an individual lived, worked, or was most active

fut.(ure)

FLV = future less vivid (aka, future remote)

FMV = future move vivid

fut.(ure)

gen.(itive)

gen.(itive) abs.(olute)

Gk. = Greek

impera.(tive)

imperf.(ect)

indecl.(inable)

indic.(ative)

indir.(ect)

inf.(initive)

interr.(ogative)

L. Gk. = Late Greek (i.e., Greek in use from the death of Alexander the Great [323 BCE] to the beginning of the Middle Ages [*c.* 500 CE])

masc.(uline)

mid.(dle voice)

ms. = manuscript

mss. = manuscripts

neut.(er)

nom.(inative)

obj.(ject)

opt.(ative)

p./pp. page(s)

part.(iciple)

pass.(ive voice)

perf.(ect)

pl.(ural)

pluperf.(ect)

pres.(ent)

pron.(oun)

quest.(ion)

reflex.(ive) pron.(oun)

rel.(ative) cl.(ause)

rel.(ative) pron.(oun)

sc. (*scilicet* < *scire licet*, Latin "it is permitted to know") = supply or understand

sing.(ular)

subj.(ect)

subju.(nctive)

superl.(ative)

s.v. (*sub verbo*, Latin, "under the word") [used to refer to an entry in a dictionary or encyclopedia]

usu.(ally)

vb. = verb

vb. adj. = verbal adjective

w/ = with

Bibliographic Abbreviations

Banchich — Banchich, T. *Cebes' Pinax*. Bryn Mawr (PA), 2002

BDAG — Bauer, W. *A Greek-English Lexicon of the New Testament and Other Early Christian Literature*[3], rev. and ed. by F. W. Danker. Chicago, 2000

BDF — Blass, F. and A. Debrunner. *A Greek Grammar of the New Testament and Other Early Christian Literature*, trans. and rev. by R. Funk. Chicago, 1962

BrDAG — Montanari, F. *The Brill Dictionary of Ancient Greek*, edd. of the English edition, M. Goh and C. Schroeder. Leiden, 2015

Denniston — Denniston, J. D. *The Greek Particles*[2]. Oxford, 1954

Fitzgerald and White — Fitzgerald, J. T. and L. M. White. *The Tabula of Cebes*. Chico (California), 1983

Jerram — Jerram, C. S. Κέβετος πίναξ. *Cebetis Tabula with Introduction and Notes*. Oxford, 1878

LSJ — *A Greek-English Lexicon*[9], eds. H. G. Liddell, R. Scott, J. Stuart Jones, R. Mackenzie. Oxford, 1968

King — Lawall, G. and J. F. Johnson, C. King, and J. Morwood. *Athenaze: An Introduction to Ancient Greek: Workbook II*. 3rd ed. New York, 2015

Mayhew — Mayhew, R. *Prodicus the Sophist: Texts, Translations, and Commentary*. Oxford, 2011

Parsons — Parsons, R. Κέβετος πίναξ. *Cebes' Tablet, with Introduction, Notes, Vocabulary, and Grammatical Questions*. Boston, 1887

Smith — Smith, J. R. *Xenophon: Memorabilia*. Boston, 1903.

Smyth — Smyth, H. W. *Greek Grammar*, rev. G. M. Messing. Cambridge (MA), 1956

Seddon — Seddon, K. *Epictetus' Handbook and the Tablet of Cebes: Guides to Stoic Living*. London and New York, 2005

Steadman — Steadman, G. D. *Cebes' Tablet: Greek Text with Facing Vocabulary and Commentary*. 2011 (available only as a PDF: https://geoffreysteadman.files.wordpress.com/2011/01/cebestablet-jan2011.pdf)

Cebes' Tablet

INTRODUCTION

Though ascribed to Cebes (*c.* 430-350 BCE), a Pythagorean philosopher from Thebes who was a disciple of Socrates (*c.* 470-399 BCE), *Cebes' Tablet* is most likely a pseudonymous text probably composed sometime in the first century CE.[2]

Primarily told in dialogue form, the *Tablet* presents an allegorical interpretation of a picture on a tablet dedicated in a temple decades ago by a mysterious individual "who adopted a certain Pythagorean and Parmenidean way of life in both word and deed" (*Tablet* 2). Structurally, its narrative is tripartite: (1) a basic narratological frame that introduces (i) a group of young men (one of whom will function as the narrator of the text) intrigued by a votive tablet located in a temple dedicated to Cronus that is inscribed or painted with an enigmatic composition and (ii) an old man who volunteers to explain the meaning of the tablet to the young men (1-4.1); (2) a dialogue between the old man and the young narrator, in which the former points at the picture throughout his exegesis of its various details as he answers the latter's questions (4.2-36.1); (3) a Socratic-style question-and-answer section modeled after that of Plato's early *Dialogues* in which the old man discusses with his young interlocutor two issues that have arisen from the previous interpretation of the picture (36.2-43).

The principal literary technique employed in the *Tablet* is allegorical, as the picture is said by the old man to represent in its entirety "Life" ($\acute{o}$ Βίος). The picture includes a large number of symbolic figures, nearly all of which are female, that depict various virtues, vices, and epistemological states (e.g., Truth, True Education, Courage, Freedom, Justice, Endurance, Opinions, Pleasures, Deceit, Folly, False Education, etc.) that inhabit different parts of a landscape ringed by several enclosures. Actual life is thus pictorially and metaphorically represented as a journey through a world in which dangers and temptations are ever present, and in which one of the goals is to recognize these and avoid them to the best of one's ability. But perhaps even more important than this is the claim of the *Tablet* that true education consists not in acquiring the knowledge one would receive from studying traditional academic disciplines, but in developing one's moral and ethical character, for only by doing the latter can one become happy. It is thus made clear that the allegorical nature of the *Tablet* is the handmaiden to its primary function as a protreptic (< Gk. προτρέπω, "turn or direct to," "urge on,"

---

[2] The figure of Cebes is best known as one of Socrates' interlocutors in Plato's *Phaedo* (whose narrative is set in 399 BCE). In this dialogue, Socrates, in prison and just before he is to drink the hemlock that will end his life, investigates with several of his close friends whether or not the soul is immortal. The attribution to Cebes was probably meant to grant the work a prestigious pedigree, thus ensuring it of being treated more seriously. For the date of the *Tablet*, see **Language and Style** below.

"persuade") work, i.e., one meant to turn or direct the reader to the true path of wisdom.[3]

For much of the nineteenth and twentienth centuries, the principal debate among scholars concerning the *Tablet* was over which philosophical school (or schools) it belonged to (e.g., Stoic, Neo-Pythagorean, Cynic—or possibly some combination of these?).[4] This approach to the work, however, is increasingly seen as unhelpful, since the *Tablet* is, preeminently, an allegorical text that espouses a *general* approach to life that seems mostly "Socratic," at least in the broadest sense of that term in that it embraces aspects of the Socrates who appears in Plato's early *Dialogues* as well as those of the more practically-minded moralist of Xenophon's sketches.

ALLEGORY

I. Definition.

Etymologically, the word ἀλληγορία has evinced almost no semantic and phonological change throughout its long history. The English word "allegory" < Middle English *allegorie* < Old French *allegorie* < Latin *allegoria* < Greek ἡ ἀλληγορία [ἄλλη + -ἀγορία, lit., "other speaking," i.e., speaking about something else], "allegory," "allegorical language"; "allegorical explanation"[5] (< ἀλληγορέω, "say or interpret allegorically"; "speak in allegories"; (pass.) "be expressed by way of allegory").[6]

---

[3] Cf. J. Elsner, *Art and the Roman Viewer* (Cambridge, 1995), 47: "The goal of art in the *Tabula* is not to imitate the viewers' world at all, but rather to initiate viewers out of their ordinary assumptions into a new exegetic reality, a truth that brings salvation." And Elsner, 33: "In the *Tabula of Cebes*, a philosophical allegory of a picture drawing on eclectic sources and purporting to offer salvation both to the viewers of the image and the readers of the text, the viewers' initial aporia ["confusion"] before the subject-matter of a picture is presented as a reflection of their aporia before the problem of life itself (from which a correct understanding of the image is going to save them)."

[4] For a summary of this debate, see Fitzgerald and White, 16-27.

[5] In ancient, medieval, and Renaissance Europe, allegorical explanations were a common way of understanding the meaning of many (apparently to us modern readers, at least) non-allegorically composed texts. Examples of such allegorical readings include Porphyry's *On the Cave of the Nymphs in the* Odyssey (late 3rd century CE) and John Tzetzes' *Allegories of the* Iliad (*c*. 1140s-*c*. 1150s). Although allegorical interpretation of literary texts continued to be a viable option in the early modern period and lasted into the first decades of the 19th century, it became more infrequent as time went on.

[6] The first appearance of ἀλληγορία with the meaning "allegory" is in the Hellenistic period. For a more detailed history of the term "allegory," see J. Whitman, *Allegory: The Dynamics of an Ancient and Medieval Technique* (Cambridge [MA], 1987), 264-8.

Wiktionary defines "allegory" as:[7]

1. The representation of abstract principles by characters or figures.

2. A picture, book, or other form of communication using such representation.

3. A symbolic representation which can be interpreted to reveal a hidden meaning, usually a moral or political one.

4. (mathematics, category theory) A category that retains some of the structure of the category of binary relations between sets, representing a high-level generalisation of that category.[8]

Cebes' Tablet embraces the first three of these definitions by recounting in its text a detailed description of a picture that has an almost entirely female cast of figures[9] representing abstract principles located within an elaborately schematized landscape that is designed to convey the possible journeys available to each person in life in terms of attaining philosophical wisdom and happiness.

II. History in Greek Literature.

Allegory appears in the very first works of Greek literature, but only in small-scale "embryonic" forms (e.g., Hesiod, *Works and Days* 286-292 [see **Appendix A**], Homer, *Iliad* 24.522-551 [Achilles' story of Zeus' two jars]). Later, as the use of allegory became more common, it began to be employed in more elaborately composed pieces, either those that are self-contained, such as Prodicus' "Choice of Heracles" (*c.* 425-420 BCE; see pp. 79ff.), or (more often) those that are integrated into longer works, such as Plato's "Allegory of the Cave" from *Republic* 514a-520a (*c.* 380 BCE). In fact, it was Plato's use of allegory in his *Dialogues* (especially the *Republic*, *Phaedrus*, and *Phaedo*) that probably had the

---

[7] https://en.wiktionary.org/wiki/allegory#Noun

[8] This definition, in essence, is simply one that applies the conceptual power of definition 1 to the mathematical field of category theory, which was co-founded in 1945 by Saunders Mac Lane and Samuel Eilenberg.

[9] Abstract concepts in Greek are almost entirely represented by feminine nouns. The one exception to the multitude of female allegorical figures that inhabit "Life" in the *Tablet* is ὁ Ὀδυρμός ("Lamentation"). Other masculine allegorical figures and concepts that appear in the *Tablet* but not within the landscape of "Life" are ὁ Δαίμων ("the God or Divine Being"; though more often cited in the text as τὸ Δαιμόνιον, "the Divine Power or Divinity") and ὁ Βίος ("Life").

greatest influence on later authors' use of this technique, for it became a fairly common one utilized by philosophers and moralists throughout Antiquity.[10]

As an example of a post-Prodicean self-contained allegorical work, *Cebes' Tablet* (perhaps 1st century CE) is rather unique, and only has parallels in much later (and often much longer) works of Antiquity (e.g., Prudentius' *Psychomachia* ["Soul-Battle"; c. 400 CE]), the Middle Ages (*Le Roman de la Rose* ["The Romance of the Rose"; composed in two parts by Guillaume de Lorris (*c.* 1230) and Jean de Meun (*c.* 1275)], Dante's *Divine Comedy* [1320], William Langland's *Piers Plowman* [*c.* 1370-90], the anonymous *Pearl* [*c.* 1375-1400]), the Renaissance (e.g., Spenser's *The Faerie Queene* [1596]), and more recent periods (e.g., Bunyan's *The Pilgrim's Progress* [1678], Orwell's *Animal Farm* [1945]).

III. Literary Function.

The attraction of allegory as a literary technique is that it has the power to illustrate often complex ideas and concepts (especially those of a moral, spiritual, or political nature) in ways that are easily comprehensible to its readers/listeners since it conveys such ideas in striking, schematically-structured tableaus filled with (generally simplified) personifications and/or symbolic representations. Because of this, allegory can be seen as a type of "royal road" used by the author to communicate his/her meaning. Such a short-cut, however, often creates its own problems, for allegory, in its pursuit of immediacy and vividness, can be seen to disregard the complexities of much philosophical, spiritual and political discourse.

NACHLEBEN ("AFTERLIFE")

The *Tablet*, which seemed to be fairly well-known in the ancient world—it was mentioned by Lucian (*c.* 125-after 180 CE) twice, and by the Christian apologist Tertullian (*c.* 155-*c.* 240 CE), who says that one of his relatives made a paraphrase of it from verses in Vergil's *Aeneid*[11]—largely disappeared during the medieval (i.e., Byzantine) period. However, an Arabic paraphrase was made of it by the Persian Neoplatonist philosopher and historian Ibn Miskawayh (932-1030), of which we have a Latin translation made by Johannes Elichmann (1601/1602-1639) in the 17th century (the paraphrase includes a longer ending than that found in the

---

[10] M. B. Trapp, s.v. allegory, Greek, in *The Oxford Classical Dictionary*, 3rd ed., edd. S. Hornblower and A. Spaworth (Oxford/New York, 1996).

[11] Lucian, *De mercede conductis* ("On Salaried Posts in Great Houses") 42; *Rhetorum praeceptor* ("A Professor of Public Speaking") 6; Tertullian, *De praescriptione haereticorum* ("on the Prescription of Heretics") 39. Cf. also Julius Pollux (*fl.* 2nd century CE), *Onomasticon* 3.95, and see Fitzgerald and White, 7-8.

extant Greek manuscripts; this ending is included—translated into English from Elichmann's Latin translation of the Arabic—in this edition).

The first printed version in Greek was probably published in Florence in 1502 in Aldus Manutius' edition of the *Erotemata*, a Greek grammar by Constantine Lascaris (1434-1501).[12] Within a century of this publication, the *Tablet* had been translated into Latin at least half a dozen times, as well as into Spanish (4x), German (3x), French (2x), English (1x), Italian (1x), Dutch (1x), and Polish (1x). The extraordinary popularity that the *Tablet* enjoyed from 1502 to the first decades of the nineteenth century, was especially due to its double utility: it was commonly employed as a "bridge-text" to help students of Ancient Greek transition from grammar to reading complete texts while simultaneously offering a useful moral lesson about the nature of life and happiness.[13] Prominent intellectuals were proponents of its potential pedagogical uses. For example, in his 1644 treatise "Of Education," John Milton (1608-74) included the *Tablet* in a select group of Greek texts (described as "easie and delightful Book[s] of Education") that would be employed "to make [students] expert in the usefullest points of Grammar, and withall to season them, and win them early to the love of vertue and true labour, ere any flattering seducement, or vain principle seise them wandering."[14] The German polymath Gottfried Wilhelm Leibniz (1646-1716), on the other hand, recommended the *Tablet* in his *Nova Methodus Discendae Docendaeque Iurisprudentiae* ("New Method of Teaching and Learning Jurisprudence"; 1667) as "a shorthand example of using diagrams to elucidate philosophical thought."[15] Beyond its use in pedagogical, moral, and philosophical instruction, the *Tablet* also exerted varying degrees of influence on such English authors who made extensive use of allegory as Spenser, Pope, and Johnson.[16]

---

[12] Cf. S. Sider, *Cebes' Tablet: Facsimiles of the Greek Text, and of Selected Latin, French, English, Spanish, Italian, German, Dutch, and Polish Translations* (New York, 1979), 3. Lascaris was probably responsible for editing that 1502? text of the *Tablet* before his death. Sider also notes that (6): "Lascaris' *Tablet* was issued with minor changes at least fourteen times more during the sixteenth century."

[13] Cf. E. Dwyer, 297 (review of R. Schleier, *Tabula Cebetis, oder "Spiegel des Menschlichen Lebens darin Tugent und untugent abgemalet ist"* [Berlin, 1973] in *Art Bulletin*, Vol. 58, No. 2 [1976], 295-7): "As a didactic work of art with Classical authority and nearly Christian content, the *Tablet* was a perfect subject for the edification of the young."

[14] https://www.dartmouth.edu/~milton/reading_room/of_education/text.shtml

[15] Squire, M. and J. Grethlein, ""Counterfeit in Character but Persuasive in Appearance": Reviewing the Ainigma of the *Tabula Cebetis*." *Classical Philology* 109 (2014), 285.

[16] For Spenser, see C. S. Lewis, "Genius and Genius," *The Review of English Studies* Vol. 12, No. 46 (1936), 189-94; for Pope, see A. Williams, "Literary Backgrounds to Book Four of the *Dunciad*," *PMLA*, Vol. 68, No. 4 (1953), 806-13; for Johnson, see L. Lipking, "Learning to Read Johnson: *The Vision of Theodore* and *The Vanity of Human Wishes*," *ELH* Vol. 43, No. 4 (1976), 517-37.

In the visual arts, numerous illustrations and paintings either of the *Tablet* or inspired by it, were made between the 16th and early 20th centuries.[17]

Beginning in the nineteenth century, the high regard in which the *Tablet* was held both in education and the popular imagination began to wane. After a short-lived resurgence in interest between *c.* 1870-1910, the *Tablet*, with the exception of a few studies (most of which involved manuscript and textual issues), was relatively neglected until the last decades of the twentieth century. Today, *Cebes' Tablet* is once again being used as a "bridge-text" (e.g., Cynthia King's selections, first published in 1996 and later included in *Athenaze: An Introduction to Ancient Greek: Workbook II*; this edition). In addition, it has recently received some sophisticated scholarly analysis.[18] The latter, though some time coming, is not unexpected, since the *Tablet*'s influence (in the original and in translation) on writers and educators of the 16th and 17th centuries, as well as its unusual nature (i.e., its combination of didactic, exegetic, allegorical, philosophical and visual elements), are invitations to scholars to engage its text from various disciplinary and interdisciplinary perspectives.[19]

---

[17] For three examples included in this edition, see **Appendix B** (Kenneth Sylvan Guthrie, *The Greek Pilgrim's Progress, Generally Known as the Picture of Kebes, a Disciple of Socrates?*), **Appendix C** (Matham and Goltzius, *TABVLA CEBETIS*), and **Appendix D** (West, "Allegorical Sketch"). For woodcuts and engravings (easily found online), see, e.g., those of David Kandel (*c.* 1535-60) and Romeyn de Hooghe (1670); for paintings, see, e.g., Frans Francken II, *Mankind's Eternal Dilemma: The Choice Beween Virtue and Vice* (1633), a fascinating work that combine aspects of the *Tablet*, Prodicus' "Choice of Heracles," the Judgment of Paris, and Christian symbolic elements, and Tadeus Kuntze, *Fortune* (1754). The definitive study of the many woodcut and copper-engraved print images of the *Tablet* in the 16th and 17th centuries is R. Schleier, *Tabula Cebetis, oder "Spiegel des Menschlichen Lebens darin Tugent und untugent abgemalet ist"* (Berlin, 1973).

[18] In English, see especially Trapp 1997 and Squire and Grethlein 2014 (listed in the **Bibliography** below); in German, see Hirsch-Luipold, R., R. Feldmeier, B. Hirsch, L. Koch, and H. G. Nesselrath, *Die Bildtafel des Kebes. Allergorie des Lebens. Eingeleitet, übersetzt und mit interpretierenden Essays versehen.* (SAPERE: Scripta Antiquitatis Posterioris ad Ethicam Religionemque pertinentia 8.) Darmstadt, 2005.

[19] Cf., e.g., the exhortation of Sandra Sider: "Those of us concerned with literary criticism, iconography, or the history of ideas need to acquaint ourselves with the *Tablet*." (*Cebes' Tablet: Facsimiles of the Greek Text, and of Selected Latin, French, English, Spanish, Italian, German, Dutch, and Polish Translations* [New York, 1979], 3) and the observation of Christian Kaesser, who notes "that [the fact that] the *Tabula* presents an exegete who interprets an ehrastic allegorical image makes the text an object of study for those working at the intersection of semiotics, image theory and hermeneutics." (C. Kaesser, 318 [in *The Classical Review*, Vol. 56, No. 2 (2006), 318-20; review of Hirsch-Luipold, R., R. Feldmeier, B. Hirsch, L. Koch, and H. G. Nesselrath, *Die Bildtafel des Kebes. Allergorie des Lebens. Eingeleitet, übersetzt und mit interpretierenden Essays versehen.* (SAPERE: Scripta Antiquitatis Posterioris ad Ethicam Religionemque pertinentia 8.) Darmstadt, 2005]).

In the first and second centuries CE, there primarily existed two forms of Greek: (1) Koine (ἡ κοινὴ διάλεκτος, "the common dialect [sc. of Greek]"), the common language of spoken discourse and of written communication employed by Greek speakers in the eastern half of the Roman empire; (2) Atticizing Greek, a movement by the educated elite to return to the Attic Greek used by writers of the fifth and fourth centuries (in prose especially that of Thucydides, Plato, and Demosthenes; in verse, Euripides, Aristophanes and Menander).

Koine Greek developed in the years following the conquests of Alexander the Great (d. 323 BCE) from the Attic Greek of the fifth and fourth centuries. It shared certain elements with non-Attic dialects (especially Ionic), and had developed many (mostly minor) grammatical, syntactical, and lexical differences from Attic Greek in its linguistic evolution from that language. Koine was the language of literary texts as diverse as those of the biographer and essayist Plutarch (*c.* 46-120 CE) and the various works that make up the New Testament (*c.* 51-*c.* 100 CE). It was also the language of government and day-to-day life as revealed by such surviving materials as imperial decrees, legal contracts, and personal letters.

Atticism was an attempt in the first, second and third centuries CE to purify the Koine of its non-Attic elements and reintroduce long-lost aspects of the grammar, syntax and vocabulary of Attic literary discourse from the fifth and fourth centuries BCE. Atticists ranged from extremists, who banished all deviant lexical forms and grammatical constructions, to those who wrote very good Attic prose with an occasional admixture of Koine elements.

The text of *Cebes' Tablet* was apparently written by a fairly strict and talented Atticist—so talented, in fact, that a majority of earlier scholars believed it was composed in the first half of the fourth century by Socrates' disciple, Cebes of Thebes.[20] The tell-tale signs of its late composition are primarily lexical: a handful of words that do not appear in Attic texts of the fifth and fourth centuries BCE are employed in the *Tablet* (see F. Drosihn, Κέβετος πίναξ. *Cebetis Tabula* [Leipzig, 1871], 37-9 for a list of these words, as well as Jerram's [xii-xiii] annotated correction of Drosihn's list and Parsons' [11-18] spirited defense of its Theban origins). The work's syntax is relatively simple, however, and, with the exception of the use of ellipse (very common in conversational dialogue), the *Tablet* seems to share the straightforward paratactic clauses (e.g., ones joined by καί and τὲ . . .

---

[20] Only a handful of scholars from the 15th-18th centuries doubted the attribution; foremost among them was the great scholar Hieronymous Wolf (1516-1580), who made a Latin translation of the text in 1561 (included in Sider's collection of facsimiles [see **Bibliography** below]). In the introduction to his edition of the *Tablet*, Jerram concludes that (xxxiii), "it is nevertheless classical in style and diction, and a good imitation of the best specimens of Attic prose."

καί) that one finds, for example, in Attic prose texts such as Xenophon (especially certain sections of the *Memorabilia* and *Anabasis*) as well as in Koine texts such as the gospels of Mark, Matthew, Luke, and John.

THE TEXT

The text used in this edition is:

> Praechter, Karl (= Carolus). Κέβετος πίναξ. *Cebetis Tabula*. Lipsiae (Leipzig), 1893

Differences between my text and that of Praechter's are as follows:

3 [p. 19 line 4] Ἀφροσύνη **for** ἀφροσύνη

3 [p. 20 line 4] Ἀφροσύνη **for** ἀφροσύνη

7 [p. 26 line 7] ἐστὶ **for** ἔστι

16 [p. 41 line 3] οὕτω προθύμως **for** προθύμως οὕτως

19 [p. 45 line 5] πρὸς ἰατρὸν δήπου γενόμενος πρότερον καθαρτικοῖς ἂν **for** πρὸς ἰατρὸν ἂν δήπου γενόμενος πρότερον καθαρτικοῖς

20 [p. 48 line 6] προσέξομεν **for** ποσέξομεν [a misprint]

24 [p. 52 line 11] ἕτεροι δὲ ὑφ' ἑτέρων **for** οἱ δὲ ὑφ' ἑτέρων

25 [p. 54 line 4] πράττουσιν **for** πράσσουσιν

26 [p. 55 line 8] ἐχιόδηκτοι **for** ἐχιοδεῖκται

33 [p. 64 line 11] συντομώτερον **for** συντομωτέρως

33 [p. 65 line 5] ἄχρηστον ἂν ἦν **for** ἄχρηστον ἦν

33 [p. 67 line 5] Ὅτι οἱ ἐν τῷ δευτέρῳ περιβόλῳ **for** Ὅτι οἱ <μὲν> ἐν τῷ πρώτῳ περιβόλῳ . . . . . . , <οἱ δ' ἐν τῷ δευτέρῳ περιβόλῳ,>

37 [p. 71 line 5] καὶ τοῖς ζῶσι **for** τοῖς ζῶσι

BIBLIOGRAPHY

Extensive bibliographies are supplied by Fitzgerald and White (49-58) and Seddon (244-5, 252-66). The following list, which does not include those works cited in the **Bibliographic Abbreviations** section above (p. xvi), includes the English-language items from their bibliographies that I believe offer the most stimulating and interesting approaches to the *Tablet* (marked with an *), as well as works they do not include (either because they appeared after their editions were in print or they were overlooked):

Bartsch, S. *Decoding the Ancient Novel: The Reader and the Role of Description in Heliodorus and Achilles Tatius*. Princeton, 1989, 14-40*

Elsner, J. *Art and the Roman Viewer*. Cambridge, 1995, 39-46*

Ong, W. J. "From Allegory to Diagram in the Renaissance Mind: A Study in the Significance of the Allegorical Tableau." *The Journal of Aesthetics and Art Criticism*, Vol. 17, No. 4 (1959) 423-40

Sider, S. *Cebes' Tablet: Facsimiles of the Greek Text, and of Selected Latin, French, English, Spanish, Italian, German, Dutch, and Polish Translations*. New York, 1979*

Squire, M. and J. Grethlein, ""Counterfeit in Character but Persuasive in Appearance": Reviewing the *Ainigma* of the *Tabula Cebetis*." *Classical Philology* 109 (2014), 285-324

Trapp, M. B. "The Tablet of Cebes." In *Aristotle and After*, ed. R. Sorabji (London, 1997), 159-80*

Tucker, G. H. *Homo Viator: Itineraries of Exile, Displacement and Writing in Renaissance Europe*. Geneva, 2003

Wasserman, E. R. "The Inherent Values of Eighteenth-Century Personification." *PMLA*, Vol. 65, No. 4 (1950), 435-63

Whitman, J. *Allegory: The Dynamics of an Ancient and Medieval Technique*. Cambridge (MA), 1987

ENGLISH TRANSLATIONS

There are dozens of English translations of *Cebes' Tablet*, the first published *c.* 1530 by Sir Francis Poyntz and the most recent in 2005 by Keith Seddon. The vast majority of which were made in the 17th and 18th centuries when the *Tablet* was at the peak of its popularity. Kenneth Sylvan Guthrie's translation, *The Greek Pilgrim's Progress, Generally Known as the Picture of Kebes, a disciple of Socrates?*, is included in facsimile form in this edition in **Appendix B**. The following are a select sample of the English translations of the *Tablet* published in the last five centuries.

Fitzgerald, J. T. and L. M. White. *The Tabula of Cebes*. Chico (California), 1983

Guthrie, K. S. *The Greek Pilgrim's Progress, Generally Known as the Picture of Kebes, a disciple of Socrates?* London and Philadelphia, 1910

Orgel, S. *Cebes in England: English Translations of the Tablet of Cebes from Three Centuries, with Related Materials*. New York, 1980. [Includes translations by Francis Poyntz (*c.* 1530), John Healey (1616), Jeremy Collier (1708), and Anthony Cooper, 3rd Earl of Shaftesbury (1914)]

Seddon, K. *Epictetus' Handbook and the Tablet of Cebes: Guides to Stoic Living*. London and New York, 2005

Seebohm, H. E. *The Picture of Kebes the Theban*. Chipping Campden (Gloucestershire, England), 1906

ΚΕΒΗΤΟΣ ΠΙΝΑΞ

1   [1] Ἐτυγχάνομεν περιπατοῦντες ἐν τῷ τοῦ Κρόνου ἱερῷ, ἐν ᾧ πολλὰ μὲν

2   καὶ ἄλλα ἀναθήματα ἐθεωροῦμεν· ἀνέκειτο δὲ καὶ πίναξ τις ἔμπροσθεν τοῦ νεώ,

3   ἐν ᾧ ἦν γραφὴ ξένη τις καὶ μύθους ἔχουσα ἰδίους, οὓς οὐκ ἠδυνάμεθα συμβαλεῖν,

---

ἄλλος, -η, -ο, other

ἀνάθημα, -ατος, τό, [< ἀνατίθημι, set up, erect, dedicate] object set up in a temple, votive or temple offering (dedicated in thanks for a victory or for deliverance from some illness or misfortune)

ἀνάκειμαι, [used as pass. of ἀνατίθημι, set up, erect, dedicate], be set up, be dedicated

γραφή, ἡ, painting, picture, drawing

δέ, (conj.) but, yet, and, on the other hand

δύναμαι, be able (+ inf.)

ἐν, (prep. + dat.) in, within

ἔμπροσθεν, (adv./prep. + gen.) before, in front of

ἔχω, have, possess; (pres. part. often =) with

θεωρέω, look at, view, observe

ἴδιος, -ία, -ον, peculiar

ἱερός, -ά, -όν, holy; τὸ ἱερόν, temple, sanctuary

καί, (conj.) and; (adv.) also

Κέβης, Κέβητος, ὁ, Cebes

Κρόνος, ὁ, Cronus

μέν, (conj. + δέ) indeed, on the one hand

μῦθος, -ου, ὁ, fable, myth, allegory

νεώς, -ώ, ὁ, shrine, temple

ξένος, -η, -ον, strange, foreign, unusual

ὅς, ἥ, ὅ, (rel. pron.) who, which

οὐ (οὐκ, οὐχ, οὐχί), (adv.) not

περιπατέω, -ήσω, walk about

πίναξ, πίνακος, ὁ, (votive) tablet or plaque

πολύς, πολλή, πολύ, much, great; (pl.) many

συμβάλλω, [συν- + βάλλω] gather together; figure out, apprehend

τις, τι, (indef. adj. and pron.) anyone/thing, someone/something, (a) certain

τυγχάνω, (+ supplementary part.) happen to X/to be X-ing

---

1 τοῦ Κρόνου Cronus was the father of Zeus and king of the pre-Olympian gods (he was identified by the Romans w/ their god Saturn). There is a common pun in Gk. on Κρόνος and χρόνος ("time"), an identification first made by the mythographer Pherecydes of Leros in the mid 5th century BCE, and frequent in later allegorical interpretations of the gods (e.g., Plutarch, *Isis and Osiris* 363d). As *Cebes' Tablet* is in many ways an allegory on human life, the pun fits

1-2 πολλά...καὶ ἄλλα in Gk., adjs. of quantity (e.g., πολύς, πολλή, πολύ) in the pl. are often joined to another adj. by καί in the same construction (both often modifying a substantive), whereas in English the second adj. is taken w/ the substantive and treated as a unit modified by the first adj. (w/ καί not translated into English) (Smyth § 2879)

2 τοῦ νεώ, usu. the "shrine" or inner part, as distinguished from the ἱερόν, the temple generally, but these terms are often interchangeable (esp. in later Gk. prose works)

3 ἦν 3rd sing. imperf. act. indic. < εἰμί, which has either a copulative function (e.g., A *is/was* B) or an existential sense (e.g., *there is/was*); here it is the latter

γραφὴ ξένη τις καὶ...ἔχουσα w/ adjs., τις has a restrictive sense and is best translated into English as "kind (of)" or "sort (of); καί here serves to introduce a clarification of a statement that has just been made ("a strange sort of tablet, that is/namely, [one] having/with...) (Smyth § 2869a)

ἠδυνάμεθα 1st pl. imperf. mid. (dep.) < δύναμαι, here w/ double augment (ε + ε = η)

συμβαλεῖν aor. act. inf. < συμβάλλω, here introducing an indir. quest.

τίνες καί ποτε ἦσαν. οὔτε γὰρ πόλις ἐδόκει ἡμῖν εἶναι τὸ γεγραμμένον οὔτε **1**

στρατόπεδον, ἀλλὰ περίβολος ἦν ἐν αὑτῷ ἔχων ἑτέρους περιβόλους δύο, τὸν **2**

μὲν μείζω, τὸν δὲ ἐλάττω. ἦν δὲ καὶ πύλη ἐπὶ τοῦ πρώτου περιβόλου. πρὸς δὲ **3**

τῇ πύλῃ ὄχλος ἐδόκει ἡμῖν πολὺς ἐφεστάναι, καὶ ἔνδον δὲ ἐν τῷ περιβόλῳ **4**

ἀλλά, (conj.) but (rather)

γάρ, (conj.) for

γράφω, portray, draw, paint

δέ, (conj.) but, yet, and, on the other hand

δοκέω, seem (often w/ dat. of person + pres. inf.)

δύο, (indecl.) two

ἑαυτοῦ, -ῆς, -οῦ, himself, herself, itself; (pl.) themselves

ἐγώ, I

ἐλάττων, -ον, [used as comp. of μικρός, -ά, -όν] smaller

ἔνδον, (adv.) within, inside

ἐπί, (prep. + gen.) on, upon

ἕτερος, -έρα, -ερον, one or the other (of two); other, another

ἐφίστημι, set by or near to; (perf. act., mid./pass.) stand at or near

μείζων, -ον, [comp. of μέγας, μεγάλη, μέγα] bigger, greater, larger

οὔτε, (conj.) and not; οὔτε...οὔτε, neither... nor

ὄχλος, ὁ, crowd

ποτε, (enclit. part.) ever, once; (makes a directly preceding interr. indef.) who/what in the world

περίβολος, ὁ, enclosure

πόλις, -εως, ἡ, city

πρός, (prep. + dat.) near

πρῶτος, -η, -ον, first

πύλη, ἡ, gate

στρατόπεδον, τό, military camp

τίς, τί, (interr. pron.) who? which? what?

---

1 τίνες καί ποτε ἦσαν "Adverbial καί...influences single words or whole clauses....[and] stresses an important idea; usually the idea set forth in the word that follows..." (Smyth § 2881); lit., "what they *ever* were," i.e., what in the world they were; cf. the English expression: "What *ever* are you doing?" "What they *ever* were is better expressed [in English] by "what they might possibly be." (Parsons, 68) or "what they could *possibly* be" (Jerram, 25)

ἦσαν 3rd pl. imperf. act. indic. < εἰμί

ἡμῖν dat. pl. of ἐγώ

εἶναι pres. act. inf. < εἰμί

τὸ γεγραμμένον the article often marks the subj.; γεγραμμένον neut. nom. sing. perf. pass. part. < γράφω

2 αὑτῷ = ἑαυτῷ

2-3 τὸν μεν...τὸν δέ "one...and the other" (Smyth § 1107)

3 μείζω syncopated (Smyth § 293b) alternative form (which occurs more frequently in everyday speech than literature) of masc. acc. sing. μείζονα, formed from μείζο(σ)α -> μείζοα -> μείζω, comp. of μέγας

ἐλάττω syncopated (Smyth § 293b) alternative form of acc. sing. ἐλάττονα, formed from ἐλάττο(σ)α-> ἐλάττοα -> ἐλάττω, comp. of μίκρος

ἐπὶ τοῦ πρώτου περιβόλου English prefers to translate the prep. as "in"

4 ἐφεστάναι perf. act. inf. < ἐφίστημι

καὶ...δέ "and also," "and moreover"; "Here καί emphasizes the important intervening word or words, while δέ connects." (Smyth § 2891)

1 πλῆθός τι γυναικῶν ἑωρᾶτο. ἐπὶ δὲ [τῆς εἰσόδου] τοῦ [πρώτου] πυλῶνος [καὶ

2 περιβόλου] γέρων τις ἑστὼς ἔμφασιν ἐποίει, ὡς προστάττων τι τῷ εἰσιόντι

3 ὄχλῳ.

γέρων, -οντος, ὁ, old man
γυνή, γυναικός, ἡ, woman
εἴσειμι/εἰσέρχομαι, go or enter into
εἴσοδος, -ου, ἡ, entrance, entry way
ἔμφασις, -εως, ἡ, exposition, setting forth, narration; gesture
ἵστημι, make X (acc.) stand; (perf. act., mid./pass.) stand
ὁράω/ὁρῶ, see

πλῆθος, -ους, τό, multitude, number, crowd
ποιέω, make
προστάττω, command, given an order
πυλών, -ῶνος, ὁ, great gate; gate tower
ὡς (conj.) as (if) (used w/ a part. to give a subj.'s real or probable reason [Smyth § 2086])

---

1 ἑωρᾶτο 3rd sing. imperf. pass. < ὁράω, w/ apparent double augment (in actuality, ὁράω was originally spelled ϝοράω, w/ a digamma [ϝ], which represented the sound of English "w", a sound that was lost in most Gk. dialects before the classical period; after the disappearance of the digamma, the temporal augment, which was ἠ [i.e. ἐε] not ἐ in this case, apparently transferred some of its quantity to the omicron, while the ἐ acquired the aspiration of the digamma, thus becoming ἑ. There is no prep. phrase expressing the agent, but "by us" is easily understood

1-2 [τῆς εἰσόδου] τοῦ [πρώτου] πυλῶνος [καὶ περιβόλου] the bracketed words were added by the 19th-century classicist Hermann Sauppe, who suspected that they had dropped out; however, the sense of ἐπὶ δὲ τοῦ πυλῶνος ("on/upon the tower of the gate") is quite clear

2 ἑστώς masc. nom. sing. perf. (w/ pres. sense) act. part. < ἵστημι; the perf. of this vb. (ἑστώς = lit., "having stood (oneself up)" = "[and therefore still currently in a] standing [position]") has a pres. sense, since it "marks the enduring result rather than the completed act" (Smyth § 1946)
εἰσιόντι masc. dat. sing. pres. act. part. < εἴσειμι/εἰσέρχομαι; in the indic. pres, εἶμι and its compounds serves as the fut. of ἔρχομαι in Ionic prose and in Attic Gk., while its pres. part. (ἰών, ἰοῦσα, ἰόν) and inf. (ἰέναι) forms retain their pres. sense

[2] Ἀπορούντων οὖν ἡμῶν περὶ τῆς μυθολογίας πρὸς ἀλλήλους πολὺν 1
χρόνον, πρεσβύτης τις παρεστώς, Οὐδὲν δεινὸν πάσχετε, ὦ ξένοι, ἔφη, 2
ἀπορούντες περὶ τῆς γραφῆς ταύτης. οὐδὲ γὰρ τῶν ἐπιχωρίων πολλοὶ οἴδασι, τί 3
ποτε αὕτη ἡ μυθολογία δύναται· οὐδὲ γάρ ἐστι πολιτικὸν ἀνάθημα· ἀλλὰ ξένος 4

ἀλλά, (conj.) but (rather)

ἀλλήλων, (of/to) another; πρὸς ἀλλήλους, among one another

ἀνάθημα, -ατος, τό, [< ἀνατίθημι, set up, erect, dedicate] object set up in a temple, votive or temple offering (dedicated in thanks for a victory or for deliverance from some illness or misfortune)

ἀπορέω, be perplexed or confused, be at a loss, be uncertain, not know

γάρ, (conj.) for, since

δεινός, -ή, -όν, strange; powerful, skilled (+ περί) in or w/ regard to X (acc. or gen.)

δύναμαι, be able (+ inf.); signify, mean

ἐπιχώριος, -ία, -ιον, native; οἱ ἐπιχώριοι, natives, local people

ἱερός, -ά, -όν, holy; τὸ ἱερόν, temple, sanctuary

μυθολογία, ἡ, narrative (of a fable), tale, account; significance or meaning of a story or picture

ξένος, -η, -ον, strange, foreign, unusual; ὁ ξένος, stranger, foreigner; guest-friend

οἶδα, (2nd perf. w/ pres. sense, i.e., I have seen therefore I now) know

ὅς, ἥ, ὅ, (rel. pron.) who, which, what

οὐδέ, (conj.) and not, nor yet; οὐδέ...οὐδέ, neither...nor

οὐδείς, οὐδεμία, οὐδέν, no one, nothing; no

οὖν, (conj.) therefore, then

οὗτος, αὕτη, τοῦτο, (dem. pron.) this

παρίστημι, make to stand or place beside; (perf. act. = pass.) stand by

πάσχω, experience; suffer

πολιτικός, -ή, -όν, pertaining or belonging to a city or state, local, native

πολύς, πολλή, πολύ, much, great; (pl.) many

ποτε, (enclit. part.) ever, once; (makes a directly preceding interr. indef.) who/what in the world

πρεσβύτης, -ου, ὁ, old man

πρός, (prep. + acc.) to, with

τίς, τί, (interr. pron.) who? which? what?

φημί, φήσω, ἔφην (imperf.), say

χρόνος, -ου, ὁ, time; πολὺν χρόνον, for a long time

---

1 ἀπορούντων....ἡμῶν...πρὸς ἀλλήλους gen. abs. (Smyth § 2070); lit., "while we were at a loss to one another," i.e., while we were puzzling among ourselves

1-2 πολὺν χρόνον acc. of extent of time (Smyth § 1582)

2 παρεστώς (= παρά + ἑστώς) < παρίστημι; cf. ἑστώς on the previous page
ἔφη 3rd sing. act. imperf. indic. < φημί; the imperf. of this vb. often has an aoristic force (Smyth § 788)

3 οἴδασι 3rd pl. perf. (w/ pres. sense) act. indic. < οἶδα; the form οἴδασι (more common is the Attic ἴσασι) is sometimes found in Ionic and in later Attic, and is relatively common in Koine Gk.

1   τις πάλαι ποτὲ ἀφίκετο δεῦρο, ἀνὴρ ἔμφρων καὶ δεινὸς περὶ σοφίαν, λόγῳ τε

2   καὶ ἔργῳ Πυθαγόρειόν τινα καὶ Παρμενίδειον ἐζηλωκὼς βίον, ὃς τό τε ἱερὸν

3   τοῦτο καὶ τὴν γραφὴν ἀνέθηκε τῷ Κρόνῳ.

4   **Ξένος:** Πότερον οὖν, ἔφην ἐγώ, καὶ αὐτὸν τὸν ἄνδρα γινώσκεις ἑωρακώς;

5   **Πρεσβύτης:** Καὶ ἐθαύμασά γε, ἔφη, αὐτὸν πολυχρονιώτατον νεώτερος

ἀνατίθημι, ἀναθήσω, ἀνέθηκα, set up
ἀνήρ, ἀνδρός, ὁ, man
αὐτός, -ή, -όν, he, she, it; himself, herself, itself
ἀφικνέομαι, ἀφίξομαι, ἀφικόμην, arrive
βίος, ὁ, life
γε, (particle) certainly, indeed
γι(γ)νώσκω, know
γραφή, ἡ, painting, picture, drawing
ἔμφρων, -ον, sensible, intelligent
ἔργον, τό, work, deed
ζηλόω, emulate; praise, approve
θαυμάζω, θαυμάσομαι, ἐθαύμασα, marvel at
ἱερός, -ά, -όν, holy; τὸ ἱερόν, temple, sanctuary
λόγος, ὁ, reason, speech, word

νεός, -α, -ον, young
ὁράω/ὁρῶ, see
ὅς, ἥ, ὅ, (rel. pron.) who, which, what
πάλαι, (adv.) long ago
Παρμενίδειος, -α, -ον, Parmenidean
περί, (prep. + acc.) in the case of, w/ respect to, in regard to, in
πολυχρόνιος, -ον, long-lived, ancient
πότερος, -έρα, -ερον, which of the two?
   πότερον...ἤ, whether...or; πότερον, (as an interr. adv. introducing a dir. quest., it is not translated)
Πυθαγόρειος, -α, -ον, Pythagorean
σοφία, ἡ, wisdom
τέ, (conj.) and; τε καί / τε...καί, (both)...and
τις, τι, (indef. adj. and pron.) anyone/thing, someone/something, (a) certain

---

1-2 λόγῳ...ἔργῳ dats. of respect (Smyth § 1516); for the Gk. *logos-ergon* phrase, cf. the English expression "a person who not only talked the talk, but walked the walk"

2 Πυθαγόρειόν...Παρμενίδειον...βίον Pythagoras (*fl.* late sixth century BCE) and Parmenides (*fl.* first half of the fifth century BCE) were pre-Socratic philosophers ἐζηλωκὼς masc. nom. sing. perf. (w/ pres. sense) act. part. < ζηλόω; Jerram (26) notes that: "ζηλόω is (1) 'I emulate,' (2) 'I praise' or 'approve,' hence 'adopt' a course of life or set of opinions."

3 ἀνέθηκε 3rd sing. aor. act. indic. < ἀνατίθημι

4 αὐτὸν intensive in the predicate position
γινώσκεις γινώσκω is the usu. spelling of γιγνώσκω in Ionic and in post-fourth century BCE Gk.
ἑωρακώς < ὁράω; for the form, cf. ἐζηλωκὼς above

5 καὶ...γε "Yes, and...", a common idiom used in replies (Smyth § 2825); "the γε emphasizes ἐθαύμασα, the καὶ connects this sentence with the preceding one." (Jerram 26)
πολυχρονιώτατον superl. of πολυχρόνιος, -ον. "The superlative expresses either the highest degree of a quality (the *relative* superlative: ὁ σοφώτατος ἀνήρ *the wisest man*) or a very high degree of a quality (the *absolutist* superlative, which does not take the article: ἀνὴρ σοφώτατος *a very wise man*)." (Smyth § 1085)
νεώτερος comp. of νεός, -α, -ον

ὤν. πολλὰ γὰρ καὶ σπουδαῖα διεγέλετο. τότε δὴ καὶ περὶ ταύτης [δὲ] τῆς   **1**
μυθολογίας πολλάκις αὐτοῦ ἠκηκόειν διεξιόντος.   **2**

[3] Ξένος: Πρὸς Διὸς τοίνυν, ἔφην ἐγὼ, εἰ μή τίς σοι μεγάλη ἀσχολία   **3**
τυγχάνει οὖσα, διήγησαι ἡμῖν· πάνυ γὰρ ἐπιθυμοῦμεν ἀκοῦσαι, τί ποτέ ἐστιν ὁ   **4**
μῦθος.   **5**

ἀκούω, hear (+ gen. of person)
ἀσχολία, ἡ [ἀ- + σχολή, leisure], lack of leisure; business
δή, (particle) now, quite, particularly, certainly
διαλέγομαι, discuss, discourse
διέξειμι/διεξέρχομαι, [lit., I go out through/completely], go through (thoroughly), explain or describe (in detail)
διηγέομαι, narrate, explain, or describe (in detail)
εἰ, (conj.) if; + μή, unless, if...not
ἐπιθυμέω, desire (to + inf.)
Ζεύς, Διός, ὁ, Zeus
μέγας, μεγάλη, μέγα, great; important
μυθολογία, ἡ, narrative (of a fable), tale, account; significance or meaning of a story or picture
μῦθος, ὁ, fable, myth, story, allegory

πάνυ, (adv.) very, very much
περί, (prep. + gen.) about, concerning, regarding
πολλάκις, (adv.) often, many times
πρός, (prep. + gen. [in swearing]) by
σπουδαῖος, -αία, -αῖον, serious, weighty, excellent
σύ, (pron.) you
τις, τι, (indef. adj. and pron.) any one/thing, someone/something, (a) certain
τίς, τί, (interr. pron.) who? which? what?
τοίνυν, (particle) [τοι + νυν], therefore, accordingly; in dialogue, to introduce an answer) well then
τότε, (adv.) then, at that time
τυγχάνω, (+ supplementary part.) happen to X
φημί, φήσω, ἔφην (imperf.), say

---

1 ὤν masc. nom. sing. pres. act. part. < εἰμί

πολλά...καὶ σπουδαῖα for καὶ not being translated into English, see note to πολλά...καὶ ἄλλα on p. 12, lines 1-2

2 ἠκηκόειν 1st sing. pluperf. (w/ imperf. sense) act. indic. < ἀκούω; the pluperf. of ἀκούω is known as the so-called Attic reduplication, in which the initial vowel and consonant of the stem on which the perf. is based (here ἀκ-) are repeated, and what was originally the intitial vowel is lengthened. The form ἠκηκόειν (the Cl. Gk. form is ἠκηκόη) is found in some fourth-century authors (e.g., Xenophon) and in later Gk. For the pluperf. w/ imperf. sense, see Smyth § 1952

διεξιόντος masc. gen. sing. pres. act. part. < διέξειμι/διεξέρχομαι; agreeing with αὐτοῦ, the object of ἠκηκόειν. For the tense, cf. the note to εἰσιόντι on p. 14, line 2

4 διήγησαι 2nd sing. aor. mid. (dep.) impera. < διηγέομαι

1   **Πρεσβύτης:** Οὐδεὶς φθόνος, ὦ ξένοι, ἔφη. ἀλλὰ τουτὶ πρῶτον δεῖ ὑμᾶς

2 ἀκοῦσαι, ὅτι ἐπικίνδυνόν τι ἔχει ἡ ἐξήγησις.

3   **Ξένος:** Οἷον τί; ἔφην ἐγώ.

4   **Πρεσβύτης:** Ὅτι, εἰ μὲν προσέξετε, ἔφη, καὶ συνήσετε τὰ λεγόμενα,

5 φρόνιμοι καὶ εὐδαίμονες ἔσεσθε· εἰ δὲ μὴ, ἄφρονες καὶ κακοδαίμονες καὶ πικροὶ

ἄφρων, -ον, mindless, foolish

δεῖ, (impers. vb.) it is necessary, one should (+ acc. and inf.)

ἐξήγησις, -εως, ἡ, explanation

ἐπικίνδυνος, -ον, dangerous, connected w/ danger

εὐδαίμων, -ον, [lit., (with) a good (εὐ) spirit/divinity (δαίμων)] happy, fortunate

κακοδαίμων, -ον, [lit., (with) a bad (κακός) spirit/divinity (δαίμων)] unhappy, unfortunate, wretched

λέγω, say, speak

ξένος, -η, -ον, strange, foreign, unusual; ὁ ξένος, stranger, foreigner

οἷος, οἵα, οἷον, of which kind or sort, such as; οἷον, (acc. of respect as adv.) such as, like, for example; οἷον τί, like what

ὅτι, (conj.) that

οὐδείς, οὐδεμία, οὐδέν, no one, nothing; no

οὗτος, αὕτη, τοῦτο, (dem. pron.) this

πικρός, -ή, -όν, bitter, embittered, spiteful, mean, morose, ill-tempered

προσέχω, προσέξω (+ τὸν νοῦν, stated or implied), hold (your mind) toward, pay attention (to)

πρῶτος, -η, -ον, first; πρῶτον, (adv.) first, first of all

συνίημι, συνήσω, put together; understand

τις, τι, (indef. adj. and pron.) any one/thing, someone/something, (a) certain

φθόνος, ὁ, envy; grudging; ill-will; + οὐδείς, no refusal, no objection, no reluctance

φρόνιμος, -ον, wise, prudent

---

1 οὐδεὶς φθόνος sc. ἔστι μοι; Parsons (69) notes that this is "a conventional expression"

τουτὶ = τοῦτο + -ι (a long iota, here functioning as a "deictic" marker; cf. δείκνυμι, I show, point out); the suffix gets the accent and causes the omicron to be elided because it is short; this long accented iota can be added to any form of a demonstrative pronoun to make it more emphatic (Smyth § 333g)

4 Ὅτι "[Just this,] that…"

4-5 εἰ…προσέξετε…συνήσετε…ἔσεσθε the so-called "emotional" fut. condit. (aka the fut. minatory), used when the protasis (i.e., the "if" cl.) expresses strong feeling (Smyth § 2328)

ἔσεσθε 2nd pl. fut. mid. (dep.) indic. < εἰμί

5 πικροὶ Jerram (26) notes that: "In Aristotle, Ethics, ii. 7, πικρός is the sulky man, who retains his anger long and is hard to reconcile."

καὶ ἀμαθεῖς γενόμενοι, κακῶς βιώσεσθε. ἔστι γὰρ ἡ ἐξήγησις ἐοικυῖα τῷ τῆς **1**
Σφιγγὸς αἰνίγματι, ὃ ἐκείνη προεβάλλετο τοῖς ἀνθρώποις. εἰ μὲν οὖν αὐτὸ **2**
συνίει τις, ἐσώζετο· εἰ δὲ μὴ συνίει, ἀπώλετο ὑπὸ τῆς Σφιγγός. ὡσαύτως δὲ καὶ **3**
ἐπὶ τῆς ἐξηγήσεως ἔχει ταύτης. ἡ γὰρ Ἀφροσύνη τοῖς ἀνθρώποις Σφίγξ ἐστιν. **4**
αἰνίττεται δὲ τάδε, τί ἀγαθόν, τί κακόν, τί οὔτε ἀγαθὸν οὔτε κακόν ἐστιν ἐν τῷ βίῳ. **5**

ἀγαθός, -ή, -όν, good
αἴνιγμα, -τος, τό, riddle
αἰνίττομαι, speak in riddles, put forth a riddle
ἀμαθής, -ές, ignorant, stupid
ἄνθρωπος, ὁ, human being; (pl. often =) humanity
ἀπόλλυμι, ἀπολέσω/ἀπολῶ, ἀπώλεσα, destroy, kill; (mid.) perish, die
αὐτός, -ή, -όν, he, she, it; himself, herself, itself
ἀφροσύνη, ἡ, folly, foolishness; mindlessness
βίος, ὁ, life
βιόω, βιώσομαι, live
γί(γ)νομαι, γενήσομαι, ἐγενόμην, become, be
εἰ, (conj.) if; + μή, unless, if...not
ἐκεῖνος, ἐκείνη, ἐκεῖνο, that, he, she, it; (pl.) those, they
ἐξήγησις, -εως, ἡ, explanation

ἐοικώς, ἐοικυῖα, ἐοικός, (+ dat.) like, similar (to)
ἐπί, (prep. + gen.) in the case of; for
ἔχω, have, hold
κακός, -ή, -όν, bad
κακῶς, (adv.) badly, poorly
ὅδε, ἥδε, τόδε, (dem. pron.) he, she, that one/thing
ὅς, ἥ, ὅ, (rel. pron.) who, which, what
οὖν, (conj.) therefore
οὔτε, (conj.) and not; οὔτε...οὔτε, neither...nor
προβάλλω, (mid. = act.) put forward, propose
συνίημι, συνήσω, put together; understand
Σφίγξ, Σφιγγός, ἡ, Sphinx
τίς, τί, (interr. pron.) who? which? what?
ὑπό, (prep. + gen.) by, at the hands of
ὡσαύτως, (adv.) in the same way, likewise, similarly

---

2 Σφιγγὸς mythical Theban monster with a human head and the body of a lion; it destroyed those who could not answer its riddle (in its best known formulation: "What walks on four legs in the morning, two legs in the afternoon, and three legs in the evening?" The solution, provided by Oedipus, was "a human being" [i.e., four "legs" as an infant who crawls on all fours, two legs as a young person/adult, and three "legs" as an elderly individual who has to employ a cane or staff])

2-3 εἰ...συνίει...ἐσώζετο, εἰ...μὴ συνίει, ἀπώλετο two past particular condits. (Smyth § 2298)

3 συνίει 3rd sing. imperf. act. indic. < συνίημι

3-4 ὡσαύτως...ἔχει ἔχω + adv. = (at least in terms of their English equivalent) εἰμί + adj. (Smyth § 1438); thus, "it holds in the same manner" = it's the same thing

4 ἡ...Ἀφροσύνη...Σφίγξ ἐστιν "in Gk. moralizing texts of the post-Classical period, the Sphinx was seen as a symbol of human foolishness or folly" (King, 24; and cf. also Fitzgerald and White, 137)

5 αἰνίττεται sc. ἡ...Ἀφροσύνη as subj.

1 ταῦτ᾽ οὖν ἐὰν μέν τις μὴ συνιῇ ἀπόλλυται ὑπ᾽ αὐτῆς· οὐκ εἰσάπαξ, ὥσπερ ὁ ὑπὸ

2 τῆς Σφιγγὸς καταβρωθεὶς ἀπέθνησκεν· ἀλλὰ κατὰ μικρὸν ἐν ὅλῳ τῷ βίῳ

3 καταφθείρεται καθάπερ οἱ ἐπὶ τιμωρίᾳ παραδιδόμενοι. ἐὰν δέ τις γνῷ,

4 ἀνάπαλιν ἡ μὲν Ἀφροσύνη ἀπόλλυται, αὐτὸς δὲ σώζεται, καὶ μακάριος καὶ

5 εὐδαίμων γίνεται ἐν παντὶ τῷ βίῳ. ὑμεῖς οὖν προσέχετε καὶ μὴ παρακούετε.

6 **[4] Ξένος:** Ὦ Ἡράκλεις, ὡς εἰς μεγάλην τινὰ ἐπιθυμίαν ἐμβέβληκας

7 ἡμᾶς, εἰ ταῦθ᾽ οὕτως ἔχει.

ἀλλά, (conj.) but (rather), yet
ἀνάπαλιν, (adv.) instead; on the contrary
ἀποθνήσκω, die
γι(γ)νώσκω, know
ἐάν, (conj. =) εἰ ἄν, if (ever) (+ subju.)
εἰσάπαξ, (adv.) [εἰς + ἅπαξ, once], at once
κατά, (prep. + acc. distributively) by..., in...
[καταβιβρώσκω] (pres. not found; in Cl.
  Gk., ἐσθίω is used as the pres.; in L. Gk.,
  τρώγω), devour, eat up
εἰς, (prep. + acc.) into
ἐμβάλλω, put in, incite, inspire
ἐπί, (prep. + gen.) in the case of; for
ἐπιθυμία, ἡ, desire, longing
ἔχω, have; οὕτως ἔχειν, to be so
Ἡρακλέης/Ἡρακλῆς, -έους, ὁ, Heracles;
  (when used in the voc., the name functions
  as an exclamation of surprise, anger, or
  disgust)
καθάπερ, (conj.) just as, as
καταφθείρω, destroy

μέγας, μεγάλη, μέγα, great
μή, (adv.) not; (in commands) don't
μικρός, -ά, -όν, small; κατὰ μικρόν, little
  by little, gradually
ὅλος, -η, -ον, entire, whole
οὕτω(ς), (adv.) so, thus, in this state, manner
  or condition
παραδίδωμι, hand over, deliver
παρακούω, [παρα-, amiss, wrong + ἀκούω],
  lit., hear in passing, i.e., hear wrongly/
  carelessly; hear or understand poorly,
  misunderstand; take no heed of, not to
  listen, not to take account
πᾶς, πᾶσα, πᾶν, all, (the) whole
προσέχω, προσέξω (+ τὸν νοῦν, mind
  [stated or implied]), hold (your mind)
  toward, pay attention (to)
τιμωρία, ἡ, punishment
Ὦ, ὦ, (exclamation) oh!, O!; (w/ voc.,
  simply an address)
ὡς, (conj.) how (heading an exclamation)
ὥσπερ, (adv.) just as (if)

---

1 ταῦτ᾽ = ταῦτα
  ἐὰν...μὴ συνιῇ ἀπόλλυται pres. gen. condit. (protasis [i.e., the "if" cl.] = ἐάν + aor.
  or pres. subju.; apodosis = pres. indic.; i.e., if he/she does not [ever] understand...he/she
  perishes)
  συνιῇ 3rd sing. pres. act. subju. < συνίημι
  ὑπ᾽ αὐτῆς i.e., ὑπὸ τῆς ἀφροσύνης

2 καταβρωθείς masc. nom. sing. aor. pass. part. < [καταβιβρώσκω]

3 ἐὰν...γνῷ the protasis (i.e., the "if" cl.) of another pres. gen. condit.
  γνῷ 3rd sing. aor. act. subju. < γι(γ)νώσκω

6 Ὦ Ἡράκλεις the voc., esp. at the beginning of a sentence, is emphatic (Smyth §
  1283)
  ἐμβέβληκας 2nd sing. perf. act. indic. < ἐμβάλλω

7 ταῦθ᾽ (= ταῦτα) οὕτως ἔχει another example of ἔχω + adv. = εἰμί + adj. (see note
  to ὡσαύτως...ἔχει on p. 21); lit., "these things hold thus," i.e., these things are so

Πρεσβύτης: Ἀλλ᾽ ἔστιν, ἔφη, οὕτως ἔχοντα.　　　　　1

Ξένος: Οὐκ ἂν φθάνοις τοίνυν διηγούμενος ὡς ἡμῶν προσεξόντων οὐ　2
παρέργως, ἐπείπερ καὶ τὸ ἐπιτίμιον τοιοῦτον ἐστίν.　　　　　3

Πρεσβύτης: Ἀναλαβὼν οὖν ῥάβδον τινὰ καὶ ἐκτείνας πρὸς τὴν γραφήν,　4
Ὁρᾶτε, ἔφη, τὸν περίβολον τοῦτον;　　　　　5

Ξένος: Ὁρῶμεν.　　　　　6

ἀναλαμβάνω, ἀναλήψομαι, ἀνέλαβον, take up

γραφή, ἡ, painting, picture, drawing

διηγέομαι, narrate, explain, or describe (in detail)

ἐκτείνω, ἐκτενῶ, ἐξέτεινα, stretch out or forth, extend

ἐπείπερ, (conj.) since indeed

ἐπιτίμιον, τό, penalty, consequence (either way, reward in one case, punishment/penalty in the other)

ὁράω/ὁρῶ, see

οὐ (οὐκ, οὐχ, οὐχί), (adv.) not

οὖν, (conj.) therefore

οὗτος, αὕτη, τοῦτο, this; he, she, it; (pl.) these

παρέργως [παρα- + ἔργον = a work alongside, a side-project], (adv.) lit., as a by-work/side-project, i.e., carelessly, passively, secondarily, i.e., of secondary importance

περίβολος, ὁ, enclosure

πρός, (prep. + acc.) to, toward

ῥάβδος, -ου, ἡ, staff

τοίνυν [τοι + νυν], (particle) therefore, accordingly; (in dialogue, to introduce an answer) well then

τοιοῦτος, -αύτη, -οῦτο/οῦτον, such, of such a sort, of that kind

φημί, φήσω, ἔφην (imperf.), say

φθάνω, do *something* (acc.) before *someone* (acc.), anticipate

ὡς, (conj.) as (if) (used w/ a part. to give a subj.'s real or probable reason [Smyth § 2086]);

---

1 ἔχοντα picking up ταῦθ᾽; ἔχοντα + οὕτως = "(these) things holding thus (i.e., being so)" and is the subj. of ἔστιν (neut. pl. subjects usu. take sing. vbs.; Smyth § 958), w/ the entire phrase meaning "(these) things being so are (so)." Note that the accent on ἔστι shows that εἰμί is being used in its existential sense (cf. the note to ἦν in 1)

2 οὐκ ἂν φθάνοις...διηγούμενος lit., "you could not anticipate describing," i.e., you could not be too quick in describing (almost w/ the force of an impera., i.e., "hurry up and..." or "describe it!"). φθάνοις 2nd sing. pres. act. opt. < φθάνω; w/ ἄν, a potential opt. (Smyth § 1824). φθάνω often takes a supplementary part.

3 ὡς ἡμῶν προσεξόντων gen. abs.; lit., "we [being regarded] as about to pay attention [to you]," i.e., for *be sure* we will pay attention to you

4 ἐκτείνας This gesture marks the beginning of an extended ecphrasis (ἔκφρασις), a vivid verbal description of a visual work of art whether real or imagined (of the latter, the most famous in Gk. literature being that of Achilles' shield in *Iliad* 18:478-608)

1 Πρεσβύτης: τοῦτο πρῶτον δεῖ εἰδέναι ὑμᾶς, ὅτι καλεῖται οὗτος ὁ τόπος
2 Βίος. καὶ ὁ ὄχλος ὁ πολὺς ὁ παρὰ τὴν πύλην ἐφεστὼς οἱ μέλλοντες
3 εἰσπορεύεσθαι εἰς τὸν βίον οὗτοί εἰσιν. ὁ δὲ γέρων ὁ ἄνω ἑστηκὼς ἔχων χάρτην
4 τινὰ ἐν τῇ χειρὶ καὶ τῇ ἑτέρᾳ ὥσπερ δεικνύων τι, οὗτος Δαίμων καλεῖται·
5 προστάττει δὲ τοῖς εἰσπορευομένοις τί δεῖ αὐτοὺς ποιεῖν, ὡς ἂν εἰσέλθωσιν εἰς
6 τὸν Βίον· δεικνύει δὲ ποίαν ὁδὸν αὐτοὺς δεῖ βαδίζειν, εἰ μέλλουσιν σώζεσθαι ἐν
7 τῷ Βίῳ.

ἄνω, (adv.) upward, up (there)
αὐτός, -ή, -όν, he, she, it; himself, herself, itself
βαδίζω, walk, go; + ὁδόν, take a road
βίος, ὁ, life
γέρων, -οντος, ὁ, old man
δαίμων, -ονος, ὁ, god, divine being
δεῖ, (impers. vb.) it is necessary, one should (+ acc. and inf.)
δεικνύω, show, point out
εἰ, (conj.) if
εἰς, (prep. + acc.) into
εἰσέρχομαι, εἰσελεύσομαι, εἰσῆλθον, go or enter into
εἰσπορεύω, lead in; (pass.) enter
ἐν, (prep. + dat.) in
ἕτερος, -έρα, -ερον, other
ἐφίστημι, set by or near to; (perf. act., mid./pass.) stand at or near
ἔχω, have, hold
ἵστημι, make X (acc.) stand; (perf. act., mid./pass.) stand
καλέω, call, name
μέλλω, intend, be about or likely to (+ inf.)

ὁδός, -οῦ, ἡ, way, path, road
ὅτι, (conj.) that
ὄχλος, ὁ, crowd
παρά, (prep. + acc.) beside, near, by
ποιέω, do
ποῖος, -οία, -οῖον, what sort of, what kind of
πολύς, πολλή, πολύ, much, great; (pl.) many
προστάττω, command, given an order, enjoin upon
πρῶτος, -η, -ον, first; πρῶτον, (adv.) first, first of all
πύλη, ἡ, gate
σῴζω/σώζω, save (from death), keep alive
τις, τι, (indef. adj. and pron.) any one/thing, someone/something, (a) certain
τίς, τί, (interr. pron.) who? which? what?
τόπος, ὁ, place
χάρτης, -ου, ὁ, (papyrus) roll, scroll; (papyrus) sheet
χείρ, χειρός, ἡ, hand
ὡς, (conj. + ἄν [+ subju.]) when(ever), as soon as

---

1 δεῖ + acc. (ὑμᾶς) and inf. (εἰδέναι < οἶδα) construction

2 ἐφεστὼς (= ἐπί + ἑστώς) < ἐφίστημι; cf. note to ἑστώς on p. 14, line 2

3 ἑστηκὼς < ἵστημι; ἑστηκὼς = (an alternative form of) ἑστώς, though the former rarely occurs in earlier Gk. texts

4 τῇ ἑτέρᾳ sc. χειρὶ; dat. of means (Smyth § 1506-7)
   Δαίμων Parsons (70) notes that: "This word generally refers, not to the person of a particular god, but to the Divine Power, or a disembodied spirit." Jerram (27) states that: "(afterwards called Δαιμόνιον, Chap. xxxiii.) [Δαίμων] is the...presiding deity of a man's life, like the Guardian Angel." Seddon (234) notes that: "Daimon is the Deity, the power that controls the destiny of all individuals."

5 ὡς ἂν εἰσέλθωσιν an indef. temporal cl. (Smyth § 2394; ὡς is almost never used in Cl. Gk. w/ subju. or opt.); εἰσέλθωσιν 3rd pl. aor. act. subju. < εἰσέρχομαι

[5] Ξένος: Ποίαν οὖν ὁδὸν κελεύει βαδίζειν, ἢ πῶς; ἔφην ἐγώ.   **1**

Πρεσβύτης: Ὁρᾷς οὖν, εἶπε, παρὰ τὴν πύλην θρόνον τινὰ κείμενον κατὰ   **2**
τὸν τόπον, καθ' ὃν εἰσπορεύεται ὁ ὄχλος, ἐφ' οὗ κάθηται γυνὴ πεπλασμένη τῷ   **3**
ἤθει καὶ πιθανὴ φαινομένη, ἢ ἐν τῇ χειρὶ ἔχει ποτήριόν τι;   **4**

Ξένος: Ὁρῶ. ἀλλὰ τίς ἐστιν αὕτη; ἔφην.   **5**

Πρεσβύτης: Ἀπάτη καλεῖται, φησὶν, ἡ πάντας τοὺς ἀνθρώπους   **6**
πλανῶσα.   **7**

Ξένος: Εἶτα τί πράττει αὕτη;   **8**

Πρεσβύτης: Τοὺς εἰσπορευομένους εἰς τὸν Βίον ποτίζει τῇ ἑαυτῆς   **9**
δυνάμει.   **10**

ἀλλά, (conj.) but (rather), yet
ἄνθρωπος, ὁ, human being
ἀπάτη, ἡ, deceit, deception
γυνή, γυναικός, ἡ, woman
εἶπον, (2nd aor.; pres in use is φήμι, λέγω, ἀγορεύω) said, spoke
δύναμις, -εως, ἡ, power
ἑαυτοῦ, -ῆς, -οῦ, himself, herself, itself; (pl.) themselves
εἶτα, (adv.) and so, then, therefore; (used in questions to express surprise or sarcasm) and then...? and so...?
ἐπί, (prep. + gen.) on, upon
ἤ, (conj.) or
ἦθος, -ους, τό, character
θρόνος, ὁ, throne
κάθημαι, sit
κατά, (prep. + acc.) (down) by, at
κεῖμαι, lie
κελεύω, command; urge

ὁράω/ὁρῶ, see
ὅς, ἥ, ὅ, (rel. pron.) who, which
οὖν, (conj.) therefore, then
οὗτος, αὕτη, τοῦτο, this, he, she, it; (pl.) these
πᾶς, πᾶσα, πᾶν, every, all
πιθανός, -ή, -όν, persuasive, alluring
πλανάω, make X (acc.) wander; lead X (acc.) astray; deceive X (acc.)
πλάττω, form, shape, make up
ποτίζω, make X (acc.) drink of Y (dat.), give X (acc.) Y (dat.) to drink (a double acc. is the more usu. construction)
ποτήριον, τό, cup
πράττω, do
πῶς, (adv.) how? in what manner?
τόπος, ὁ, place
φαίνω, bring to light; (pass.) be seen, seem, appear
φημί, φήσω, ἔφην (imperf.), say

---

1 ἤ can introduce a question parallel to a preceding one or supplemental to it; in English this function of ἤ is often best translated as "and"

3 καθ' ὅν = κατὰ ὅν
ἐφ' = ἐπί
πεπλασμένη fem. nom. sing. perf. pass. part. < πλάττω; lit., "having been made up (so as to be deceptive)," i.e., counterfeit or fake

3-4 τῷ ἤθει dat. of respect (Smyth § 1516). In Cl. Gk., more common would be an acc. of respect (Smyth § 1600-1603). Jerram has "affected in manner" for πεπλασμένη ἤθει

5 αὕτη "this woman," "she"; in later passages, αὗται may be translated "these women" or "they," οὗτος "this man" or "he," and οὗτοι "these men" or "they"

6 φησὶν one expects imperf.

1 Ξένος: Τοῦτο δὲ τί ἐστι τὸ ποτόν;

2 Πρεσβύτης: Πλάνος, ἔφη, καὶ Ἄγνοια.

3 Ξένος: Εἶτα τί;

4 Πρεσβύτης: Πιόντες τοῦτο πορεύονται εἰς τὸν Βίον.

5 Ξένος: Πότερον οὖν πάντες πίνουσι τὸν πλάνον ἢ οὔ;

6 [6] Πρεσβύτης: Πάντες πίνουσιν, ἔφη, ἀλλ' οἱ μὲν πλεῖον, οἱ δὲ ἧττον.

7 Ἔτι δὲ οὐχ ὁρᾷς ἔνδον τῆς πύλης πλῆθός γυναικῶν ἑτέρων παντοδαπὰς

8 μορφὰς ἐχουσῶν;

9 Ξένος: Ὁρῶ.

10 Πρεσβύτης: Αὗται τοίνυν Δόξαι καὶ Ἐπιθυμίαι καὶ Ἡδοναὶ καλοῦνται.

11 ὅταν οὖν εἰσπορεύηται ὁ ὄχλος, ἀναπηδῶσιν αὗται καὶ πλέκονται πρὸς

ἄγνοια, ἡ, ignorance
ἀναπηδάω, ἀναπηδήσω, ἀνεπήδησα, jump or leap up
βαδίζω, walk, go; + ὁδόν, take a road
βίος, ὁ, life
δόξα, ἡ, opinion
εἰσπορεύω, lead in; (pass.) enter
ἐν, (prep. + dat.) in
ἔνδον, (adv./prep. + gen.) within, inside
ἐπιθυμία, ἡ, desire
ἕτερος, -έρα, -ερον, other
ἔτι, (adv.) still, further, moreover
ἔχω, have
ἡδονή, ἡ, pleasure, sense-gratification
ἥσσων/ἥττων, ἧσσον/ἧττον, less, weaker; (neut. acc. sing. as adv.) less
καλέω, call, name
μορφή, ἡ, form
ὅταν, ([ὅτε + ἄν], conj. adv.) whenever (+ subju.)
οὐ (οὐκ, οὐχ, οὐχί), (adv.) not
ὄχλος, ὁ, crowd

παντοδαπός, -ή, -όν, of all kinds, of every kind
πᾶς, πᾶσα, πᾶν, every, all
πίνω, πίομαι, ἔπιον, drink
πλάνος, ὁ, error
πλείων/πλέων, πλεῖον/πλέον, more, greater; (neut. acc. sing. as adv.) more
πλέκω, weave, twine, entwine; (mid. + πρός + acc.) embrace
πλῆθος, -ους, τό, multitude, number, crowd
πορεύω, -εύσω, carry, convey; (pass.) go (across), pass, enter
πότερος, -έρα, -ερον, which of the two? πότερον...ἤ, whether...or; πότερον, (as an interr. adv. introducing a dir. quest., it is not translated)
ποτόν, τό, drink
τοίνυν, (particle) [τοι + νυν], therefore, accordingly; (in dialogue, to introduce an answer) well then

---

1 τοῦτο w/ τὸ ποτόν

4 πιόντες masc. nom. sing. aor. act. part. < πίνω
   οἱ μὲν...οἱ δέ "some...others..." (Smyth § 1107)

11 εἰσπορεύηται 3rd sing. pres. pass. subju. < εἰσπορεύω; subju. in a pres. general temp. cl. introduced by ὅταν
   ἀναπηδῶσιν (α-contract; ἀναπηδά + ουσιν) 3rd pl. pres. act. indic. < ἀναπηδάω

ἕκαστον, εἶτα ἀπάγουσι.   **1**

    Ξένος: Ποῦ δὲ ἀπάγουσιν αὐτούς;   **2**

    Πρεσβύτης: Αἱ μὲν εἰς τὸ σῴζεσθαι, ἔφη, αἱ δὲ εἰς τὸ ἀπόλλυσθαι διὰ τὴν   **3**
ἀπάτην.   **4**

    Ξένος: Ὦ δαιμόνιε, ὡς χαλεπὸν τὸ πόμα λέγεις.   **5**

    Πρεσβύτης: Καὶ πᾶσαί γε, ἔφη, ἐπαγγέλλονται ὡς ἐπὶ τὰ βέλτιστα   **6**
ἄξουσαι καὶ εἰς βίον εὐδαίμονα καὶ λυσιτελῆ. οἱ δὲ διὰ τὴν ἄγνοιαν καὶ τὸν   **7**

ἄγω, ἄξω, ἤγαγον, lead
ἀπάγω, lead away
ἀπόλλυμι, destroy, kill; (mid.) perish, die; (pass.) be ruined or destroyed
αὐτός, -ή, -όν, he, she, it; himself, herself, itself; (pl.) them; themselves
βέλτιστος, -η, -ον, best
γε, (particle) indeed
δαιμόνιος, -ον, belonging to a divine being (δαίμων), strange; (as direct address expressing admiration or surprise), sir
διά, (prep. + acc.) through, by means of; because of, on account of
εἰς, (prep. + acc.) into, to; in regard to
εἶτα, (adv.) then, next
ἕκαστος, ἑκάστη, ἕκαστον, each, every

ἐπαγγέλλω, proclaim, announce; (mid.) promise (unasked); offer (of one's own free will)
ἐπί, (prep. + acc.; expressing the goal) to
εὐδαίμων, -ον, happy, fortunate
λέγω, speak or tell of
λυσιτελής, -ές, profitable, advantageous
ποῖ, (adv.) to what place?
πόμα, -τος, τό, drink
ποῦ, (adv.) where?
σῴζω/σώζω, save (from death)
χαλεπός, -ή, -όν, hard, grievous, difficult; dangerous
Ὦ, ὤ, (exclamation) oh!, O!; (w/ voc., simply an address)
ὡς, (conj.) how (heading an exclamation); (+ fut. part. expresses [the alleged] purp.)

---

1 ἀπάγουσι sc. αὐτούς; note that some later Gk. texts, like this one, do not always have movable ν where one would usu. expect it

2 ποῦ = ποῖ; in later Gk., the adv. of place where (ποῦ) absorbed the meaning of the adv. of place to which (ποῖ) (cf. BDF § 103); cf. archaic English "whither" w/ "where"

3 αἱ μὲν...αἱ δὲ sc. ἀπάγουσιν αὐτούς w/ both cls. Jerram (28) notes that they do this "because, though some opinions may be right, they are mere opinions, not knowledge. So desires (ἐπιθυμίαι) may be good or bad, but they are dangerous because of their uncertainty."
εἰς τὸ σῴζεσθαι...τὸ ἀπόλλυσθαι εἰς + acc. (here, two articular infs.; Smyth § 2025, 2034b) can express purp. (Smyth § 1686d); lit., "for the purpose of salvation...for the purpose of destruction," i.e., to save (them)...to destroy (them)

5 ὡς χαλεπὸν τὸ πόμα sc. ἐστί

6-7 ὡς...ἄξουσαι sc. αὐτούς; ὡς + fut. part. expresses purp. and "sets forth the ground of belief on which the agent acts, and denotes the thought, assertion, real or presumed intention, in the mind of the subject of the principal verb or of some other person mentioned prominently in the sentence, without implicating the speaker or writer." (Smyth § 2086); often ὡς, as in this case, may be rendered as "allegedly," "as if intending," "w/ the avowed intention of," etc.

1 πλάνον, ὃν πεπώκασι παρὰ τῆς Ἀπάτης, οὐχ εὑρίσκουσι ποία ἐστὶν ἡ ἀληθινὴ

2 ὁδὸς ἡ ἐν τῷ Βίῳ, ἀλλὰ πλανῶνται εἰκῆ, ὥσπερ ὁρᾷς καὶ τοὺς πρότερον

3 εἰσπορευομένους, ὡς περιάγονται ὅποι ἂν τύχῃ.

4 [7] Ξένος: Ὁρῶ τούτους, ἔφην. ἡ δὲ γυνὴ ἐκείνη τίς ἐστιν, ἡ ὥσπερ

5 τυφλή καὶ μαινομένη τις εἶναι δοκοῦσα, καὶ ἑστηκυῖα ἐπὶ λίθου τινὸς

6 στρογγύλου;

7 Πρεσβύτης: Καλεῖται μὲν, ἔφη, Τύχη· ἐστὶ δὲ οὐ μόνον τυφλὴ καὶ

8 μαινομένη, ἀλλὰ καὶ κωφή.

9 Ξένος: Αὕτη οὖν τί ἔργον ἔχει;

ἀληθινός, -όν, true
ἀπάτη, ἡ, deceit, deception
βίος, ὁ, life
γυνή, γυναικός, ἡ, woman
δοκέω, seem to (+ inf.)
εἰκῆ, (adv.) recklessly, rashly, w/out plan or purpose, aimlessly
εἰσπορεύω, lead in; (pass.) enter
ἐκεῖνος, ἐκείνη, ἐκεῖνο, that, he, she, it; (pl.) those, they
ἐπί, (prep. + gen.) on, upon
ἔργον, τό, work, task
εὑρίσκω, find, discover
ἵστημι, make X (acc.) stand; (perf. act., mid./pass.) stand
καλέω, call, name
κωφός, -ή, -όν, mute, deaf
λίθος, ὁ, stone
μαίνομαι, rave, be mad or insane
μόνος, -η, -ον, alone; μόνον, (adv.) only
ὁδός, -οῦ, ἡ, way, path, road

ὅποι, (adv.) to which place, to what place, where
ὁράω/ὁρῶ, see
ὅς, ἥ, ὅ, (rel. pron.) who, whose, whom,
παρά, (prep. + gen.) from
περιάγω, lead X (acc.) around; (mid.) travel about in various directions
πλανάω, make X wander; lead X astray; deceive X; (pass.), wander, stray
πλάνος, ὁ, error
ποῖος, -οία, -οῖον, of what sort or kind?
πρότερος, -έρα, -ερον, former; πρότερον/τὸ πρότερον, (adv.) previously
στρογγύλος, -η, -ον, round
τυγχάνω, τεύξομαι, ἔτυχον, happen to be at (a place); (3rd sing. often is used impersonally) it happens, it chances (to be)
τυφλός, -ή, -όν, blind
τύχη, ἡ, fortune, luck, chance
ὡς, (conj.) that; how (i.e., in what manner)
ὥσπερ, (adv.) as, just as, in the way in which; as if; like

---

1 πεπώκασι 3rd pl. perf. act. indic. < πίνω

2-3 τοὺς πρότερον εἰσπορευομένους "those who have previously entered"; the pres. part. is here thrown temporally backward by the force of the adv., making a perf. tense

3 ὅποι ἂν τύχῃ pres. general cl. w/ ἄν + aor. subju.; lit., "to wherever it happens (to them)," i.e., at random

5 ἑστηκυῖα fem. nom. sing. perf. (w/ pres sense) act. part. < ἵστημι; for the force of the tense, see note to ἑστώς on p. 14, lines 2-3

7 Τύχη beginning in the Hellenistic period, the cult of Τύχη (Latin *Fortuna*) became increasingly popular. At first venerated as a city deity, responsible for its fortune and prosperity, Τύχη's influence was soon believed to also extend to individuals. A survivor

Πρεσβύτης: Περιπορεύεται πανταχοῦ, ἔφη· καὶ παρ' ὧν μὲν ἁρπάζει τὰ 1
ὑπάρχοντα καὶ ἑτέροις δίδωσι· παρὰ δὲ τῶν αὐτῶν πάλιν ἀφαιρεῖται 2
παραχρῆμα ἃ δέδωκε καὶ ἄλλοις δίδωσιν εἰκῇ καὶ ἀβεβαίως. διὸ καὶ τὸ σημεῖον 3
καλῶς μηνύει τὴν φύσιν αὐτῆς. 4

Ξένος: Ποῖον τοῦτο; ἔφην ἐγώ. 5

Πρεσβύτης: Ὅτι ἐπὶ λίθου στρογγύλου ἕστηκεν. 6

Ξένος: Εἶτα τί τοῦτο σημαίνει; 7

Πρεσβύτης: Οὐκ ἀσφαλὴς οὐδὲ βεβαία ἐστὶν ἡ παρ' αὐτῆς δόσις. 8
ἐκπτώσεις γὰρ μεγάλαι καὶ σκληραὶ γίνονται, ὅταν τις αὐτῇ πιστεύσῃ. 9

ἀβεβαίως, (adv.) in a fickle manner, unreliably, w/ no security
ἄλλος, -η, -ο, other
ἁρπάζω, -άσω, snatch (away), rob, steal
ἀσφαλής, -ές, safe, secure
αὐτός, -ή, -όν, he, she, it; himself, herself, itself; (pl.) they; themselves; ὁ αὐτός, the same
ἀφαιρέω, take away, rob; (mid.) take away (for oneself)
βέβαιος, -αία, -ον, stable, constant, secure, certain
γί(γ)νομαι, take place, come to pass, happen
δίδωμι, give
διό, (conj.; = δι[ά] ὅ, on account of which thing) wherefore, for which reason, therefore
δόσις, -εως, ἡ, gift
εἶτα, (adv.) and so, then, therefore; (used in questions to express surprise or sarcasm) and then...? and so...?

ἔκπτωσις, -εως, ἡ, falling out (of one's hope), disappointment; failure; calamity
ἕτερος, -έρα, -ερον, other
καλῶς, (adv.) rightly, aptly
μέγας, μεγάλη, μέγα, great
μηνύω, reveal
ὅταν, ([ὅτε + ἄν], conj. adv.) whenever (+ subju.)
ὅτι, (conj.) that
οὐδέ, (conj.) and not
πάλιν, (adv.) back, again, in turn
πανταχοῦ, (adv.) everywhere
παραχρῆμα, (adv.) immediately
περιπορεύομαι, go around
σημαίνω, signify
σημεῖον, -ου, τό, sign
σκληρός, -ά, -όν, hard, harsh, bitter
ὑπάρχω, begin; belong; τὰ ὑπάρχοντα, goods, belongings, possessions
φύσις, -εως, ἡ, nature, natural disposition, inherent character

---

of Christianity, Τύχη/*Fortuna* was a popular (allegorical) figure in the Middle Ages and Renaissance. Note that verb forms of this noun have already appeared throughout the *Tablet* (e.g., on this page, τύχῃ; as the very first word of the text, Ἐτυγχάνομεν)

1 παρ' ὧν μέν lit., "from which ones some [of these]," i.e., from some of these

2 παρὰ...τῶν αὐτῶν "from the same people/ones" (referring to ἑτέροις); αὐτός, -ή, -όν in the attributive position = "the same" (Smyth § 1163, 1173, 1204, 1210)

3 ἃ sc. ἐκεῖνα as antecedent (the demonstrative pron. antecedent to a rel. pron. is often omitted; Smyth § 2509)
δέδωκε 3rd sing. perf. act. indic. < δίδωμι

6 ἕστηκεν 3rd sing. perf. (w/ pres. sense) act. indic. < ἵστημι

9 πιστεύῃ pres. act. subju. in a pres. indef./gen. temp. cl.

1   [8] **Ξένος:** Ὁ δὲ [τῶν ἀνθρώπων] πολὺς ὄχλος οὗτος, ὁ περὶ αὐτὴν

2 ἑστηκὼς, τί βούλεται καὶ τίνες καλοῦνται;

3   **Πρεσβύτης:** Καλοῦνται μὲν οὗτοι Ἀπροβούλευτοι· αἰτοῦσι δὲ ἕκαστος

4 αὐτῶν ἃ ῥίπτει.

5   **Ξένος:** Πῶς οὖν οὐχ ὁμοίαν ἔχουσι τὴν μορφήν, αλλ' οἱ μὲν αὐτῶν δοκοῦσι

6 χαίρειν, οἱ δὲ ἀθυμοῦσιν ἐκτετακότες τὰς χεῖρας;

7   **Πρεσβύτης:** Οἱ μὲν δοκοῦντες, ἔφη, χαίρειν καὶ γελᾶν αὐτῶν, οἱ εἰληφότες

8 τι παρ' αὐτῆς εἰσίν· οὗτοι δὲ καὶ Ἀγαθὴν Τύχην αὐτὴν καλοῦσιν. οἱ δὲ δοκοῦντες

ἀγαθός, -ή, -όν, good
ἀθυμέω, be discouraged or disheartened, despair
αἰτέω, beg
ἀπροβούλευτος, -ον [ἀ-, not + προ-, before + βουλεύω, deliberate, plan], not planning or deliberating ahead, w/out forethought, heedless
βούλομαι, want
γελάω/γελῶ, laugh
δοκέω, seem to (+ inf.)
ἕκαστος, -η, -ον, each
ἐκτείνω, stretch out
ἵστημι, make X (acc.) stand; (perf. act., mid./pass.) stand

καλέω, call
λαμβάνω, take, receive
μορφή, ἡ, form, shape, appearance
ὅμοιος, -οία, -οιον, same, similar
ὄχλος, ὁ, crowd
παρά, (prep. + gen.) from
περί, (prep. + acc.) around
πολύς, πολλή, πολύ, much, great; (pl.) many
πῶς, (adv.) how?
ῥίπτω, throw
τύχη, ἡ, fortune
χαίρω, rejoice
χείρ, χειρός, ἡ, hand

---

2 ἑστηκώς see note to ἑστηκώς on p. 24, line 3

3 Ἀπροβούλευτοι Jerram (29) notes that: "According to Aristotle, Ethics iii. 3, βούλευσις, 'deliberation,' requires, first, the assumption of some end to be attained, secondly, the choice and pursuit of the best means thereto. These people, trusting merely to Fortune, have no definite aim in life, hence they are careless also as to means."

     αἰτοῦσι...ἕκαστος "with singular collective substantives denoting persons and with like words implying a plural, the verb may stand in the plural" (Smyth § 950-952); lit., "they beg, each one (of them)..."

4 ἃ sc. ἐκεῖνα as antecedent (see note to ἃ on preceding page, line 3)

5-6 οἱ μὲν αὐτῶν...οἱ δὲ "some of them...others"; αὐτῶν is partitive gen. (Smyth § 1306, 1310)

6 ἐκτετακότες masc. nom. pl. perf. act. part. < ἐκτείνω

7 γελᾶν (α-contract; γελά + ειν) pres. act. inf. < γελάω/γελῶ

     εἰληφότες masc. nom. pl. perf. act. part. < λαμβάνω

κλαίειν [καὶ ἐκτετακότες] εἰσὶ παρ' ὧν ἀφείλετο ἃ δέδωκε πρότερον αὐτοῖς.　　**1**

οὗτοι δὲ πάλιν αὐτὴν Κακὴν Τύχην καλοῦσι.　　**2**

Ξένος: Τίνα οὖν ἔστιν ἃ δίδωσιν αὐτοῖς, ὅτι οὕτως οἱ μὲν λαμβάνοντες　　**3**
χαίρουσιν, οἱ δὲ ἀποβάλλοντες κλαίουσι;　　**4**

Πρεσβύτης: Ταῦτα, ἔφη, ἃ παρὰ τοῖς πολλοῖς ἀνθρώποις δοκεῖ εἶναι　　**5**
ἀγαθά.　　**6**

Ξένος: Ταῦτ' οὖν τίνα ἐστί;　　**7**

Πρεσβύτης: Πλοῦτος δηλονότι καὶ δόξα καὶ εὐγένεια καὶ τέκνα καὶ　　**8**
τυραννίδες καὶ βασιλεῖαι καὶ τἆλλα ὅσα τούτοις παραπλήσια.　　**9**

Ξένος: Ταῦτα οὖν πῶς οὐκ ἔστιν ἀγαθά;　　**10**

Πρεσβύτης: Περὶ μὲν τούτων, ἔφη, καὶ αὖθις ἐκποιήσει διαλέγεσθαι. νῦν δὲ　　**11**
περὶ τὴν μυθολογίαν γινώμεθα.　　**12**

ἄλλος, -η, -ο, other; τὰ ἄλλα, (all) the other things, the rest
ἄνθρωπος, -ου, ὁ, human being
ἀποβάλλω, lose
αὖθις, (adv.) (of fut. time) later, again
ἀφαιρέω, ἀφαιρήσω, ἀφεῖλον, take away; (mid.) take away (for oneself)
βασιλεία, ἡ, kingdom
γί(γ)νομαι, become, be
δηλονότι [= δῆλόν (ἐστιν) ὅτι, it is quite clear that], (adv.) quite clearly, manifestly, plainly
διαλέγομαι, discuss
δίδωμι, give
δόξα, ἡ, (good) reputation
ἐκποιέω, make out of, bring out; (impers.) it suffices
εὐγένεια, ἡ, high birth, nobility
κακός, -ή, -όν, bad
κλαίω, cry, wail, lament

μυθολογία, ἡ, narrative (of a fable), tale, account; significance of a story or picture
νῦν, (adv.) now
ὅσος, -η, -ον, as great as, as much as; (pl.) as many as
ὅτι, (conj.) that
οὕτω(ς), (adv.) so
πάλιν, (adv.) back, again, in turn
παρά, (prep. + dat.) in the estimation of, among
παραπλήσιος, -ον, like, resembling (+ dat.)
περί, (prep. + gen.) concerning, about; (+ acc.) concerned w/
πλοῦτος, ὁ, wealth, riches
πρότερος, -έρα, -ερον, former; πρότερον/ τὸ πρότερον, (adv.) previously, earlier
πῶς, (adv.) how?
τέκνον, τό, child
τυραννίς, -ίδος, ἡ, sovereignty; despotism, despotic rule, tyranny

---

1 παρ' ὧν sc. ἐκεῖνοι as antecedent
ἀφείλετο sc. Τύχη as subj.
ἃ sc. ἐκεῖνα as antecedent (and in the following sentence as well)
δέδωκε see note to δέδωκε on p. 29, line 3

3 τίνα nom. neut. pl. subj. w/ sing. vb. (see note to ἔχοντα on p. 23, line 1)

9 τἆλλα = τὰ ἄλλα.

10 γινώμεθα 1st pl. pres. mid. (dep.) subju. < γί(γ)νομαι; hortatory subju. (Smyth § 1797): "let us be!" Take this vb. closely w/ περὶ

1   Ξένος: Ἔστω οὕτως.

2   [9] Πρεσβύτης: Ὁρᾷς οὖν, ὡς ἂν παρέλθῃς τὴν πύλην ταύτην, ἀνωτέρω

3   ἄλλον περίβολον, καὶ γυναῖκας ἔξω τοῦ περιβόλου ἑστηκυίας, κεκοσμημένας

4   ὥσπερ ἑταῖραι εἰώθασι;

5   Ξένος: Καὶ μάλα.

6   Πρεσβύτης: Αὗται τοίνυν, ἡ μὲν Ἀκρασία καλεῖται, ἡ δὲ Ἀσωτία, ἡ δὲ

7   Ἀπληστία, ἡ δὲ Κολακεία.

8   Ξένος: Τί οὖν ὧδε ἑστήκασιν αὗται;

9   Πρεσβύτης: Παρατηροῦσιν, ἔφη, τοὺς εἰληφότας τι παρὰ τῆς Τύχης.

10   Ξένος: Εἶτα τί;

ἀκρασία, ἡ, [ἀ-, w/out + κράτος, power]
    intemperance; lack of power or control
    over one's passions/desires
ἄλλος, -η, -ο, other, another
ἀνωτέρω, (comp. adv.) higher up
ἀσωτία, ἡ, [ἀ-, w/out + σῴζω, save or
    preserve] profligacy, wastefulness
ἔθω, εἴωθα (perf. as pres.) I am accustomed
εἶτα, (adv.) then, next
ἔξω, (adv./prep. + gen.) outside (of)
ἑταίρα, ἡ, [lit., female companion]
    courtesan
ἵστημι, make X (acc.) stand; (perf. act.,
    mid./pass.) stand
κοσμέω, adorn

μάλα, (adv.) very, extremely; καὶ μάλα,
    certainly, yes
παρά, (prep. + gen.) from
παρατηρέω, watch closely
παρέρχομαι, παρελεύσομαι,
    παρῆλθον, pass by
περίβολος, ὁ, enclosure
πύλη, ἡ, gate
τοίνυν, (particle; in dialogue, to introduce an
    answer) well then
τύχη, ἡ, fortune
ὧδε, (adv.) here
ὡς, (conj.) + ἄν (+ subju.) when(ever), as
    soon as
ὥσπερ, (adv.) just as

---

1 ἔστω 3rd sing. pres. act. impera. < εἰμί: "let it be!"

2 ὡς ἂν παρέλθῃς an indef. temporal cl. (Smyth § 2394; ὡς is almost never used in
   Cl. Gk. w/ subju. or opt.)
   παρέλθῃς 2nd sing. aor. act. subju. < παρέρχομαι

3 ἑστηκυίας fem. acc. pl. perf. (w/ pres. sense) act. part. < ἵστημι
   κεκοσμημένας fem. acc. pl. perf. pass. part. < κοσμέω

4 εἰώθασι 3rd pl. perf. (w/ pres. sense) act. indic. < ἔθω

6 Ἀσωτία Jerram (29) notes that this is: "a very strong word, = utter 'profligacy,' past
   all hope of deliverance..."

8 ὧδε Jerram (29) notes that this word: "is properly an adverb of manner = 'thus,' but
   with verbs denoting *locality* it easily passes into an adverb of place."
   ἑστήκασιν 3rd pl. perf. (w/ pres. sense) act. indic. < ἵστημι

9 εἰληφότας cf. note to εἰληφότες on p. 30, line 7

10 Εἶτα τί; lit., "What then?", i.e., "What do they do next?," "Then what do they do?"

Πρεσβύτης: Ἀναπηδῶσι καὶ συμπλέκονται αὐτοῖς καὶ κολακεύουσι καὶ **1**
ἀξιοῦσι παρ' αὐταῖς μένειν, λέγουσαι ὅτι βίον ἕξουσιν ἡδύν τε καὶ ἄπονον καὶ **2**
κακοπάθειαν ἔχοντα οὐδεμίαν. ἐὰν οὖν τις πεισθῇ ὑπ' αὐτῶν εἰσελθεῖν εἰς τὴν **3**
Ἡδυπάθειαν, μέχρι μέν τινος ἡδεῖα δοκεῖ εἶναι ἡ διατριβή, ἕως ἂν γαργαλίζῃ **4**
τὸν ἄνθρωπον· εἶτ' οὐκέτι. ὅταν γὰρ ἀνανήψῃ, αἰσθάνεται ὅτι οὐκ ἤσθιεν, ἀλλ' **5**
ὑπ' αὐτῆς κατησθίετο καὶ ὑβρίζετο. διὸ καὶ ὅταν ἀναλώσῃ πάντα ὅσα ἔλαβε **6**

αἰσθάνομαι, perceive, realize
ἀναλίσκω, ἀναλώσω, ἀνήλωσα,
  squander, used up, spend
ἀνανήφω, ἀνανήψω, ἀνένηψα, regain
  one's senses, come to one's senses; become
  sober again
ἀναπηδάω, jump or leap up
ἄνθρωπος, ὁ, human being
ἀξιόω, urge, ask, think X (acc.) worthy
ἄπονος, -ον, free from toil, painless
γαργαλίζω, tickle, titillate
διατριβή, -ῆς, ἡ, way of spending time;
  pastime, diversion, amusement
διό, (conj.; = δι[ά] ὅ, on account of which
  thing) wherefore, for which reason,
  therefore
δοκέω, seem to (+ inf.)
ἐάν, (conj. =) εἰ ἄν, if (ever) (+ subju.)
εἰσέρχομαι, εἰσελεύσομαι, εἰσῆλθον, go
  or enter into
ἐσθίω, eat
ἔχω, ἕξω, ἔσχον, have
ἕως, (conj.) until, as long as; (+ ἄν w/ subju.
  = a gen. temporal cl.), as long as, so long as
ἡδυπάθεια, ἡ, [lit., pleasant experience]
  luxury

ἡδύς, -εῖα, -ύ, sweet, pleasant
κακοπάθεια, ἡ, [lit., bad experience]
  distress, misery, hardship
κατεσθίω, devour
κολακεύω, flatter
λαμβάνω, λήψομαι, ἔλαβον, take
λέγω, say
μένω, remain
μέχρι, (adv./prep. + gen.) until
ὅσος, -η, -ον, as great as, as much as; (pl.)
  as many as; πάντα ὅσα, all that
ὅταν, (conj. adv.) whenever (+ subju.; a gen.
  temporal cl.)
ὅτι, (conj.) that
οὐδείς, οὐδεμία, οὐδέν, no one, nothing;
  no
οὐκέτι, (adv.) no longer
παρά, (prep. + gen.) from; (+ dat.) among,
  with
πείθω, persuade
συμπλέκω, twine together; (mid./pass.)
  embrace (+ dat.)
ὑβρίζω, violate, maltreat, outrage, treat
  insultingly
ὑπό, (prep. + gen.) by

---

2 αὐταῖς = ἑαυταῖς

3-4 ἐάν...πεισθῇ...δοκεῖ pres. gen. condit. (see note to ἐάν...μὴ συνιῇ ἀπόλλυται
on p. 22, line 1)
πεισθῇ 3rd sing. aor. pass. subju. < πείθω

4 μέχρι μέν τινος sc. χρόνου: "up to a certain (time)," i.e., up to a certain point; μέν
here is answered not by a δέ, but by εἶτ' (= εἶτα)

5 ἀνανήψῃ 3rd sing. aor. act. subju. < ἀνανήφω; subju. in a pres. gen. temp. cl.
introduced by ὅταν (so too ἐπιλίπῃ later in this paragraph)

1 παρὰ τῆς Τύχης, ἀναγκάζεται ταύταις ταῖς γυναιξὶ δουλεύειν καὶ πάνθ'

2 ὑπομένειν καὶ ἀσχημονεῖν καὶ ποιεῖν ἕνεκεν τούτων πάνθ' ὅσα ἐστὶ βλαβερά,

3 οἶον ἀποστερεῖν, ἱεροσυλεῖν, ἐπιορκεῖν, προδιδόναι, ληΐζεσθαι, καὶ πάνθ' ὅσα

4 τούτοις παραπλήσια. ὅταν οὖν πάντα αὐτοῖς ἐπιλίπῃ, παραδίδονται τῇ

5 Τιμωρίᾳ.

6 **[10] Ξένος:** Ποία δέ ἐστιν αὕτη;

7 **Πρεσβύτης:** Ὁρᾷς ὀπίσω τι, ἔφη, αὐτῶν ἄνω ὥσπερ θυρίον μικρὸν καὶ

8 τόπον στενόν τινα καὶ σκοτεινόν;

9 **Ξένος:** [Καὶ μάλα.]

10 **Πρεσβύτης:** Οὐκοῦν καὶ γυναῖκες αἰσχραὶ καὶ ῥυπαραὶ καὶ ῥάκη

11 ἠμφιεσμέναι δοκοῦσι συνεῖναι;

αἰσχρός, -ά, -όν, shameful; ugly
ἀμφιέννυμι, put around or on; (pass.) clothed in, wearing
ἀναγκάζω, force, constrain, compel
ἄνω, (adv.) upward, up above
ἀποστερέω, plunder; rob, steal; defraud
ἀσχημονέω, behave indecently, behave in an unseemly manner, act disgracefully
βλαβερός, -ά, -όν, harmful, injurious
δουλεύω, be a slave to X (dat.), serve X (dat.) as a slave
ἕνεκα/ἕνεκεν, (prep. + gen.) for the sake of
ἐπιλείπω, ἐπιλείψω, ἐπέλιπον, fail X (dat.), run out for X (dat.)
ἐπιορκέω, commit perjury, swear falsely
θύριον, τό, [dim. of ἡ θύρα] small door
ἱεροσυλέω, -ήσω, rob a temple, desecrate
ληΐζομαι, plunder, despoil, pillage
μάλα, (adv.) very, extremely; καὶ μάλα, certainly, yes
μικρός, -ά, -όν, small
οἶος, οἴα, οἶον, of which kind or sort, οἶον, (acc. of respect as adv.) such as, for example

ὀπίσω, (adv./prep. + gen.) behind
οὐκοῦν, (adv.) then...don't...? (introducing a question that expects the answer "yes" and carries the thought forward from a previous assent; cf. οὔκουν, certainly not; so...not)
παρά, (prep. + gen.) from
παραδίδωμι, deliver
παραπλήσιος, -ον, like, similar to (+ dat.)
ποιέω, do
ποῖος, -οία, -οῖον, what sort or kind of?, of what sort or kind?
προδίδωμι, betray, commit treason
ῥάκος, -ους, τό, rag
ῥυπαρός, -ά, -όν, filthy, dirty
σκοτεινός, -ή, -όν, dark
στενός, -ή, -όν, narrow
σύνειμι, be together, congregate
τιμωρία, ἡ, retribution, punishment
τόπος, ὁ, place
τύχη, ἡ, fortune
ὑπομένω, submit to, endure
ὥσπερ, (adv.) like

---

4 πάντα nom. neut. pl. subj. w/ sing. vb. (see note to ἔχοντα on p. 23, line 1)

6 αὕτη i.e., ἡ Τιμωρία

7 τι could be either adv. ("somewhat," "a little," "a bit") w/ ὀπίσω or indef. pron. dir. obj. of Ὁρᾷς; here, both work

11 ἠμφιεσμέναι fem. nom. pl. perf. pass. part. < ἀμφιέννυμι; this vb. augments its prefix, not its stem, something which happens w/ vbs. that are not often used except as compounds (Smyth § 450)

Ξένος: Καὶ μάλα.　　1

Πρεσβύτης: Αὗται τοίνυν, ἔφη, ἡ μὲν τὴν μάστιγα ἔχουσα καλεῖται　2
Τιμωρία, ἡ δὲ τὴν κεφαλὴν ἐν τοῖς γόνασιν ἔχουσα Λύπη, ἡ δὲ τὰς τρίχας　3
τίλλουσα ἑαυτῆς Ὀδύνη.　4

Ξένος: Ὁ δὲ ἄλλος οὗτος, ὁ παρεστηκὼς αὐταῖς, δυσειδής τις καὶ λεπτὸς　5
καὶ γυμνός, καὶ μετ᾽ αὐτοῦ τις ἄλλη ὁμοία αὐτῷ, αἰσχρὰ καὶ λεπτή· τίς ἐστιν;　6

Πρεσβύτης: Ὁ μὲν Ὀδυρμὸς καλεῖται, ἔφη, ἡ δὲ Ἀθυμία· ἀδελφὴ δ᾽ ἐστὶν　7
αὕτη αὐτοῦ. τούτοις οὖν παραδίδοται καὶ μετὰ τούτων συμβιοῖ τιμωρούμενος.　8
εἶτα ἐνταῦθα πάλιν εἰς τὸν ἕτερον οἶκον ῥίπτεται, εἰς τὴν Κακοδαιμονίαν, καὶ　9
ὧδε τὸν λοιπὸν βίον καταστρέφει ἐν πάσῃ κακοδαιμονίᾳ, ἂν μὴ ἡ Μετάνοια　10
αὐτῷ ἐπιτύχῃ ἐκ προαιρέσεως συναντήσασα.　11

ἀδελφή, ἡ, sister
ἀθυμία, ἡ, dejection, despair, despondency, discouragement
ἄλλος, -η, -ο, other
ἄν, (contraction of εἰ ἄν); + μή, unless, if...does not
γόνυ, γόνατος, τό, knee
γυμνός, -ή, -όν, naked
δυσειδής, -ές, [δυσ-, un-, mis-, bad + εἶδος, form, figure] misshapen, deformed, ugly
ἑαυτοῦ, -ῆς, -οῦ, himself, herself, itself; (pl.) themselves
εἶτα, (adv.) then, next
ἐνταῦθα, (adv.) at this point, then
ἐπιτυγχάνω, ἐπιτεύξομαι, ἐπέτυχον, meet up w/ (+ dat.); (+ supplementary part.) succeed in X, happen to X
θρίξ, τριχός, ἡ, hair
κακοδαιμονία, ἡ, [lit., bad-spiritedness, bad fortune] unhappiness
καταστρέφω, bring to an end
κεφαλή, ἡ, head
λεπτός, -ή, -όν, thin, gaunt, emaciated
λοιπός, -ή, -όν, remaining, the rest

λύπη, ἡ, pain (of body or mind); grief
μάστιξ, -γος, ἡ, whip, lash
μετά, (prep. + gen.) with
μετάνοια, ἡ, [μετα-, change + νοῦς, mind] repentance
ὀδύνη, ἡ, pain (of body or mind); grief; distress
ὀδυρμός, ὁ, lamentation, complaining
ὅμοιος, -οία, -οιον, like, similar to (+ dat.)
παρίστημι, make to stand by or alongside; (perf. act., pass.) stand by, beside, or near X (dat.)
προαίρεσις, -εως, ἡ, choosing (one thing) before (another); choice; purpose
συμβιόω, live w/
συναντάω, συναντήσω, συνήντησα, encounter, meet or meet w/ (+ dat.)
τίλλω, pull or pluck out
τιμωρέω, punish
τοίνυν, (particle) [τοι + νυν], therefore, accordingly; (in dialogue, to introduce an answer) well then
ὧδε, (adv.) here

---

2 Αὗται "(Of) these"; this is an example of the partitive apposition (Smyth § 981)

5 παρεστηκὼς masc. nom. sing. perf. (w/ pres. sense) act. part. < παρίστημι

8-9 παραδίδοται...συμβιοῖ...ῥίπτεται sc. one/a person as subj.

10-11 ἂν...ἐπιτύχῃ protasis (i.e., the "if" cl.) of a pres. gen. condit.

10 Μετάνοια later called Μεταμέλεια in 35

11 ἐκ προαιρέσεως lit., "from [her own] choice," i.e., purposely, deliberately

1   **[11] Ξένος:** Εἶτα τί γίνεται, ἐὰν ἡ Μετάνοια αὐτῷ συναντήσῃ;

2   **Πρεσβύτης:** Ἐξαιρεῖ αὐτὸν ἐκ τῶν κακῶν καὶ συνίστησιν αὐτῷ ἑτέραν

3   Δόξαν [καὶ Ἐπιθυμίαν] τὴν εἰς τὴν Ἀληθινὴν Παιδείαν ἄγουσαν, ἅμα δὲ καὶ τὴν

4   εἰς τὴν Ψευδοπαιδείαν καλουμένην.

5   **Ξένος:** Εἶτα τί γίνεται;

6   **Πρεσβύτης:** Ἐὰν μὲν, φησὶ, τὴν Δόξαν ταύτην προσδέξηται, τὴν ἄξουσαν

7   αὐτὸν εἰς τὴν Ἀληθινὴν Παιδείαν, καθαρθεὶς ὑπ' αὐτῆς σώζεται, καὶ μακάριος

8   καὶ εὐδαίμων γίνεται ἐν τῷ βίῳ· εἰ δὲ μὴ, πάλιν πλανᾶται ὑπὸ τῆς

9   Ψευδοδοξίας.

ἄγω, ἄξω, ἤγαγον, lead
ἀληθινός, -όν, true
ἅμα, (adv.) at the same time
γί(γ)νομαι, become, be; (3rd sing. often =)
  happens
δόξα, ἡ, opinion
ἐάν, (conj. =) εἰ ἄν, if (ever) (+ subju.)
ἐκ/ἐξ, (prep. + gen.) from
ἐξαιρέω, remove, take or pull out
ἐπιθυμία, ἡ, desire
ἕτερος, -έρα, -ερον, another
εὐδαίμων, -ον, happy
καθαίρω, καθαρῶ, ἐκάθηρα, cleanse,
  purify
κακός, -ή, -όν, bad, evil; τὰ κακά, evils,
  ills

μακάριος, -ία, -ον, blessed
μετάνοια, ἡ, [μετα-, change + νοῦς, mind]
  repentance
παιδεία, ἡ, education
πάλιν, (adv.) back, again, in turn
πλανάω, make X (acc.) wander; lead X
  (acc.) astray
προσδέχομαι, προσδέξομαι,
  προσεδεξάμην, receive (favorably),
  accept
συναντάω, συναντήσω, συνήντησα,
  encounter, meet or meet w/ (+ dat.)
συνίστημι, introduce to Y (dat.) X (acc.)
σῴζω/σώζω, save
ὑπό, (prep. + gen.) by
Ψευδοπαιδεία, ἡ, False Education

---

1 συναντήσῃ 3rd sing. aor. act. subju. < συναντάω; subju. in the protasis of a pres. gen. condit.

2-3 ἑτέραν δόξαν i.e., a *good* opinion, as opposed to the bad one, mentioned in the next line, afterwards called Ψευδοπαιδεία

3-4 τὴν εἰς τὴν Ψευδοπαιδείαν καλουμένην = [sc. συνίστησιν αὐτῷ ἑτέραν Δόξαν καὶ Ἐπιθυμίαν] τὴν [sc. ἄγουσαν αὐτὸν] εἰς τὴν Ψευδοπαιδείαν καλουμένην καλουμένην the pass. part. of καλέω often has the sense of "so-called," or is used to introduce a new word (here, e.g., "her whom we will call")
Ψευδοπαιδείαν the first appearance of this word in Gk.

6 προσδέξηται 3rd sing. aor. act. subju. < προσδέχομαι; subju. in the protasis of a pres. gen. condit.

[12] Ξένος: Ὦ Ἡράκλεις, ὡς μέγας ὁ κίνδυνος ἄλλος οὗτος. Ἡ δὲ 1
Ψευδοπαιδεία, ποία ἐστίν; ἔφην ἐγώ. 2

Πρεσβύτης: Οὐχ ὁρᾷς τὸν ἕτερον περίβολον ἐκεῖνον; 3

Ξένος: Καὶ μάλα, ἔφην ἐγώ. 4

Πρεσβύτης: Οὐκοῦν ἔξω τοῦ περιβόλου παρὰ τὴν εἴσοδον γυνή ἔστηκεν, ἣ 5
δοκεῖ πάνυ καθάριος καὶ εὔτακτος εἶναι; 6

Ξένος: Καὶ μάλα. 7

Πρεσβύτης: Ταύτην τοίνυν οἱ πολλοὶ καὶ εἰκαῖοι τῶν ἀνδρῶν Παιδείαν 8
καλοῦσιν· οὐκ ἔστι δὲ, ἀλλὰ Ψευδοπαιδεία, ἔφη. οἱ μέν τοι σωζόμενοι, ὁπόταν 9
βούλωνται εἰς τὴν Ἀληθινὴν Παιδείαν ἐλθεῖν, ὧδε πρῶτον παραγίνονται. 10

ἀληθινός, -όν, true
βούλομαι, wish, want (+ inf.)
εἰκαῖος, -αία, -αῖον, heedless, reckless,
  purposeless, rash
εἴσοδος, ἡ, entrance
ἐκεῖνος, ἐκείνη, ἐκεῖνο, that, he, she, it;
  (pl.) those, they
ἔξω, (adv./prep. + gen.) outside (of)
ἐπί, (prep. + acc.) to, toward
ἔρχομαι, ἐλεύσομαι, ἦλθον, go, come
εὔτακτος, (lit., well-ordered, well-arranged)
  well-behaved, disciplined
καθάριος, -ον, clean, pure; elegant,
  refined; decent, respectable
κίνδυνος, ὁ, danger
μάλα, (adv.) very, altogether; καὶ μάλα,
  certainly, yes
μέγας, μεγάλη, μέγα, great
ὁπόταν, (adv. conj.) [ὁπότε + ἄν] whenever
  (+ subju.)

οὐκοῦν, (adv.) then...don't...? (introducing a
  question that expects the answer "yes" and
  carries the thought forward from a previous
  assent; cf. οὔκουν, certainly not; so...not)
παιδεία, ἡ, education
παρά, (prep. + acc.) beside, near, by
παραγί(γ)νομαι, arrive
περίβολος, -ου, ὁ, enclosure
πρῶτος, -η, -ον, first; πρῶτον, (adv.)
  first, first of all
σώζω/σῴζω, save
τοι, (particle) in truth, indeed
τοίνυν, (particle) [τοι + νυν], therefore,
  accordingly; (in dialogue, to introduce an
  answer) well then
Ὦ, ὤ, oh!, O!
ὧδε, (adv.) here
ὡς, (conj.) how (heading an exclamation)

---

1 ὡς μέγας...οὗτος sc. ἐστί

5 ἕστηκεν 3rd sing. perf. (w/ pres. sense) act. indic. < ἵστημι

8 οἱ πολλοὶ καὶ εἰκαῖοι τῶν ἀνδρῶν in Gk., adjs. of quantity (e.g., πολύς, πολλή,
πολύ) in the pl. are often joined to another adj. by καί in the same construction,
whereas in English καί is not translated (Smyth § 2879). τῶν ἀνδρῶν partitive gen.;
in English, οἱ πολλοὶ καὶ εἰκαῖοι τῶν ἀνδρῶν = οἱ πολλοὶ εἰκαῖοι ἄνδρες

9 οὐκ ἔστι "She is not *really* so"; Jerram (31), who notes that when ἔστι is used in its
existential sense [note accent on the first syllable, as opposed to the enclitic ἐστί], it
either signifies existence [i.e., "X exists"] or else has a marked emphasis, as here

10 ἐλθεῖν aor. act. inf. < ἔρχομαι

1   Πρεσβύτης: [Οὐκ] ἔστιν, ἔφη.

2   Ξένος: Πότερον οὖν ἄλλη ὁδὸς οὐκ ἔστιν ἐπὶ τὴν Ἀληθινὴν Παιδείαν
3   ἄγουσα;

4   [13] Ξένος: Οὗτοι δὲ οἱ ἄνθρωποι, οἱ ἔσω τοῦ περιβόλου ἀνακάμπτοντες,
5   τίνες εἰσίν;

6   Πρεσβύτης: Οἱ τῆς Ψευδοπαιδείας, ἔφη, ἐρασταὶ, ἠπατημένοι καὶ οἰόμενοι
7   μετὰ τῆς Ἀληθινῆς Παιδείας συνομιλεῖν.

8   Ξένος: Τίνες οὖν καλοῦνται οὗτοι;

9   Πρεσβύτης: Οἱ μὲν Ποιηταί, ἔφη, οἱ δὲ Ῥήτορες, οἱ δὲ Διαλεκτικοί, οἱ δὲ
10   Μουσικοί, οἱ δὲ Ἀριθμητικοί, οἱ δὲ Γεωμέτραι, οἱ δὲ Ἀστρολόγοι, οἱ δὲ Κριτικοί,

---

ἀληθινός, -όν, true
ἀνακάμπτω, walk back and forth, wander
ἄνθρωπος, ὁ, human being
ἀπατάω, deceive
ἀριθμητικός, ὁ, one skilled in numbers,
   mathematician
ἀστρολόγος, ὁ, one skilled in astronomy,
   astronomer.
γεωμέτρης, γεωμέτρου, ὁ, measurer of
   land; one skilled in geometry, geometer,
   geometrician
διαλεκτικός, διαλεκτικοῦ, ὁ, one skilled
   in logical argument, dialectician
ἐραστής, -οῦ, ὁ, lover, devotee
ἔσω, (adv./prep. + gen.) inside
κριτικός, ὁ, one skilled in judging; scholar;
   grammarian; literary critic

μετά, (prep. + gen.) with
μουσικός, ὁ, one skilled in music, musician
ὁδός, ἡ, way, path, road
οἴομαι, think
παιδεία, ἡ, education
περίβολος, ὁ, enclosure
ποιητής, -οῦ, ὁ, poet
πότερος, -έρα, -ερον, which of the two?
   πότερον...ἤ, whether...or; πότερον,
   (as an interr. adv. introducing a dir. quest., it
   is not translated)
ῥήτωρ, -ορος, ὁ, orator, professional
   teacher of oratory
συνομιλέω, associate (w/)
Ψευδοπαιδεία, ἡ, False Education

---

6 ἠπατημένοι masc. nom. pl. perf. pass. part. < ἀπατάω

9-10 οἱ μὲν...οἱ δὲ...οἱ δὲ... "some (are called)...others (are called)...etc." Jerram (31) notes that: "...the exclusion of poets, orators, etc., from the highest place is consistent with what is said in Chap. XXXIII, that the arts and sciences do not make men *good*. And since Virtue dwells with True Learning (Chap. XVII, XVIII, XX) these men of science, so long as they seek nothing beyond, are necessarily companions of False Learning." The list provided in this section, excepting the last two types (Ἡδονικοί, Περιπατητικοί), made up the traditional Hellenistic "liberal arts and sciences" (called in Gk. ἐγκύκλιος παιδεία, lit., "in a circle education" < ἐγκύκλιος = "circular," "recurrent" [i.e., required regularly, general] + παιδεία, "education," "child-rearing"; through a Latin copyist's error, this two-word Gk. phrase was written as a single word: "encyclopedia").

οἱ δὲ Ἡδονικοί, οἱ δὲ Περιπατητικοὶ καὶ ὅσοι ἄλλοι τούτοις εἰσὶ παραπλήσιοι.　　**1**

[14] **Ξένος**: Αἱ δὲ γυναῖκες ἐκεῖναι, αἱ δοκοῦσαι περιτρέχειν ὅμοιαι ταῖς　　**2**

πρώταις, ἐν αἷς ἔφης εἶναι τὴν Ἀκρασίαν [καὶ ἄλλαι αἱ μετ' αὐτῶν], τίνες εἰσίν;　　**3**

　　Πρεσβύτης: Αὗται ἐκεῖναί εἰσιν, ἔφη.　　**4**

　　Ξένος: Πότερον οὖν καὶ ὧδε εἰσπορεύονται;　　**5**

　　Πρεσβύτης: Νὴ Δία, καὶ ὧδε· σπανίως δὲ, καὶ οὐχὶ ὥσπερ ἐν τῷ πρώτῳ　　**6**

περιβόλῳ.　　**7**

　　Ξένος: Πότερον οὖν καὶ αἱ Δόξαι; ἔφην.　　**8**

　　Πρεσβύτης: Μένει γὰρ καὶ ἐν τούτοις τὸ πόμα, ὃ ἔπιον παρὰ τῆς Ἀπάτης,　　**9**

ἀκρασία, ἡ, intemperance; lack of power or control over one's passions/desires
ἀπάτη, ἡ, deceit, deception
δόξα, ἡ, opinion
εἰσπορεύω, lead in; (pass.) enter
ἐκεῖνος, ἐκείνη, ἐκεῖνο, that, he, she, it; (pl.) those, they
Ζεύς, Διός, ὁ, Zeus
ἡδονικός, ὁ, one skilled in pleasures; hedonist; member of the Cyrenaic or the Epicurean school of philosophy
μένω, remain
μετά, (prep. + gen.) with
νή, (adv. of swearing) yes, by X! (acc.)

ὅμοιος, -οία, -οιον, like, similar to (+ dat.)
ὅσος, -η, -ον, as great as, as much as; (pl.) as many as
παρά, (prep. + gen.) from
παραπλήσιος, -ον, like, similar to (+ dat.)
περιπατητικός, ὁ, one walking about (while teaching); peripatetic; member of the Aristotelian school of philosophy
περιτρέχω, run around
πίνω, πίομαι, ἔπιον, drink
πόμα, -τος, τό, drink
πρῶτος, -η, -ον, first
σπανίως, (adv.) seldom, rarely
ὧδε, (adv.) here

---

1 Ἡδονικοί the Cyrenaic school of philosophy was founded by Aristippus, a disciple of Socrates, c. 370 BCE, and the addressee of Socrates' paraphrase of Prodicus' "Choice of Heracles" in Xenophon's *Memorabilia* 2.1.21-34 (see pp. 81ff.)

3 εἶναι τὴν Ἀκρασίαν acc. + inf. construction after a vb. of saying; the pres. inf. (εἶναι) represents the imperf. in indir. discourse after a past tense main vb. (Smyth § 2019)

4 αὗται ἐκεῖναί εἰσιν ἐκεῖναί is predicate: "They themselves are those women," i.e., They are those very same women (you just mentioned)

9 γὰρ "(yes,) for/because" (Denniston, 73)

1   καὶ ἡ ἄγνοια μένει [ἐν τούτοις, νὴ Δία,] καὶ μετ' αὐτῆς γε ἡ ἀφροσύνη· καὶ οὐ

2   μὴ ἀπέλθῃ ἀπ' αὐτῶν οὔθ' ἡ δόξα οὔθ' ἡ λοιπὴ κακία, μέχρις ἂν ἀπογνόντες τῆς

3   Ψευδοπαιδείας εἰσέλθωσιν εἰς τὴν ἀληθινὴν ὁδὸν καὶ πίωσι τὰς τούτων

4   καθαρτικὰς δυνάμεις. εἶτα, ὅταν καθαρθῶσι καὶ ἐκβάλωσι τὰ κακὰ πάνθ' ὅσα

5   ἔχουσι, καὶ τὰς δόξας καὶ τὴν ἄγνοιαν καὶ τὴν λοιπὴν κακίαν πᾶσαν, τότε δὴ

ἄγνοια, ἡ, ignorance
ἀληθινός, -όν, true
ἀπέρχομαι, ἀπελεύσομαι, ἀπῆλθον, depart, go away
ἀπό, (prep. + gen.) from
ἀπογι(γ)νώσκω, -γνώσομαι, reject, repudiate, renounce
ἀφροσύνη, ἡ, foolishness; mindlessness
γε, (particle) certainly, indeed
δή, (particle) certainly
δόξα, ἡ, opinion
δύναμις, -εως, ἡ, power
εἰσπορεύω, lead in; (pass.) enter
ἐκβάλλω, ἐκβαλῶ, ἐξέβαλον, cast forth
καθαίρω, καθαρῶ, ἐκάθηρα, cleanse, purify

καθαρτικός, -ή, -όν, purifying, purifying X (acc.) of Y (gen.)
κακία, ἡ, evil, vice, wickedness
κακός, -ή, -όν, bad, evil; τὰ κακά, evils
λοιπός, -ή, -όν, remaining
μέχρι, (conj.) until; (before a vowel =) μέχρις; (w/ ἄν + subju. = a gen. templ. cl.) until
ὁδός, -οῦ, ἡ, way, path, road
ὅσος, -η, -ον, as great as, as much as; (pl.) as many as
ὅταν, (conj. adv.) whenever (+ subju.)
οὔτε, (conj.) and not; οὔτε...οὔτε, neither...nor
παρά, (prep. + dat.) with
τότε, (adv.) then, at that time
Ψευδοπαιδεία, ἡ, False Education

1-2 οὐ μὴ ἀπέλθῃ "will *not* go away"; the subju., usu. aorist as here, is used w/ οὐ μή to express an emphatic neg. statement referring to the fut. (Smyth § 1804); note that though the subju. is a compound pl. (ἡ δόξα, ἡ λοιπὴ κακία), the vb. in Gk. can agree w/ the nearest of two or more subjs. (Smyth § 966)

2 οὔθ'...οὔθ' = οὔτε...οὔτε
  ἀπογνόντες masc. nom. pl. aor. act. part. < ἀπογι(γ)νώσκω

3 εἰσέλθωσιν 3rd pl. aor. act. subju. < εἰσέρχομαι; subju. in a gen. temp. cl. (so too πίωσι < πίνω)

3-4 τούτων καθαρτικας either "purifying (them) of these things," i.e., of the bad things mentioned in the previous lines (w/ τούτων being a gen. of separation; Smyth § 1392) or "their purifying powers" (w/ τούτων being a gen. of poss.; Smyth § 1297)

4 καθαρθῶσι 3rd pl. aor. act. subju. < καθαίρω; subju. in a gen. temp. cl. (so too ἐκβάλωσι < ἐκβάλλω)

5 τότε δὴ "at exactly this time"; "then, and not till then" (Jerram, 33); Parsons (71): "The common reading has ἄν after τότε in place of δή. Either reading makes a clear sentence, but ἄν is so rarely employed with the future indicative, that the text as given is to be preferred. With ἄν the sentence means they can on *no other condition* be saved; with δή the idea is they will be saved not until *that very time*."

οὕτω σωθήσονται. ὧδε δὲ μένοντες παρὰ τῇ Ψευδοπαιδείᾳ οὐδέποτε 1
ἀπολυθήσονται οὐδὲ ἐλλείψει αὐτοὺς κακὸν οὐδὲν ἕνεκα τούτων τῶν 2
μαθημάτων. 3

[15] **Ξένος**: Ποία οὖν αὕτη ἡ ὁδὸς ἔστιν, ἡ φέρουσα ἐπὶ τὴν Ἀληθινὴν 4
Παιδείαν; [ἔφην]. 5

Πρεσβύτης: Ὁρᾷς ἄνω, ἔφη, τόπον τινὰ ἐκεῖνον, ὅπου οὐδεὶς ἐπικατοικεῖ, 6
ἀλλ' ἔρημος δοκεῖ εἶναι; 7

Ξένος: Ὁρῶ. 8

Πρεσβύτης: Οὐκοῦν καὶ θύραν τινὰ μικρὰν καὶ ὁδόν τινα πρὸ τῆς θύρας, 9
ἥτις οὐ πολὺ ὀχλεῖται, ἀλλ' ὀλίγοι πάνυ πορεύονται, ὥσπερ δι' ἀνοδίας τινὸς 10
καὶ τραχείας καὶ πετρώδους εἶναι δοκούσης; 11

ἀνοδία, ἡ, trackless waste
ἄνω, (adv.) on high
ἀπολύω, ἀπολύσω, ἀπέλυσα, free, set
  free, release
διά, (prep. + gen.) through
ἐλλείπω, ἐλλείψω, leave
ἕνεκα, (prep. + gen.) as a result of
ἐπικατοικέω, (this word only occurs here in
  Gk.) inhabit, reside, dwell
ἔρημος, -η, -ον, desered, desolate
θύρα, ἡ, door
μάθημα, -ατος, τό, academic discipline,
  (field of) study
μένω, remain
μικρός, -ά, -όν, small
ὀλίγος, -η, -ον, few
ὅπου, (adv.) where
ὅστις, ἥτις, ὅ τι, whoever, who,
  whichever, which
οὐδέ, (conj.) and not, nor yet

οὐδείς, οὐδεμία, οὐδέν, no one, nothing;
  no
οὐδέποτε, (adv.) never
οὐκοῦν, (adv.) then...don't...? (introducing a
  question that expects the answer "yes" and
  carries the thought forward from a previous
  assent; cf. οὔκουν, certainly not; so...not)
οὕτω(ς), (adv.) thus
ὀχλέω, frequent, crowd, throng
παιδεία, ἡ, education
πάνυ, (adv.) (w/ adjs.) very
πετρώδης, -ες, rocky
πολύ, (adv.) much, very
πορεύω, carry; (pass.) travel, traverse,
  journey
πρό, (prep. + gen.) before
τόπος, ὁ, place
τραχύς, -εῖα, -ύ, rough
φέρω, bear, carry; (of roads) lead

---

2 οὐδέ...οὐδέν "nor...any"; "If in the same clause one or more *compound* negatives
  follow a negative with the same verb, the compound negative simply confirms the first
  negative." (Smyth § 2761)

2-3 τούτων τῶν μαθημάτων i.e., the teachings offered by those listed in Chaper 13

9 οὐκοῦν sc. ὁρᾷς

10 ἥτις = ἥ (BDAG s.v. ὅστις 3: "Quite often, ὅστις takes the place of the simple rel. ὅς,
  ἥ, ὅ ; this occurs occasionally in ancient Gk. usage..., but more frequently in later Gk.")

1   Ξένος: Καὶ μάλα, ἔφην.

2   Πρεσβύτης: Οὐκοῦν καὶ βουνός τις ὑψηλὸς δοκεῖ εἶναι καὶ ἀνάβασις στενὴ

3 πάνυ καὶ κρημνοὺς ἔχουσα ἔνθεν καὶ ἔνθεν βαθεῖς;

4   Ξένος: Ὁρῶ.

5   Πρεσβύτης: Αὕτη τοίνυν ἐστὶν ἡ ὁδός, ἔφη, ἡ ἄγουσα πρὸς τὴν Ἀληθινὴν

6 Παιδείαν.

7   Ξένος: Καὶ μάλα γε χαλεπὴ προσιδεῖν.

8   Πρεσβύτης: Οὐκοῦν καὶ ἄνω ἐπὶ τοῦ βουνοῦ ὁρᾷς πέτραν τινὰ μεγάλην

9 καὶ ὑψηλὴν καὶ κύκλῳ ἀπόκρημνον;

10   Ξένος: Ὁρῶ, ἔφην.

11 [16] Πρεσβύτης: Ὁρᾷς οὖν καὶ γυναῖκας δύο ἑστηκυίας ἐπὶ τῆς πέτρας,

12 λιπαρὰς καὶ εὐεκτούσας τῷ σώματι, ὡς ἐκτετάκασι τὰς χεῖρας προθύμως;

13   Ξένος: Ὁρῶ· ἀλλὰ τίνες καλοῦνται, ἔφην, αὗται;

ἀνάβασις, -εως, ἡ, ascent
ἄνω, (adv.) up, upward
ἀπόκρημνος, -ον, [ἀπο- + ὁ κρημνός, precipice] steep, precipitous
βαθύς, -εία, -ύ, deep, high, steep
βουνός, ὁ, hill
γε, (particle) certainly, indeed
δύο, two
ἐκτείνω, stretch out
ἔνθεν, (adv.) on the one side; ἔνθεν καὶ ἔνθεν, on this side and on that side, on both sides
ἐπί, (prep. + gen.) on, upon
εὐκεκτέω, be in good health or good condition, be healthy
κρημνός, ὁ, precipice
κύκλος, ὁ, circle; κύκλῳ, (adv.) in a circle, all around

λιπαρός, -ά, -όν, shining, radiant
μάλα, (adv.) very; καὶ μάλα, (lit., very much indeed [w/ καὶ as adv.]) certainly, yes
μέγας, μεγάλη, μέγα, great, big
παιδεία, ἡ, education
πέτρα, ἡ, rock, mass of rock, boulder, cliff
προθύμως, (adv.) eagerly
προσοράω, προσόψομαι, προσεῖδον, look at or upon
στενός, -ή, -όν, narrow
σῶμα, ατος, τό, body
ὑψηλός, -ή, -όν, high, lofty, towering
χαλεπός, -ή, -όν, hard, difficult
χείρ, χειρός, ἡ, hand
ὡς, (conj.) how (i.e., in what manner); that

---

7 χαλεπὴ προσιδεῖν sc. ἐστί; προσιδεῖν aor. act. epexegetic (i.e., "explanatory"/ limiting) inf. (Smyth § 2005) aor. < προσοράω, προσόψομαι, προσεῖδον, limiting the adj. χαλεπή: "it is difficult to look at/upon," i.e., it looks difficult

11 ἑστηκυίας fem. acc. pl. perf. (w/ pres. sense) act. part. < ἵστημι

12 τῷ σώματι dat. of respect (Smyth § 1516). In Cl. Gk., more common would be an acc. of respect (Smyth § 1600-1603)
ἐκτετάκασι 3rd pl. perf. (w/ pres. sense) act. indic. < ἐκτείνω

Πρεσβύτης: Ἡ μὲν Ἐγκράτεια καλεῖται, ἔφη, ἡ δὲ Καρτερία· εἰσι δὲ **1**
ἀδελφαί. **2**

Ξένος: Τί οὖν τὰς χεῖρας ἐκτετάκασιν οὕτω προθύμως; **3**

Πρεσβύτης: Παρακαλοῦσιν, ἔφη, τοὺς παραγινομένους ἐπὶ τὸν τόπον **4**
θαρρεῖν καὶ μὴ ἀποδειλιᾶν, λέγουσαι ὅτι βραχὺ ἔτι δεῖ καρτερῆσαι αὐτούς, εἶτα **5**
ἥξουσιν εἰς ὁδὸν καλήν. **6**

Ξένος: Ὅταν οὖν παραγένωνται ἐπὶ τὴν πέτραν, πῶς ἀναβαίνουσιν; ὁρῶ **7**
γὰρ ὁδὸν φέρουσαν οὐδεμίαν ἐπ᾽ αὐτάς. **8**

Πρεσβύτης: Αὗται ἀπὸ τοῦ κρημνοῦ προσκαταβαίνουσι καὶ ἕλκουσιν **9**
αὐτοὺς ἄνω πρὸς αὐτάς. εἶτα κελεύουσιν αὐτοὺς διαναπαύσασθαι· καὶ μετὰ **10**
μικρὸν διδόασιν ἰσχὺν καὶ θάρσος καὶ ἐπαγγέλονται αὐτοὺς καταστήσειν πρὸς **11**
τὴν Ἀληθινὴν Παιδείαν· καὶ δεικνύουσιν αὐτοῖς τὴν ὁδόν, ὡς ἔστι καλή τε καὶ **12**
ὁμαλὴ καὶ εὐπόρευτος καὶ καθαρὰ παντὸς κακοῦ, ὥσπερ ὁρᾷς. **13**

ἀδελφή, ἡ, sister
ἀναβαίνω, go up, ascend
ἀποδειλιάω, shrink back
βραχύ, (adv.) for a short time
δεῖ, (impers. vb.) it is necessary, one should (+ acc. and inf.)
δεικνύω, show
διαναπαύω, rest a while
δίδωμι, give
ἐγκράτεια, ἡ, self-control (esp. w/ regard to pleasure)
ἕλκω, pull, drag
ἐπαγγέλλω, announce, proclaim; (mid.) promise (unasked) (+ fut. inf.)
ἐπί, (prep. + acc.) to
ἔτι, (adv.) still, yet
εὐπόρευτος, -ον, easy to travel
ἥκω, ἥξω, (mostly w/ εἰς) have come to, be present at
θαρρέω, be confident
θάρσος, -ους, τό, daring, courage
ἰσχύς, -ύος, ἡ, strength, might

καθαρός, -ά, -όν, clean, pure; free of or from (+ gen.)
καθίστημι, καταστήσω, bring, bring back
καλός, -ή, -όν, good; beautiful
καρτερέω, be strong, endure
καρτερία, -ας, ἡ, endurance, patience; fortitude (in enduring pain)
κελεύω, bid, urge, command
λέγω, say
μετά, (prep. + acc.) after
μικρός, -ά, -όν, small; μετὰ μικρόν, a little after, after a short time
ὁμαλός, -ή, -όν, even, smooth
ὅταν, (conj. adv.) whenever (+ subju.)
παραγί(γ)νομαι, παραγενήσομαι, παρεγενόμην, arrive at, come to (+ ἐπί)
παρακαλέω, encourage, exhort
πέτρα, ἡ, rock, mass of rock, boulder, cliff
προσκαταβαίνω, descend (further); go down to meet
πῶς, (adv.) how?
φέρω, bear, carry; (of roads) lead

---

5 ἀποδειλιᾶν (α-contract; ἀποδειλιά + ειν) pres. act. inf. < ἀποδειλιάω

8 αὐτάς i.e., Ἐγκράτειαν and Καρτερίαν

10 αὐτάς = ἑαυτάς

11 καταστήσειν fut. act. inf. < καθίστημι; inf. in indir. statement w/ αὐτοὺς as its object

1   Ξένος: Ἐμφαίνει, νὴ Δία.

2   [17] Πρεσβύτης: Ὁρᾷς οὖν, ἔφη, καὶ ἔμπροσθεν τοῦ ἄλσους ἐκείνου

3   τόπον τινά, ὃς δοκεῖ καλός τε εἶναι καὶ λειμωνοειδὴς καὶ φωτὶ πολλῷ

4   καταλαμπόμενος;

5   Ξένος: Καὶ μάλα.

6   Πρεσβύτης: Κατανοεῖς οὖν ἐν μέσῳ τῷ λειμῶνι περίβολον ἕτερον καὶ

7   πύλην ἑτέραν;

8   Ξένος: Ἔστιν οὕτως. ἀλλὰ τίς καλεῖται ὁ τόπος οὗτος;

9   Πρεσβύτης: Εὐδαιμόνων οἰκητήριον, ἔφη· ὧδε γὰρ διατρίβουσιν αἱ Ἀρεταὶ

10   πᾶσαι καὶ ἡ Εὐδαιμονία.

11   Ξένος: Εἶεν, ἔφην ἐγώ, ὡς καλὸν λέγεις τὸν τόπον εἶναι.

ἄλσος, -ους, τό, grove
ἀρετή, ἡ, courage, virtue, manliness
διατρίβω, spend or pass time
εἶεν, (3rd sing. pres. opt. of εἰμί [lit., "be it so"], used as a particle/interjection in dialogue, esp. to mark transitions), well! so! come now!
ἐκεῖνος, ἐκείνη, ἐκεῖνο, that, he, she, it; (pl.) those, they
ἔμπροσθεν, (adv./prep. + gen.) before, in front of
ἐμφαίνω, show, make evident; (impers.) it is manifest, plain, or clear
ἕτερος, -έρα, -ερον, other
εὐδαιμονία, ἡ, [lit., well-spiritedness] happiness
εὐδαίμων, -ον, happy, fortunate
Ζεύς, Διός, ὁ, Zeus

καλός, -ή, -όν, beautiful
καταλάμπω, illuminate
κατανοέω, -ήσω, observe, perceive
λειμών, -ῶνος, ὁ, meadow
λειμωνοειδής, -ές, [ὁ λειμών, meadow + εἶδος, form, shape] meadow-like, grassy and flowery
μάλα, (adv.) very; καὶ μάλα, certainly, yes
μέσος, -η, -ον, middle (of)
νή, (adv. of swearing) yes, by X! (acc.)
οἰκητήριον, -ου, τό, dwelling
οὕτω(ς), (adv.) thus
πύλη, ἡ, gate
τέ, (conj.) and; τε καί / τε...καί, (both)...and
τόπος, ὁ, place
φῶς, φωτός, τό, light
ὧδε, (adv.) here
ὡς, (conj.) how (heading an exclamation)

---

3 φωτὶ πολλῷ dat. of means (Smyth § 1506-7)

11 λέγεις perhaps distinguishing between the real beauty of the place and its apparent beauty noted in XVII.1." (Banchich, 36)

[18] Πρεσβύτης: Οὐκοῦν παρὰ τὴν πύλην ὁρᾷς, ἔφη, ὅτι γυνή τις ἐστὶ, 1
καλὴ καὶ καθεστηκυῖα τὸ πρόσωπον, μέση δὲ καὶ κεκριμένη ἤδη τῇ ἡλικίᾳ, 2
στολὴν δ' ἔχουσα ἁπλῆν τε καὶ ἀκαλλώπιστον; ἔστηκε δὲ οὐκ ἐπὶ στρογγύλου 3
λίθου, ἀλλ' ἐπὶ τετραγώνου, ἀσφαλῶς κειμένου. καὶ μετὰ ταύτης ἄλλαι δύο εἰσὶ, 4
θυγατέρες τινὲς δοκοῦσαι εἶναι. 5

Ξένος: Ἐμφαίνει οὕτως ἔχειν. 6

Πρεσβύτης: Τούτων τοίνυν ἡ μὲν ἐν τῷ μέσῳ Παιδεία ἐστίν, ἡ δὲ 7
Ἀλήθεια, ἡ δὲ Πειθώ. 8

Ξένος: Τί δὲ ἔστηκεν ἐπὶ λίθου τετραγώνου αὕτη; 9

ἀκαλλώπιστος, -ον [ἀ-, not, un- + κάλλος, beauty + ὤψ, face], unadorned
ἀλήθεια, ἡ, truth
ἁπλοῦς, -ῆ, -οῦν, simple
ἀσφαλῶς, (adv.) securely
δύο, two
θυγάτηρ, -τρός, ἡ, daughter
καθίστημι, καταστήσω, bring, bring back, bring into a certain state; (2nd aor., perf., and pluperf. act.) settle, be calm
κεῖμαι, κείσομαι, be placed, be set
κρίνω, distinguish, judge
λίθος, ὁ, stone
μετά, (prep. + gen.) with

οὐκοῦν, (adv.) then…don't…? (introducing a question that expects the answer "yes" and carries the thought forward from a previous assent; cf. οὔκουν, certainly not; so…not)
παρά, (prep. + acc.) beside, near, by, alongside
πειθώ, -οῦς, ἡ, persuasion
πρόσωπον, τό, face
στολή, ἡ, robe
στρογγύλος, -η, -ον, round
τετράγωνος, -ον, [τετράς, the number four + γωνία, corner, angle] four-angled, square
τί, (interr. pron.) why?

---

2 καθεστηκυῖα fem. nom. sing. perf. act. part. < καθίστημι; lit., "settled," i.e., calm, composed, dignified

τὸ πρόσωπον acc. of respect (Smyth § 1600, 1601a)

μέσῃ…κεκριμένῃ…τῇ ἡλικίᾳ dat. of time when (Smyth § 1539-1540); lit., "at the age/time of life already having been judged the middle," i.e., in the prime of life. Parsons (71) translates as: "and now, having come to an age of maturity and discretion." and notes that: "ἤδη gives a force like "having attained.""

κεκριμένῃ fem. dat. sing. perf. pass. part. < κρίνω

3 ἔστηκε 3rd sing. perf. (w/ pres. sense) act. indic. < ἵστημι

6 οὕτως ἔχειν another example of ἔχω + adv. = (at least in terms of their English equivalent) εἰμί + adj. (see note to ὡσαύτως…ἔχει on p. 21, lines 3-4 and note to ταῦθ' (= ταῦτα) οὕτως ἔχει on p. 22, line 7); lit., "to hold thus," i.e., to be so, to be the case

7 Τούτων partitive gen.

7-8 ἡ μὲν…ἡ δὲ…ἡ δὲ… "one…the other…the other…"

1 **Πρεσβύτης:** Σημεῖον, ἔφη, ὅτι ἀσφαλής τε καὶ βεβαία ἡ πρὸς αὐτὴν ὁδός

2 ἐστι τοῖς ἀφικνουμένοις, καὶ τῶν διδομένων ἀσφαλὴς ἡ δόσις τοῖς λαμβάνουσι.

3 **Ξένος:** Καὶ τίνα ἐστίν, ἃ δίδωσιν αὕτη;

4 **Πρεσβύτης:** Θάρσος καὶ ἀφοβία, ἔφη ἐκεῖνος.

5 **Ξένος:** Ταῦτα δὲ τίνα ἐστίν;

6 **Πρεσβύτης:** Ἐπιστήμη, ἔφη, τοῦ μηδὲν ἄν ποτε δεινὸν παθεῖν ἐν τῷ βίῳ.

7 **[19] Ξένος:** Ὦ Ἡράκλεις, ὡς καλά, ἔφην, τὰ δῶρα. ἀλλὰ τίνος ἕνεκεν

8 οὕτως ἔξω τοῦ περιβόλου ἕστηκεν;

9 **Πρεσβύτης:** Ὅπως τοὺς παραγινομένους, ἔφη, θεραπεύῃ καὶ ποτίζῃ τὴν

ἀσφαλής, -ές, safe, secure
ἀφικνέομαι, arrive
ἀφοβία, ἡ, fearlessness
βέβαιος, -αία, -ον, secure
δίδωμι, give
δόσις, -εως, ἡ, gift
δῶρον, -ου, τό, gift
ἕνεκα/ἕνεκεν, (prep. + gen., mostly after its case) for the sake of
ἔξω, (adv./prep. + gen.) outside
ἐπιστήμη, ἡ, knowledge, understanding
Ἡρακλέης/Ἡρακλῆς, -έους, ὁ, Heracles; (when used in the voc., the name functions as an exclamation of surprise, anger, or disgust)
θάρσος, -ους, τό, daring, courage
θεραπεύω, -εύσω, heal

λαμβάνω, take, receive
μηδείς, μηδεμία, μηδέν, no one, nothing
ὅπως, (adv.; introducing a purp. cl.) in order that, that (+ subju.)
παραγί(γ)νομαι, παραγενήσομαι, παρεγενόμην, arrive
πάσχω, πείσομαι, ἔπαθον, experience; suffer
ποτέ, (particle) ever
ποτίζω, make X (acc.) drink of Y (acc.), give X (acc.) Y (acc.) to drink; (sometimes) make X (acc.) drink of Y (dat.), give X (acc.) Y (dat.) to drink
σημεῖον, τό, sign
Ὦ, ὤ, (exclamation) oh!, O!; (w/ voc., simply an address)
ὡς, (conj.) how (heading an exclamation); as

---

1 Σημεῖον sc. ἐστί

2 διδομένων lit., "of the things being given (by her)," i.e., of the things that she gives; the gen. is dependent on ἡ δόσις

3 ἃ sc. ἐκεῖνα as antecedent

6 τοῦ...ἄν...παθεῖν articular inf. (Smyth § 2025-30); the object of the inf. is μηδὲν...δεινόν, while the ἄν expresses potentiality or possibility (Smyth § 2270): "Knowledge," he said, "that one would never suffer anything terrible in life."

7 ὡς καλά...τὰ δῶρα = ὡς καλά ἐστι...τὰ δῶρα
τίνος ἕνεκεν lit., "for the sake of what thing," i.e., for what reason?, for what purpose?

8 ἕστηκεν 3rd sing. perf. (w/ pres. sense) act. indic. < ἵστημι

9 ποτίζῃ sc. αὐτούς, i.e., τοὺς παραγινομένους

καθαρτικὴν δύναμιν. εἶθ', ὅταν καθαρθῶσιν, οὕτως εἰσάγει τούτους πρὸς τὰς 1
Ἀρετάς. 2

Ξένος: Πῶς τοῦτο; ἔφην ἐγώ. οὐ γὰρ συνίημι. 3

Πρεσβύτης: Ἀλλὰ συνήσεις, ἔφη. ὡς ἂν, εἴ τις φιλοτίμως κάμνων 4
ἐτύγχανε, πρὸς ἰατρὸν δήπου γενόμενος πρότερον καθαρτικοῖς ἂν ἐξέβαλλε τὰ 5
νοσοποιοῦντα· εἶτα οὕτως ἂν αὐτὸν ὁ ἰατρὸς εἰς ἀνάληψιν καὶ ὑγείαν κατέστησεν· 6

ἀνάληψις, -εως, ἡ, recovery	καθίστημι, καταστήσω, bring X (acc.)
ἀρετή, ἡ, virtue, excellence	into (εἰς/ἐς) (a state of) Y (acc.)
δήπου, (adv.) doubtless, surely	κάμνω, καμῶ, be sick, fall ill
δύναμις, -εως, ἡ, power	νοσοποιέω, cause sickness
εἰσάγω, lead in	προσγί(γ)νομαι, προσγενήσομαι,
ἐκβάλλω, ἐκβαλῶ, ἐξέβαλον, cast out,	προσεγενόμην, go or come to
expel	πρότερος, -έρα, -ερον, former;
ἰατρός, ὁ, doctor	πρότερον/τὸ πρότερον, (adv.) first
καθαίρω, καθαρῶ, ἐκάθηρα, cleanse,	συνίημι, συνήσω, understand
purify	τυγχάνω, τεύξομαι, (+ supplementary
καθαρτικός, -ή, -όν, purifying; τὰ	part.) happen to X
καθαρτικά, purgatives	ὑγίεια [late form = ὑγεία], ἡ, health
	φιλοτίμως, (adv.) extremely, critically

----

1 εἶθ' = εἶτα
καθαρθῶσιν 3rd pl. aor. pass subju. < καθαίρω; subju. in a gen. temp. cl.

4 ὡς ἂν "as if," "as it were"; introducing the comparison with a patient and his doctor in the remainder of this sentence. The premature ἄν is best explained by Jerram (34): "ἄν often...occurs twice in a sentence, the first time to show that the sentence is going to be conditional, and again with the verb which it modifies."

4-5 εἴ...ἐτύγχανε,...ἂν ἐξέβαλλε Pres. C-to-F condit. (imperf. indic. in the protasis [i.e., the "if" cl.] and imperf. indic. w/ ἄν in the apodosis ["main cl."]): "if someone were to happen..., he would..."; either abrupt shift of subj. from "sick man" (τις... κάμνων ἐτύγχανε) to "doctor" (ἐξέβαλλε), or the sick man is also the subj. of ἐξέβαλλε (in which case, sc. "by the doctor's assistance" [so Parsons, 72])

4 φιλοτίμως (adv.) lit., "ambitiously," "eagerly." Parsons (71) notes that here: "This word seems to have a strained sense, coming from the extreme to which *ambition* runs." Jerram (35) believes that the meaning of the adv. here derives: "from the idea of the overwhelming force of ambition as a motive to action."

5 γενόμενος under the influence of the prep. phrase πρὸς ἰατρὸν, has the force of προσγενόμενος
καθαρτικοῖς dat. of means (Smyth § 1506-7)

6 ἂν...κατέστησεν "he would have brought"; ἄν w/ the indic. mood of historical tenses—the "past potential"—signifies past potentiality, probability, or necessity (Smyth § 1784); this is the apodosis of a Past C-to-F condit. Since the protasis (εἴ...ἐτύγχανε) in line 4 is of a Pres. C-to-F condit., this is a mixed condit.)
κατέστησεν 3rd sing. aor. act. indic. < καθίστημι

1   εἰ δὲ μὴ ἐπείθετο οἷς ἐπέταττεν, εὐλόγως ἂν δήπου ἀπωσθεὶς ἐξώλετο ὑπὸ τῆς

2   νόσου.

3   **Ξένος**: Ταῦτα μὲν συνίημι, ἔφην ἐγώ.

4   **Πρεσβύτης**: Τὸν αὐτὸν τοίνυν τρόπον, ἔφη, καὶ πρὸς τὴν Παιδείαν ὅταν

5   τις παραγένηται, θεραπεύει αὐτὸν καὶ ποτίζει τῇ ἑαυτῆς δυνάμει, ὅπως

6   ἐκκαθάρῃ πρῶτον καὶ ἐκβάλῃ τὰ κακὰ πάντα ὅσα ἔχων ἦλθε.

7   **Ξένος**: Ποῖα ταῦτα;

8   **Πρεσβύτης**: Τὴν ἄγνοιαν καὶ τὸν πλάνον, ὃν ἐπεπώκει παρὰ τῆς

ἄγνοια, ἡ, ignorance
ἀθυμία, ἡ, despair, depression
ἀπωθέω, reject, repudiate
ἑαυτοῦ, -ῆς, -οῦ, himself, herself, itself; (pl.) themselves
ἐκκαθαίρω, cleanse, purify
ἐξόλλυμι, destroy; (2nd aor. mid. = pass.)
ἐπιτάττω, order
ἔρχομαι, ἐλεύσομαι, ἦλθον, come
εὐλόγως, (adv.) reasonably, rightly, deservedly

νόσος, -ου, ἡ, sickness, disease
ὅπως, (adv.; introducing a purp. cl.) in order that, that (+ subju.)
ὅσος, -η, -ον, as great as, as much as; (pl.) as many as; πάντα ὅσα, all that
παραγί(γ)νομαι, παραγενήσομαι, παρεγενόμην, arrive
πείθω, persuade; (mid./pass.) obey, comply w/, submit to (+ dat.)
πλάνος, ὁ, error
πρῶτος, -η, -ον, first; πρῶτον, (adv.) first
τρόπος, ὁ, manner, way

---

1 εἰ...μὴ ἐπείθετο..., ἂν...ἐξώλετο another "mixed" condit., beginning w/ a Pres. C-to-F protasis, and concluding with a Past C-to-F apodosis (again, the imperf. would be expected, and it is probably best to trans. ἐξώλετο as if it were an imperf.)
οἷς = ἐκείνοις ἅ, "those things that"; attraction of the rel. pron. to the case of the antecedent (Smyth § 2522)
ἐπέταττεν sc. ὁ ἰατρὸς as subj.
ἀπωσθείς masc. nom. sing. aor. pass. part. < ἀπωθέω; sc. by the doctor, "who will have nothing more to say to such a patient" (Jerram, 35)
ἐξώλετο 3rd sing. aor. mid. (= pass.) indic. < ἐξόλλυμι

4 τὸν αὐτὸν...τρόπον an adverbial acc. of manner (Smyth § 1608): "in the same way"; note αὐτὸν in the attributive position means "the same"

5 ποτίζει repeat αὐτον as dir. obj.; note the different construction from that earlier in this section

6 ἐκκαθάρῃ 3rd sing. aor. act. subju. < ἐκκαθαίρω

8 ὃν refers grammatically to πλάνος only, its nearest antecedent, but includes ἄγνοιαν as well
ἐπεπώκει 3rd sing. pluperf. act. indic. < πίνω

Ἀπάτης, καὶ τὴν ἀλαζονείαν καὶ τὴν ἐπιθυμίαν καὶ τὴν ἀκρασίαν καὶ τὸν θυμὸν 1

καὶ τὴν φιλαργυρίαν καὶ τὰ λοιπὰ πάντα, ὧν ἀνεπλήσθη ἐν τῷ πρώτῳ 2

περιβόλῳ. 3

[20] Ξένος: Ὅταν οὖν καθαρθῇ, ποῦ αὐτὸν ἀποστέλλει; 4

Πρεσβύτης: Ἔνδον, ἔφη, πρὸς τὴν Ἐπιστήμην καὶ πρὸς τὰς ἄλλας 5

Ἀρετάς. 6

Ξένος: Ποίας ταύτας; 7

Πρεσβύτης: Οὐχ ὁρᾷς, ἔφη, ἔσω τῆς πύλης χορὸν γυναικῶν, ὡς εὐειδεῖς 8

δοκοῦσιν εἶναι καὶ εὔτακτοι καὶ στολὴν ἀτρύφερον καὶ ἁπλῆν ἔχουσιν· ἔτι τε ὡς 9

ἄπλαστοί εἰσι, καὶ οὐδαμῶς κεκαλλωπισμέναι καθάπερ αἱ ἄλλαι; 10

Ξένος: Ὁρῶ, ἔφην· ἀλλὰ τίνες αὗται καλοῦνται; 11

ἀκρασία, ἡ, intemperance; lack of power or control over one's passions/desires

ἀλαζονεία, ἡ, pretentiousness, boastfulness

ἀναπίμπλημι, ἀναπλήσω, ἀνέπλησα, fill up; (pass.) be filled up w/ (+ gen.) be infected w/ (a disease) (+ gen.)

ἀπάτη, ἡ, deceit, deception

ἄπλαστος, -ον, not fashioned or made, natural, genuine

ἁπλοῦς, -ῆ, -οῦν, simple

ἀποστέλλω, send (away)

ἀτρύφερος, -ον, [ἀ-, not + τρύφερος, delicate, luxurious, expensive)] inexpensive; plain, simple

ἔνδον, (adv.) inside

ἐπιθυμία, ἡ, desire

ἐπιστήμη, ἡ, knowledge, understanding

ἔσω, (adv./prep. + gen.) inside

ἔτι, (adv.) still, further, moreover

εὐειδής, -ές, (lit., well-shaped, well-formed), beautiful, attractive

εὔτακτος, (lit., well-arranged, well-ordered), well-behaved, disciplined

θυμός, ὁ, passion; anger

καθαίρω, καθαρῶ, ἐκάθηρα, purify

καθάπερ, (conj.) just as, as

καλλωπίζω, embellish, beautify, adorn

λοιπός, -ή, -όν, remaining; τὰ λοιπά, the rest

οὐδαμῶς, (adv.) in no way

ποῖ, (adv.) to what place?

ποῦ, (adv.) where?

στολή, ἡ, robe

φιλαργυρία, ἡ, avarice, greed

χορός, ὁ, (lit., chorus of singing dancers) group

ὡς, (conj.) how (i.e., in what manner); how (heading an exclamation)

---

2 ἀνεπλήσθη 3rd sing. aor. pass. indic. < ἀναπίμπλημι
κα θαρθῇ 3rd sing. aor. pass subju. < καθαίρω; subju. in a gen. temp. cl.

4 ἀποστέλλει sc. Παιδεία as subj.
ποῦ = ποῖ; see note on p. 25, line 2

10 κεκαλλωπισμέναι fem. nom. pl. perf. mid./pass. part. < καλλωπίζω

1   Πρεσβύτης: Ἡ μὲν πρώτη Ἐπιστήμη, ἔφη, καλεῖται, αἱ δὲ ἄλλαι ταύτης

2   ἀδελφαὶ, Ἀνδρεία, Δικαιοσύνη, Καλοκἀγαθία, Σωφροσύνη, Εὐταξία, Ἐλευθερία,

3   Ἐγκράτεια, Πρᾳότης.

4   Ξένος: Ὦ κάλλιστε, ἔφην ἔγωγε, ὡς ἐν μεγάλῃ ἐλπίδι ἐσμέν.

5   Πρεσβύτης: Ἐὰν συνῆτε, ἔφη, καὶ ἕξιν περιποιήσησθε ὧν ἀκούετε.

6   Ξένος: Ἀλλὰ προσέξομεν, ἔφην ἔγωγε, ὡς μάλιστα.

7   Πρεσβύτης: Τοιγαροῦν, ἔφη, σωθήσεσθε.

8   [21] Ξένος: Ὅταν οὖν παραλάβωσιν αὐτὸν αὗται, ποῦ ἄγουσι;

9   Πρεσβύτης: Πρὸς τὴν μητέρα, ἔφη.

10   Ξένος: Αὕτη δὲ τίς ἐστιν;

11   Πρεσβύτης: Εὐδαιμονία, ἔφη.

12   Ξένος: Ποία δὲ ἐστὶν αὕτη;

ἄγω, lead
ἀδελφή, ἡ, sister
ἀκούω, hear (+ gen.)
ἀνδρεία, ἡ, courage, bravery
δικαιοσύνη, ἡ, justice, righteousness
ἐγκράτεια, ἡ, self-control, restraint
ἔγωγε, I, for my part, I myself
ἐλευθερία, ἡ, freedom, liberty
ἐλπίς, ἐλπίδος, ἡ, hope
ἕξις, -εως, ἡ, habit
εὐδαιμονία, ἡ, happiness
εὐταξία, ἡ, [lit., good order] orderliness,
   propriety
καλοκἀγαθία, ἡ, [καλός + καί + ἀγαθία,
   lit., (the character and conduct of) a fine and
   good (person)] goodness, rectitude, honor,
   honorable behavior

μάλιστα, (adv.; superl. of μάλα) most, most
   of all; ὡς μάλιστα, as much as possible, as
   best as one can
μήτηρ, μητρός, ἡ, mother
παραλαμβάνω, παραλήψομαι,
   παρέλαβον, receive
περιποιέω, περιποιήσω, form; (mid.)
   acquire
πρᾳότης, πρᾳότητος, ἡ, kindness;
   gentleness, mildness, modesty
προσέχω, προσέξω (+ τὸν νοῦν, mind
   [stated or implied]), hold (your mind)
   toward, pay attention (to)
συνίημι, understand
σωφροσύνη, ἡ, moderation, temperance,
   sound-mindedness
τοιγαροῦν (particle), [τοι + γάρ + οὖν] for
   that very reason, therefore

---

4 κάλλιστε voc. superl. < καλός, -ή, -όν: "most noble or honorable man"

5 Ἐὰν συνῆτε,...καὶ περιποιήσησθε the protasis of a FMV condit. (the apodosis
comes later w/ σωθήσεσθε); συνῆτε 2nd pl. aor. act. subju. < συνίημι;
περιποιήσησθε 2nd pl. aor. mid. subju. < περιποιέω
ἕξιν Jerram (36) notes that: "In Aristotle, ἕξις is a 'moral habit' formed by the
consistent practice of virtuous actions, for 'from a series of similar acts permanent
habits are formed'... Ethics II. i."
ὧν = ἐκείνων ἅ, gen. w/ ἕξιν and acc. dir. obj. of ἀκούετε, which usu. takes the acc. of
the *thing* heard and the gen. of the *person* from whom one heard it (Smyth § 1361)

8 ποῦ = ποῖ; see note on p. 25, line 2

Πρεσβύτης: Ὁρᾷς τὴν ὁδὸν ἐκείνην, τὴν φέρουσαν ἐπὶ τὸ ὑψηλὸν ἐκεῖνο, ὅ 1
ἐστιν ἀκρόπολις τῶν περιβόλων πάντων; 2

    Ξένος: Ὁρῶ. 3

Πρεσβύτης: Οὐκοῦν ἐπὶ τοῦ προπυλαίου γυνὴ καθεστηκυῖα εὐειδής τις 4
κάθηται ἐπὶ θρόνου ὑψηλοῦ, κεκοσμημένη ἐλευθέρως καὶ ἀπεριέργως καὶ 5
ἐστεφανωμένη στεφάνῳ εὐανθεῖ πάνυ καλῷ; 6

    Ξένος: Ἐμφαίνει οὕτως. 7

    Πρεσβύτης: Αὕτη τοίνυν ἐστὶν ἡ Εὐδαιμονία, ἔφη. 8

[22] Ξένος: Ὅταν οὖν ὧδέ τις παραγένηται, τί ποιεῖ; 9

ἀκρόπολις, -εως, ἡ, (high) citadel
ἀπεριέργως, (adv.) [a-, not + περι-,
  excessively + ἔργον, busy, work; a-, not +
  περίεργον, overdoing (it)], artlessly,
  simply
ἐλευθέρως, (adv.) in the manner of a free-
  born person (i.e., not as a slave or
  courtesan)
ἐμφαίνω, show, make evident; (impers.) it is
  manifest, plain, or clear
ἐπί, (prep. + gen.) in, at, near; on, upon;
  (+ acc.) to, toward
εὐανθής, -ές, [lit., well-flowered], flowery,
  made of beautiful flowers
εὐειδής, -ές, [lit., well-shaped, well-
  formed], beautiful, attractive

θρόνος, ὁ, throne
κάθημαι, sit
καθίστημι, set down, establish; (perf. act.)
  be stationed
κοσμέω, adorn
πάνυ, (adv.) (w/ adjs.) very, very much,
  exceedingly
παραγί(γ)νομαι, παραγενήσομαι,
  παρεγενόμην, arrive
ποιέω, do; make X (acc.) a Y (acc.)
προπύλαιον, τό, gateway, vestibule
στέφανος, ὁ, crown, wreath
ὑψηλός, -ή, -όν, high; τὸ ὑψηλόν, high
  place
φέρω, bear, carry; (of roads) lead

---

4 καθεστηκυῖα fem. nom. sing. perf. act. part. < καθίστημι; note that this word is used
in a different sense in Chapter 18 (p. 33, line 2)

5 κεκοσμημένη fem. nom. sing. perf. mid./pass. part. < κοσμέω

6 ἐστεφανωμένη στεφάνῳ rhetorical trope known as *figura etymologica*, in which a
vb. or part. governs its related noun
ἐστεφανωμένη fem. nom. sing. perf. mid./pass. part. < στεφανόω
στεφάνῳ dat. of means (Smyth § 1506-7)

9 παρεγένηται 3rd sing. aor. mid. (dep.) subju. < παραγί(γ)νομαι; subju. in a gen.
temp. cl.
ποιεῖ the subj. is ἡ Εὐδαιμονία

1   **Πρεσβύτης:** Στεφανοῖ αὐτόν, ἔφη, τῇ ἑαυτῆς δυνάμει ἥ τε Εὐδαιμονία καὶ

2   αἱ ἄλλαι Ἀρεταὶ πᾶσαι, ὥσπερ τοὺς νενικηκότας τοὺς μεγίστους ἀγῶνας.

3   **Ξένος:** Καὶ ποίους ἀγῶνας νενίκηκεν αὐτός; ἔφην ἐγώ.

4   **Πρεσβύτης:** Τοὺς μεγίστους, ἔφη, καὶ τὰ μέγιστα θηρία, ἃ πρότερον αὐτὸν

5   κατήσθιε καὶ ἐκόλαζε καὶ ἐποίει δοῦλον. ταῦτα πάντα νενίκηκε καὶ ἀπέρριψεν

6   ἀφ' ἑαυτοῦ καὶ κεκράτηκεν ἑαυτοῦ, ὥστε ἐκεῖνα νῦν τούτῳ δουλεύουσι, καθάπερ

7   οὗτος ἐκείνοις πρότερον.

ἀγών, -ῶνος, ὁ, contest, competition (musical, athletic, etc.)	κατεσθίω, devour
	κολάζω, punish
ἀπορρίπτω, ἀπορρίψω, ἀπέρριψα, throw or cast away	κρατέω, master, be master of (+ gen.)
ἀρετή, ἡ, virtue, excellence	μέγιστος, -η, -ον, greatest
δύναμις, -εως, ἡ, power	νικάω, conquer, win, be victorious in
εὐδαιμονία, ἡ, happiness	πρότερος, -έρα, -ερον, former;
καθάπερ, (conj.) just as	πρότερον/τὸ πρότερον, (adv.) previously
	ὥστε, (conj.) so that

----

1 στεφανοῖ 3rd sing. pres. act. indic. < στεφανόω (στεφανό + ει); note that though the subj. is a compound pl. (ἥ...Εὐδαιμονία, αἱ ἄλλαι Ἀρεταὶ πᾶσαι), the vb. in Gk. can agree w/ the nearest of two or more subjs. (Smyth § 966)

τῇ...δυνάμει dat. of means (Smyth 1506-7); the "power" is explained in the next chapter

ἥ the def. art. w/ an acute accent from the enclitic τε

2 νενικηκότας masc. acc. pl. perf. act. part. < νικάω

τοὺς μεγίστους ἀγῶνας e.g., the Olympic Games (ὁ Ὀλυμπικός ἀγών)

3 νενίκηκεν 3rd sing. perf. act. indic. < νικάω

4 τοὺς μεγίστους,...καὶ τὰ μέγιστα θηρία, Jerram (37) notes that one should: "Observe the twofold construction of the verb νικᾶν here; (1) that of the *cognate* accus. with ἀγῶνας, 'to conquer *in* the contests,' (2) accus. of the *direct object* with θηρία."

ἃ governing singular verbs, as is usu. for neut. pls.

5 κατήσθιε καὶ ἐκόλαζε καὶ ἐποίει note the force of the imperfs.: "used to..."

ἐκόλαζε...ἐποίει sc. αὐτὸν as obj.; ποιέω takes a double acc. constr.

6 ἐκεῖνα neut. pl. subj. of δουλεύουσι, referring to the θηρία above. The pl. vb. (rather than the usu. sing. vb. w/ a neut. pl. subj.—see ἃ πρότερον αὐτὸν κατήσθιε καὶ ἐκόλαζε καὶ ἐποίει in the previous sentence) is perhaps being used here to emphasize the number of monsters now enslaved to the victor. Jerram (37) notes that: "The rule that a neuter plural takes a singular verb admits of two main exceptions; (1) where the notion of *plurality* is prominent, (2) where the things are *personified* as so many individuals. Both reasons apply here; for there are many wild passions in man, and these are presently described as persons, Ἄγνοια, Λύπη, etc., (Ch. XXIII)."

ὥστε result cl. (+ indic. = actual result; Smyth § 2257)

6-7 καθάπερ οὗτος ἐκείνοις = καθάπερ οὗτος ἐδουλέυε ἐκείνοις

50

[23] Ξένος: Ποῖα ταῦτα λέγεις τὰ θηρία; πάνυ γὰρ ἐπιποθῶ ἀκοῦσαι.　　1

Πρεσβύτης: Πρῶτον μὲν, ἔφη, τὴν Ἄγνοιαν καὶ τὸν Πλάνον. ἢ οὐ δοκεῖ　2
σοι ταῦτα θηρία;　　3

Ξένος: Καὶ πονηρά γε, ἔφην ἐγώ.　　4

Πρεσβύτης: Εἶτα τὴν Λύπην καὶ τὸν Ὀδυρμὸν καὶ τὴν Φιλαργυρίαν καὶ　5
τὴν Ἀκρασίαν καὶ τὴν λοιπὴν ἅπασαν Κακίαν. πάντων τούτων κρατεῖ καὶ οὐ　6
κρατεῖται ὥσπερ πρότερον.　　7

Ξένος: Ὦ καλῶν ἔργων, ἔφην ἐγὼ, καὶ καλλίστης νίκης. Ἀλλ᾽ ἐκεῖνο ἔτι　8
μοι εἰπέ· τίς ἡ δύναμις τοῦ στεφάνου, ᾧ ἔφης . . . στεφανοῦν αὐτόν;　　9

ἄγνοια, ἡ, ignorance
ἀκούω, ἀκούσομαι, ἤκουσα, hear
ἀκρασία, ἡ, intemperance; lack of power or
　control over one's passions/desires
ἅπας, ἅπασα, ἅπαν, every single
δύναμις, -εως, ἡ, power
εἶπον, (2nd aor.; pres in use is φήμι, λέγω,
　ἀγορεύω) said, spoke, told; (imper.) say,
　speak, tell
ἐπιποθέω/ἐπιποθῶ, desire (+ inf.)
ἔργον, τό, deed, feat
ἔτι, (adv.) still
ἤ, (conj.) or
θηρίον, τό, beast
κακία, ἡ, evil, vice, wickedness
κάλλιστος, -η, -ον, (superl. of καλός, -ή,
　-όν) fairest, most noble, most beautiful

λοιπός, -ή, -όν, remaining, the rest
λύπη, ἡ, pain (of body or mind); grief
νίκη, ἡ, victory
ὀδυρμός, ὁ, lamentation, complaining
πλάνος, ὁ, error
πονηρός, -ά, -όν, wicked, base
πρότερος, -έρα, -ερον, former;
　πρότερον/τὸ πρότερον, (adv.) previously
στέφανος, ὁ, crown, wreath
στεφανόω, crown
πρῶτος, -η, -ον, first; πρῶτον, (adv.)
　first, first of all
φιλαργυρία, ἡ, [lit., love of money]
　avarice, greed
Ὦ, ὤ, (exclamation + gen.) O! oh! What!

2-3 οὐ δοκεῖ σοι ταῦτα θηρία sc. εἶναι (w/ ταῦτα as acc. subj. and θηρία as
　predicate of the indir. statement)

8 ὦ καλῶν ἔργων...καὶ καλλίστης νίκης gen. of cause used in exclamations and
　typically preceded by an interjection (Smyth § 1407): "Noble deeds...and a most noble
　victory!"

9 τίς sc. ἐστί
　ᾧ dat. of means (Smyth § 1506-7)
　. . . the lacuna (". . .") is resolved by Praechter by the insertion of either τὴν
　Εὐδαιμονίαν or τὰς Ἀρετὰς as the subj. of the indir. statement
　στεφανοῦν pres. act. inf. < στεφανόω (στεφανό + ειν)

1   Πρεσβύτης: Εὐδαιμονικὴ, ὦ νεανίσκε. ὁ γὰρ στεφανωθεὶς ταύτῃ τῇ

2   δυνάμει εὐδαίμων γίνεται καὶ μακάριος, καὶ οὐκ ἔχει ἐν ἑτέροις τὰς ἐλπίδας τῆς

3   εὐδαιμονίας, ἀλλ᾽ ἐν αὑτῷ.

4   [24] Ξένος: Ὡς καλὸν τὸ νίκημα λέγεις. ὅταν δὲ στεφανωθῇ, τί ποιεῖ ἢ

5   ποῖ βαδίζει;

6   Πρεσβύτης: Ἄγουσιν αὐτὸν ὑπολαβοῦσαι αἱ Ἀρεταὶ πρὸς τὸν τόπον

7   ἐκεῖνον, ὅθεν ἦλθε πρῶτον, καὶ δεικνύουσιν αὐτῷ τοὺς ἐκεῖ διατρίβοντας, ὡς

8   κακῶς διατρίβουσι καὶ ἀθλίως ζῶσι, καὶ ὡς ναυαγοῦσιν ἐν τῷ βίῳ, καὶ

9   πλανῶνται καὶ ἄγονται κατακεκρατημένοι ὥσπερ ὑπὸ πολεμίων, οἱ μὲν ὑπ᾽

10   Ἀκρασίας, οἱ δὲ ὑπ᾽ Ἀλαζονείας, οἱ δὲ ὑπὸ Φιλαργυρίας, ἕτεροι δὲ ὑπὸ

11   Κενοδοξίας, ἕτεροι δὲ ὑφ᾽ ἑτέρων Κακῶν. ἐξ ὧν οὐ δύνανται ἐκλῦσαι ἑαυτοὺς

ἀθλίως, (adv.) wretchedly
ἀλαζονεία, ἡ, pretentiousness, boastfulness
βαδίζω, go
δεικνύω, show
διατρίβω, spend time
δύναμαι, be able (+ inf.)
ἐκεῖ, (adv.) there
ἐκλύω, free X (acc.) from Y (gen.)
ἐλπίς, ἐλπίδος, ἡ, hope
ἔρχομαι, ἐλεύσομαι, ἦλθον, come
εὐδαιμονικός, -ή, -όν, making one happy, conferring happiness
εὐδαίμων, -ον, happy
ζάω/ζῶ, live
κακῶς, (adv.) badly, poorly; wickedly
κατακρατέω, overpower
κενοδοξία, ἡ, vanity, conceit

μακάριος, -ία, -ον, blessed
ναυαγέω, suffer shipwreck
νεανίσκος, ὁ, young man
νίκημα, -ατος, τό, victory
ὅθεν, (adv.) from which, from where
πλανάω, make X wander; lead X astray; deceive X; (pass.), wander
ποῖ, (adv.) to what place? where?
πολέμιος, -ία, -ιον, hostile; ὁ πολέμιος, enemy
ὑπολαμβάνω, ὑπολήψομαι, ὑπέλαβον, take under one's protection, take by the hand, receive
ὡς, (conj.) how (heading an exclamation); that; how (i.e., in what manner); (+ fut. part. expresses the alleged purp.)

---

1 στεφανωθεὶς masc. nom. sing. aor. pass. part. < στεφανόω

1-2 ταύτῃ τῇ δυνάμει dat. of means (Smyth § 1506-7)

2 μακάριος denotes "the perfect undisturbed state of bliss which the gods alone fully enjoy." (Jerram, 37)

3 αὑτῷ = ἑαυτῷ

4 στεφανωθῇ 3rd sing. aor. pass. subju. < ἐστί; subju. in a gen. temp. cl.

9 κατακεκρατετημένοι masc. nom. pl. perf. pass. part. < κατακρατέω

9-10 οἱ μὲν..., οἱ δὲ..., "some...others..."

11 ἐξ ὧν take w/ τῶν δεινῶν, lit. "from which things...the terrors"; rel. for demonstrative, i.e., ἐξ ὧν = ἐξ τούτων + τῶν δεινῶν = "from these terrors" (but note how the Gk. word order makes τῶν δεινῶν emphatic)

τῶν δεινῶν, οἷς δέδενται, ὥστε σωθῆναι καὶ ἀφικέσθαι ὧδε· ἀλλὰ ταράττονται 1

διὰ παντὸς τοῦ βίου. τοῦτο δὲ πάσχουσι διὰ τὸ μὴ δύνασθαι τὴν ἐνθάδε ὁδὸν 2

εὑρεῖν· ἐπελάθοντο γὰρ τὸ παρὰ τοῦ Δαιμονίου πρόσταγμα. 3

[25] Ξένος: Ὀρθῶς μοι δοκεῖς λέγειν. ἀλλὰ καὶ τοῦτο πάλιν ἀπορῶ, διὰ τί 4

δεικνύουσιν αὐτῷ τὸν τόπον ἐκεῖνον αἱ Ἀρεταί, ὅθεν ἥκει τὸ πρότερον. 5

Πρεσβύτης: Οὐκ ἀκριβῶς ᾔδει οὐδὲ ἠπίστατο, ἔφη, οὐδὲν τῶν ἐκεῖ, ἀλλ' 6

ἀκριβῶς, (adv.) clearly
ἀπορέω/ἀπορῶ, be puzzled, perplexed or
  confused (about + acc.)
ἀφικνέομαι, ἀφίξομαι, ἀφικόμην, arrive
Δαιμόνιον, τό = Δαίμων, Δαίμονος, ὁ
δεικνύω, show
δεινός, -ή, -όν, terrible
δέω, bind
διά, (prep. + gen.) throughout; (+ acc.) on
  account of, because of
ἐκεῖ, (adv.) there
ἐνθάδε, (adv.) to this place, here

ἐπιλανθάνομαι/ἐπιλήθομαι,
  ἐπιλήσομαι, ἐπελαθόμην, forget
ἐπίσταμαι, understand
ἥκω, have come
ὅθεν, (adv.) from which, from where
οἶδα, (2nd perf. w/ pres. sense) know
ὀρθῶς, (adv.) correctly
πάλιν, (adv.) again, in turn
πάσχω, suffer
πρόσταγμα, -τος, τό, command
ταράττω, trouble
ὥστε, (conj.) so that, so as

---

1 δέδενται 3rd pl. perf. (w/ pres. force) pass. indic. < δέω
  ὥστε result cl. (+ inf. = potential result; Smyth § 2258)
  σωθῆναι aor. pass. inf. < σώζω

2-3 διὰ τὸ μὴ δύνασθαι τὴν...ὁδὸν εὑρεῖν articular inf., obj. of the prep. διά,
  negated by μή, and followed, as is often the case after forms of δύναμαι, by another
  inf., here εὑρεῖν, the obj. of which is τὴν...ὁδόν

4 τοῦτο acc. of respect ("with respect to this thing"; Smyth § 1600)/adverbial acc. of
  motive ("for this reason"; Smyth § 1610) w/ ἀπορῶ
  διὰ τί lit., "on account of what thing?", i.e., for what reason?, why?

5 ἥκει τὸ πρότερον the force of the adv. τὸ πρότερον pushes the pf. tense of ἥκει
  back to the pluperf.

6 ᾔδει 3rd sing. pluperf. (w/ imperf. sense) < οἶδα
  οὐδέ...οὐδέν "nor...any"; "If in the same clause one or more *compound* negatives
  follow a negative with the same verb, the compound negative simply confirms the first
  negative." (Smyth § 2761)
  ἠπίστατο 3rd sing. imperf. mid./pass. (dep.) < ἐπίσταμαι
  τῶν ἐκεῖ "of the things/matters there"

1 ἐνεδοίαζε· καὶ διὰ τὴν ἄγνοιαν καὶ τὸν πλάνον, ὃν δὴ ἐπεπώκει, τὰ μὴ ὄντα

2 ἀγαθὰ ἐνόμιζεν ἀγαθὰ εἶναι, καὶ τὰ μὴ ὄντα κακά, κακά. διὸ καὶ ἔζη κακῶς,

3 ὥσπερ οἱ ἄλλοι οἱ ἐκεῖ διατρίβοντες. νῦν δὲ ἀνειληφὼς τὴν ἐπιστήμην τῶν

4 συμφερόντων, αὐτός τε καλῶς ζῇ καὶ τούτους θεωρεῖ ὡς κακῶς πράττουσιν.

5 **[26] Ξένος:** Ἐπειδὰν οὖν θεωρήσῃ πάντα, τί ποιεῖ ἢ ποῦ ἔτι βαδίζει;

6 **Πρεσβύτης:** Ὅπου ἂν βούληται, ἔφη· πανταχοῦ γάρ ἐστιν αὐτῷ ἀσφάλεια,

7 ὥσπερ τῷ τὸ Κωρύκιον ἄντρον ἔχοντι. καὶ πανταχοῦ, οὗ ἂν ἀφίκηται, πάντα

ἀγαθός, -ή, -όν, good
ἄντρον, τό, cave
ἀπολαμβάνω, receive
ἀσφάλεια, ἡ, safety
βαδίζω, go
βούλομαι, wish, want (+ inf.)
δή, (particle) of course
διατρίβω, spend time
διό, (conj.; = δι[ά] ὅ, on account of which thing) wherefore, for which reason, therefore
ἐνδοιάζω, be in doubt, be at a loss, be confused
ἐπειδάν (= ἐπεί + δή + ἄν) whenever, as soon as (+ subju., = an indef. temporal cl.)
ἐπιστήμη, ἡ, knowledge
ἔτι, (adv.) afterwards, next
ζάω/ζῶ, live
θεωρέω, see, observe, perceive
κακῶς, (adv.) badly, poorly; wickedly

καλῶς, (adv.) nobly
Κωρύκιος, -α, -ον, Corycian
νομίζω, believe
νῦν, (adv.) now
οἷ, (adv.) to what place, to which place; οἷ ἄν, to whatever or whichever place (+ subju. = an indef. cl.)
ὅπου, (adv.) where; ὅπου ἄν, wherever (+ subju. = an indef. cl.)
οὗ, (adv.) where; οὗ ἄν, wherever (+ subju. = an indef. cl.)
πανταχοῦ, (adv.) everywhere
πλάνος, ὁ, error
ποῖ, (adv.) to what place? to which place?
ποῦ, (adv.) where?
πράττω, do, fare; κακῶς πράττω, fare badly or poorly
συμφέρω, serve; (as impers.) it profits; τὰ συμφερόντα, things that are advantageous, advantages

---

1 τὴν ἄγνοιαν καὶ τὸν πλάνον, ὃν δὴ ἐπεπώκει cf. p. 34 lines 8-9
ὃν δή "which, of course"; ὃν refers grammatically to πλάνος only, its nearest antecedent, but includes ἄγνοιαν as well. "The use of δή is to give an intensive and ironical force to the relative." (Parsons, 72)
ἐπεπώκει 3rd sing. pluperf. act. indic. < πίνω

1-2 τὰ μὴ ὄντα ἀγαθά "whatever things are not good"; "the participle with the article has οὐ when a definite person or thing is meant, but μή when the idea is indefinite or virtually conditional (whoever, whatever)" (Smyth § 2734). The entire phrase is the acc. subj. of the inf. εἶναι (in indir. statement after ἐνόμιζεν)

5 ποῦ = ποῖ; so too in line 6, ὅπου = ὅποι, and in line 7, οὗ ἄν = οἷ ἄν; for these adverbial substitutions (common in later Gk.), see note on p. 25, line 2

7 τὸ Κωρύκιον ἄντρον a cave on Mt. Parnassus used by the people of Delphi as a place of refuge in 480 BC when the Persians invaded Greece (Herodotus 8.36). "Proverbial for a safe retreat." (Banchich, 39)
πάντα acc. of respect (Smyth § 1601c): "with respect to all things," "in all ways"

καλῶς βιώσεται μετὰ πάσης ἀσφαλείας. ὑποδέξονται γὰρ αὐτὸν ἀσμένως 1
πάντες καθάπερ τὸν ἰατρὸν οἱ κάμνοντες. 2

Ξένος: Πότερον οὖν κἀκείνας τὰς γυναῖκας, ἃς ἔφης θηρία εἶναι, οὐκέτι 3
φοβεῖται, μή τι πάθῃ ὑπ' αὐτῶν; 4

Πρεσβύτης: Οὐ μὴ διοχληθήσεται οὐδὲν οὔτε ὑπὸ Ὀδύνης οὔτε ὑπὸ Λύπης 5
οὔτε ὑπ' Ἀκρασίας οὔτε ὑπὸ Φιλαραγυρίας οὔτε ὑπὸ Πενίας οὔτε ὑπ' ἄλλου 6
Κακοῦ οὐδενός. ἁπάντων γὰρ κυριεύει, καὶ ἐπάνω πάντων ἐστὶ τῶν πρότερον 7
αὐτὸν λυπούντων, καθάπερ οἱ ἐχιόδηκτοι. τὰ γὰρ θηρία δήπου, τὰ πάντας τοὺς 8

ἅπας, ἅπασα, ἅπαν, all
ἀσμένως, (adv.) gladly
ἀφικνέομαι, ἀφίξομαι, ἀφικόμην, arrive
βιόω, βιώσομαι, live
δήπου, (adv.) indeed, doubtless, surely, of
  course
διοχλέω, -ήσω, trouble or disturb
  (exceedingly)
ἐπάνω, (adv./prep. + gen.) above, superior to
ἐχιόδηκτος, -ον, snake-bitten
θηρίον, τό, beast
ἰατρός, ὁ, doctor
καθάπερ, (conj., κατά, "concerning" + ἅ,
  "which things" + περ, [adds force to the
  word to which it is added] = lit.,
  "concerning the very things which") just as
κάμνω, be sick
κυριεύω, -εύσω, be master of (+ gen.)
λυπέω, cause X (acc.) pain or distress

λύπη, ἡ, pain (of body or mind); grief
ὀδύνη, ἡ, pain (of body or mind); grief;
  distress
οὐδείς, οὐδεμία, οὐδέν, no one, nothing;
  no; οὐδέν, (acc. of respect used as adv.)
  not at all, in no way; (+ preceding neg.) at
  all, in any way
οὐκέτι, (adv.) no longer
πάσχω, πείσομαι, ἔπαθον, suffer
πενία, ἡ, poverty
πότερος, -έρα, -ερον, which of the two?
  πότερον...ἤ, whether...or; πότερον, (as an
  interr. adv. introducing a dir. quest., it is not
  translated)
ὑποδέχομαι, ὑποδέξομαι, receive,
  welcome
φιλαργυρία, ἡ, avarice, greed
φοβέομαι, fear

----

2 καθάπερ τὸν ἰατρὸν οἱ κάμνοντες sc. ὑποδέξονται ἀσμένως

3 κἀκείνας = καὶ ἐκείνας.

4 μή τι πάθῃ in a fear cl., trans. μή as "that" (Smyth § 2221)

5 οὐ μὴ διοχληθήσεται οὐ μή used to express an emphatic neg. statement w/ regard to
fut. time (Smyth § 2755b; cf. note on p. 28, lines 1-2 where οὐ μή is used w/ the subju.
w/ this same sense)

8 οἱ ἐχιόδηκτοι two possibilities: (1) it was thought that those who were bitten by
snakes and survived were henceforth immune from the venom of snakes; (2) the
reference is to "those who *allow* themselves to be thus bitten because they have an
antidote about them, as Indian serpent-charmers are said to have." (Jerram, 39)
τὰ...θηρία i.e., snakes

1 ἄλλους κακοποιοῦντα μέχρι θανάτου, ἐκείνους οὐ λυπεῖ διὰ τὸ ἔχειν

2 ἀντιφάρμακον αὐτούς. οὕτω καὶ τοῦτον οὐκέτι οὐδὲν λυπεῖ, διὰ τὸ ἔχειν

3 ἀντιφάρμακον.

4 [27] Ξένος: Καλῶς ἐμοὶ δοκεῖς λέγειν. ἀλλ' ἔτι τοῦτό μοι εἰπέ· τίνες εἰσὶν

5 οὗτοι οἱ δοκοῦντες ἐκεῖθεν ἀπὸ τοῦ βουνοῦ παραγίνεσθαι; καὶ οἱ μὲν αὐτῶν

6 ἐστεφανωμένοι ἔμφασιν ποιοῦσιν εὐφροσύνης τινός, οἱ δὲ ἀστεφάνωτοι λύπης

7 καὶ ταραχῆς· καὶ τὰς κνήμας καὶ τὰς κεφαλὰς δοκοῦσι τετρῖφθαι, κατέχονται

8 δὲ ὑπὸ γυναικῶν τινων.

9 Πρεσβύτης: Οἱ μὲν ἐστεφανωμένοι οἱ σεσωσμένοι εἰσὶ πρὸς τὴν Παιδείαν,

10 καὶ εὐφραίνονται τετυχηκότες αὐτῆς. οἱ δὲ ἀστεφάνωτοι, οἱ μὲν, ἀπεγνωσμένοι

11 ὑπὸ τῆς Παιδείας, ἀνακάμπτουσι, κακῶς καὶ ἀθλίως διακείμενοι· οἱ δὲ,

---

ἀθλίως, (adv.) wretchedly
ἀνακάμπτω, turn back
ἀντιφάρμακον, τό, antidote
ἀπογι(γ)νώσκω, reject
ἀστεφάνωτος, -ον, uncrowned
βουνός, ὁ, hill
διάκειμαι, be in a certain state (+ adv.);
    + κακῶς, be in a sorry, sad, or bad state
εἶπον, (2nd aor.; pres in use is φήμι, λέγω,
    ἀγορεύω) said, spoke, told; (imper.) say,
    speak, tell
ἐκεῖθεν, (adv.) from there, from that place
εὐφραίνω, delight; (pass.) be happy
εὐφροσύνη, ἡ, joy, happiness
θάνατος, ὁ, death

κακοποιέω, injure, harm, cause harm or
    injury to X (acc.)
κακῶς, (adv.) badly, poorly
κατέχω, restrain, hold back
κεφαλή, ἡ, head
κνήμη, ἡ, leg (properly, the lower leg
    between the foot and the knee)
μέχρι, (adv./prep. + gen.) up to (the point of)
παραγί(γ)νομαι, -γενήσομαι, arrive, be
    near, be present at
στεφανόω, crown
ταραχή, ἡ, confusion
τρίβω, beat, batter, bruise
τυγχάνω, meet with, happen upon, obtain
    (+ gen.)

1-2 τὸ ἔχειν ἀντιφάρμακον αὐτούς articular inf., obj. of the prep. διά, w/ an acc. subj. (αὐτούς; Smyth § 1972) and an acc. obj. (ἀντιφάρμακον): "(through [the fact of]/on account of) their having an antidote"

5-6 οἱ μὲν...οἱ δὲ "some...others..."

6 ἐστεφανωμένοι masc. nom. pl. perf. pass. part. < στεφανόω; note augmentation of ε- instead of reduplication of stem to form the perf. (Smyth § 442b)

6-7 λύπης καὶ ταραχῆς sc. ἔμφασιν ποιοῦσιν

7 κνήμας...κεφαλάς accs. of respect
τετρῖφθαι perf. pass. inf. < τρίβω

9 σεσωσμένοι masc. nom. pl. perf. mid./pass. part. < σώζω (+ πρός =) "arrive safely at"

10 τετυχηκότες masc. nom. pl. perf. act. part. < τυγχάνω
ἀπεγνωσμένοι masc. nom. pl. perf. pass. part. < ἀπογιγνώσκω; note augmentation (ε-) instead of reduplication of stem to form the perf. (Smyth § 440a)

ἀποδεδειλιακότες καὶ οὐκ ἀναβεβηκότες πρὸς τὴν Καρτερίαν, πάλιν 1

ἀνακάμπτουσι καὶ πλανῶνται ἀνοδίᾳ. 2

Ξένος: Αἱ δὲ γυναῖκες, αἱ μετ' αὐτῶν ἀκολουθοῦσαι, τίνες εἰσὶν αὗται; 3

Πρεσβύτης: Λῦπαι, ἔφη, καὶ Ὀδύναι καὶ Ἀθυμίαι καὶ Ἀδοξίαι καὶ Ἄγνοιαι. 4

[28] Ξένος: Πάντα κακὰ λέγεις αὐτοῖς ἀκολουθεῖν. 5

Πρεσβύτης: Νὴ Δία, πάντα, ἔφη, ἐπακολουθοῦσιν. ὅταν δὲ οὗτοι 6

παραγένωνται εἰς τὸν πρῶτον περίβολον πρὸς τὴν Ἡδυπάθειαν καὶ τὴν 7

Ἀκρασίαν, οὐχ ἑαυτοὺς αἰτιῶνται, ἀλλ' εὐθὺς κακῶς λέγουσι καὶ τὴν Παιδείαν 8

καὶ τοὺς ἐκεῖσε βαδίζοντας, ὡς ταλαίπωροι καὶ ἄθλιοί εἰσι καὶ κακοδαίμονες, οἳ 9

τὸν βίον τὸν παρ' αὐταῖς ἀπολιπόντες κακῶς ζῶσι καὶ οὐκ ἀπολαύνουσι τῶν 10

παρ' αὐταῖς ἀγαθῶν. 11

Ξένος: Ποῖα δὲ λέγουσιν ἀγαθὰ εἶναι;

ἀγαθός, -ή, -όν, good

ἀδοξία, ἡ, dishonor, disgrace, ill repute

ἄθλιος, -ία, -ιον, wretched

ἀθυμία, ἡ, despondency, discouragement, rejection

αἰτιάομαι/αἰτιῶμαι, blame

ἀκολουθέω, follow (often + dat.)

ἀναβαίνω, go up, ascend

ἀνοδία, ἡ, trackless waste

ἀποδειλιάω, shrink back, cower, be very fearful

ἀπολαύω, enjoy (+ gen.)

ἀπολείπω, ἀπολείψω, ἀπέλιπον, abandon

βαδίζω, go

ἐκεῖσε, (adv.) to that place

ἐπακολουθέω, follow after, pursue

εὐθύς, (adv.) immediately, at once

ζάω/ζῶ, live

ἡδυπάθεια, ἡ, [lit., pleasant experience] luxury

κακοδαίμων, -ον, unhappy

κακῶς, (adv.) wickedly; badly, poorly

καρτερία, ἡ, perseverance, patient endurance

νή, (adv. of swearing) yes, by X! (acc.)

ὀδύνη, ἡ, pain (of body or mind); grief; distress

παρά, (prep. + dat.) with

πλανάω, -ήσω, make X wander; lead X astray; deceive X; (pass.), wander

ταλαίπωρος, -ον, miserable

---

1 ἀποδεδειλιακότες masc. nom. pl. perf. act. part. < ἀποδειλιάω
ἀναβεβηκότες masc. nom. pl. perf. act. part. < ἀναβαίνω

2 ἀνοδίᾳ dat. of place where (Smyth § 1531; in Cl. Gk., the dat. of place w/out a prep. occurs only in verse)

5 Πάντα κακὰ λέγεις αὐτοῖς ἀκολουθεῖν some editors and translators take this sentence as a question

6 πάντα neut. pl. subj. of ἐπακολουθοῦσιν. The pl. vb., rather than the usu. sing. w/ a neut. pl. subj., is probably being used here because the πάντα κακὰ are to be identified w/ the personifications (αἱ γυναῖκες) in the previous chapter

8 αἰτιῶνται (α-contract; αἰτιά + ονται) 3rd pl. pres. mid./pass. (dep.) indic. < αἰτιάομαι/αἰτιῶμαι

1 **Πρεσβύτης:** Τὴν ἀσωτίαν καὶ τὴν ἀκρασίαν, ὡς εἴποι ἄν τις ἐπὶ

2 κεφαλαίου. τὸ γὰρ εὐωχεῖσθαι βοσκημάτων τρόπον ἀπόλαυσιν

3 μεγίστων ἀγαθῶν ἡγοῦνται εἶναι.

4 **[29] Ξένος:** Αἱ δὲ ἕτεραι γυναῖκες αἱ ἐκεῖθεν παραγινόμεναι,

5 ἱλαραί τε καὶ γελῶσαι, τίνες καλοῦνται;

6 **Πρεσβύτης:** Δόξαι, ἔφη, αἱ ἀγαγοῦσαι πρὸς τὴν Παιδείαν τοὺς

7 εἰσελθόντας πρὸς τὰς Ἀρετὰς ἀνακάμπτουσιν, ὅπως ἑτέρους ἀγάγωσι,

8 καὶ ἀναγγέλλουσιν ὅτι εὐδαίμονες ἤδη γεγόνασιν οὓς τότε ἀπήγαγον.

9 **Ξένος:** Πότερον οὖν, ἔφην ἐγώ, αὗται εἴσω πρὸς τὰς Ἀρετὰς

10 ⟨οὐκ⟩ εἰσπορεύονται;

ἀναγγέλλω, report, announce
ἀνακάμπτω, turn back
ἀπάγω, ἀπάξω, ἀπήγαγον, lead away
ἀπόλαυσις, -εως, ἡ, enjoyment of
  (+ gen.)
ἀσωτία, ἡ, profligacy
βόσκημα, -τος, τό, that which is fed;
  (pl.) cattle
γελάω/γελῶ, laugh
δόξα, ἡ, opinion
εἰσέρχομαι, εἰσελεύσομαι, εἰσῆλθον, go
  or enter into
εἰσπορεύω, lead in; (pass.) enter
εἴσω, (adv.) within, inside
ἐκεῖθεν, (adv.) from there
ἐξαιρέω, ἐξαιρήσω, ἐξεῖλον, take out;
  (mid., of ships) unload (their cargo)

εὐωχέω, treat well; (mid.) feast
ἡγέομαι, believe, think, consider
ἱλαρός, -ά, -όν, joyous
κεφάλαιον, τό, the substance, the main
  point, the sum of the matter; ἐπὶ κεφαλαίου,
  in a word, in short, to be brief
ἤδη, (adv.) now, already
μέγιστος, -η, -ον, greatest
ναῦς, νεώς, ἡ, ship
ὅπως, (adv.) in order that, that (+ subju.)
τότε, (adv.) then, at that time
τρόπος, ὁ, manner, way; τρόπον, (acc. [of
  respect] as adv.) in the manner of (+ gen.)
φορτίον, -ου, τό, load, burden; (pl.) wares,
  cargo

---

1 εἴποι 3rd sing. aor. act. opt. < εἶπον; w/ ἄν, a potential opt. (Smyth § 1824)

2 τὸ εὐωχεῖσθαι articular inf., here acc. subj. of εἶναι in indir. statement set up by ἡγοῦνται

5 γελῶσαι (α-contract; γελά + ουσαι) fem. nom. pl. pres. act. part. < γελάω/γελῶ

6 ἀγαγοῦσαι fem. pl. nom. aor. act. part. < ἄγω
ὅπως...ἀγάγωσι, καὶ ἀναγγέλλουσιν some editors read ἀναγγείλωσιν (i.e., within the ὅπως cl.)

8 γεγόνασιν 3rd pl. perf. act. indic. < γί(γ)νομαι
οὓς = ἐκείνους οὓς, the subj. of γεγόνασιν

Πρεσβύτης: [Ἔφη οὔ.] Οὐ γὰρ θέμις Δόξαν εἰσπορεύεσθαι πρὸς τὴν 1
Ἐπιστήμην· ἀλλὰ τῇ Παιδείᾳ παραδιδόασιν αὐτούς. εἶτα, ὅταν ἡ Παιδεία 2
παραλάβῃ, ἀνακάμπτουσιν αὗται πάλιν ἄλλους ἄξουσαι, ὥσπερ αἱ νῆες τὰ 3
φορτία ἐξελόμεναι πάλιν ἀνακάμπτουσι καὶ ἄλλων τινῶν γεμίζονται. 4

[30] Ξένος: Ταῦτα μὲν δὴ καλῶς μοι δοκεῖς, ἔφην, ἐξηγῆσθαι. ἀλλ' ἐκεῖνο 5
οὐδέπω ἡμῖν δεδήλωκας, τί προστάττει τὸ Δαιμόνιον τοῖς εἰσπορευομένοις εἰς 6
τὸν Βίον ποιεῖν. 7

Πρεσβύτης: Θαρρεῖν, ἔφη. διὸ καὶ ὑμεῖς θαρρεῖτε· πάντα γὰρ ἐξηγήσομαι 8
καὶ οὐδὲν παραλείψω. 9

Ξένος: Καλῶς λέγεις, ἔφην ἐγώ. 10

Πρεσβύτης: Ἐκτείνας οὖν τὴν χεῖρα πάλιν, Ὁρᾶτε, ἔφη, τὴν γυναῖκα 11
ἐκείνην, ἣ δοκεῖ τυφλή τις εἶναι καὶ ἐπὶ λίθου στρογγύλου ἑστάναι, ἣν καὶ ἄρτι 12
ὑμῖν εἶπον ὅτι Τύχη καλεῖται; 13

Ξένος: Ὁρῶμεν. 14

ἄρτι, (adv.) just, just now
γεμίζω, fill or load w/ (+ gen.)
Δαιμόνιον, τό = Δαίμων, Δαίμονος, ὁ
δηλόω, make clear
διό, (conj.; = δι[ά] ὅ, on account of which thing) wherefore, for which reason, therefore
εἶπον, (2nd aor.; pres in use is φήμι, λέγω, ἀγορεύω) said, spoke, told
ἐκτείνω, ἐκτενῶ, ἐξέτεινα, stretch out
ἐξηγέομαι, ἐξηγήσομαι, explain
ἐπιστήμη, ἡ, knowledge
θαρρέω, be confident; have courage

θέμις, θέμιδος, ἡ, right
καλῶς, (adv.) thoroughly; well
λίθος, ὁ, stone
οὐδέπω, (adv.) not yet
παραδίδωμι, deliver
παραλαμβάνω, παραλήψομαι, παρέλαβον, receive
παραλείπω, παραλείψω, omit, leave out
προστάττω, command X (dat.) to do Y (inf.)
στρογγύλος, -η, -ον, round
τυφλός, -ή, -όν, blind
χείρ, χειρός, ἡ, hand

---

1 [Ἔφη οὔ.] i.e., ""No," he answered." (Seddon)
οὐ θέμις sc. ἐστί (w/ acc. and inf. in indir. statement)

3 ἄξουσαι fem. nom. pl. fut. act. part. < ἄγω; fut. part. expressing purp. (Smyth § 2065)

5 μὲν δή expresses positive certainty, esp. in conclusions: "indeed, then..." (Smyth § 2900)

6 δεδήλωκας 2nd sing. perf. act. indic. < δηλόω

8 θαρρεῖν = τὸ Δαιμόνιον προστάττει τοῖς εἰσπορευομένοις εἰς τὸν βίον θαρρεῖν
ἐξηγήσομαι sc. ὑμῖν

11 τὴν χεῖρα the article is often used, where English employs a poss. pron., to mark something as belonging to a person or thing mentioned in the sentence (Smyth § 1121)

12 ἑστάναι perf. act. inf. < ἵστημι

1   **[31] Πρεσβύτης:** Ταύτῃ κελεύει, ἔφη, μὴ πιστεύειν, καὶ βέβαιον μηδὲν

2 νομίζειν μηδὲ ἀσφαλὲς εἶναι, ὅ τι ἂν παρ' αὐτῆς τις λάβῃ, μηδὲ ὡς ἴδια

3 ἡγεῖσθαι. οὐδὲν γὰρ κωλύει πάλιν ταῦτα ἀφελέσθαι καὶ ἑτέρῳ δοῦναι· πολλάκις

4 γὰρ εἴωθε τοῦτο ποιεῖν. καὶ διὰ ταύτην οὖν τὴν αἰτίαν κελεύει πρὸς τὰς παρ'

5 αὐτῆς δόσεις ἴσους γίνεσθαι καὶ μήτε χαίρειν ὅταν διδῷ μήτε ἀθυμεῖν ὅταν

6 ἀφέληται, καὶ μήτε ψέγειν αὐτὴν μήτε ἐπαινεῖν. οὐδὲν γὰρ ποιεῖ μετὰ λογισμοῦ,

7 ἀλλ' εἰκῆ καὶ ὡς ἔτυχε πάντα, ὥσπερ πρότερον ὑμῖν ἔλεξα. διὰ τοῦτο οὖν τὸ

ἀθυμέω, be disheartened, discouraged or despondent; despair

αἰτία, ἡ, cause, reason

ἀσφαλής, -ές, safe, secure

ἀφαιρέω, ἀφαιρήσω, ἀφεῖλον, take away; (mid.) take away (for oneself)

βέβαιος, -αία, -ον, stable, constant, secure, certain

διά, (prep. + acc.) on account of, because of, for

δίδωμι, give

δόσις, -εως, ἡ, gift

ἔθω, εἴωθα (perf. as pres.), be accustomed

εἰκῆ, (adv.) randomly, at random; recklessly, w/out plan or purpose

ἐπαινέω, praise

ἡγέομαι, believe, think, consider

ἴδιος, -ία, -ον, private, one's own; τὰ ἴδια, private property, one's own property

ἴσος, -η, -ον, indifferent

κελεύω, command, order, urge

κωλύω, prevent X (acc.) from doing Y (inf.)

λαμβάνω, λήψομαι, ἔλαβον, take, receive

λέγω, λέξω, ἔλεξα, say, speak, tell

λογισμός, ὁ, reason, reflection, consideration

μηδέ, (conj.) and not, nor yet, neither; μηδέ...μηδέ, neither...nor

μηδείς, μηδεμία, μηδέν, no one, nothing

μήτε, (particle) and not; (mostly doubled) neither...nor

νομίζω, believe

πιστεύω, put one's trust in X (dat.), believe (in) X (dat.)

πολλάκις, (adv.) often, many times

πρός, (+ acc.) to, toward; pertaining to, in reference to

τυγχάνω, τεύξομαι, ἔτυχον, happen to one (dat.); ὡς/ὥσπερ ἔτυχεν, as it chances, as chance or luck has it (gnomic aor.); as it chanced, as luck had it

χαίρω, rejoice

ψέγω, blame

---

1 ταύτῃ i.e., Fortune, obj. of πιστεύειν
    κελεύει the subject is ὁ Δαίμων; sc. αὐτούς, i.e., the ones entering life, as obj.

2 ὅ τι ἄν "whatever" (+ subju. = general rel. cl. [Smyth § 2567])

3 κωλύει sc. αὐτήν, i.e., Τύχην, as obj.
    ἀφελέσθαι aor. mid. inf. < ἀφαιρέω

4 εἴωθε sc. Τύχη as subj.
    κελεύει sc. τὸ Δαιμόνιον as subj. and αὐτούς as object

5-6 διδῷ, ἀφέληται 3rd pres. act. subju. and 3rd aor. mid. subju. of δίδωμι and ἀφαιρέω, respectively, in a general temporal cl.

6 ποιεῖ sc. Τύχη as subj.

7 ἔτυχε punning on the understood subj. of this paragraph, Τύχη
    πάντα sc. ποιεῖ w/ πάντα as its dir. obj.

Δαιμόνιον κελεύει μὴ θαυμάζειν ὅ τι ἂν πράττῃ αὕτη, μηδὲ γίνεσθαι ὁμοίους   1

τοῖς κακοῖς τραπεζίταις. καὶ γὰρ ἐκεῖνοι, ὅταν μὲν λάβωσι τὸ ἀργύριον παρὰ   2

τῶν ἀνθρώπων, χαίρουσι καὶ ἴδιον νομίζουσιν εἶναι. ὅταν δὲ ἀπαιτῶνται,   3

ἀγανακτοῦσι καὶ δεινὰ οἴονται πεπονθέναι, οὐ μνημονεύοντες ὅτι ἐπὶ τούτῳ   4

ἔλαβον τὰ θέματα, ἐφ' ᾧ οὐδὲν κωλύει τὸν θέμενον πάλιν κομίσασθαι. ὡσαύτως   5

τοίνυν κελεύει ἔχειν τὸ Δαιμόνιον καὶ πρὸς τὴν παρ' αὐτῆς δόσιν καὶ   6

μνημονεύειν ὅτι τοιαύτην ἔχει φύσιν ἡ Τύχη, ὥστε ἃ δέδωκεν ἀφελέσθαι καὶ   7

ταχέως πάλιν δοῦναι πολλαπλάσια, αὖθις δὲ ἀφελέσθαι ἃ δέδωκεν· οὐ μόνον δὲ,   8

ἀγανακτέω, be annoyed, be angry
ἀπαιτέω, demand back, ask (for something)
  back; (pass.) be asked (to return something)
ἀργύριον, τό, money
Δαιμόνιον, τό = Δαίμων, Δαίμονος, ὁ
δεινός, -ή, -όν, terrible; δεινὰ παθεῖν, to
  suffer mistreatment or injuries
ἐπί, (prep. + dat.) on (the condition)
θαυμάζω, wonder at, marvel at (+ acc.)
θέμα, -τος, τό, deposit
κομίζω, κομιῶ/κομίσω, ἐκόμισα, carry;
  (mid.) receive again, recover
λαμβάνω, λήψομαι, ἔλαβον, take,
  receive
μνημονεύω, recall, remember

μόνος, -η, -ον, alone; μόνον, (adv.) only
ὅμοιος, -οία, -οιον, like (+ dat.)
πάσχω, suffer
πολλαπλάσιος, -ον, many times as many,
  many times more; πολλαπλάσια (adv.)
  many times over
πράττω, do
ταχέως, (adv.) quickly
τοιοῦτος, -αύτη, -οῦτο, such as this, of
  that kind
τραπεζίτης, -ου, ὁ, banker
φύσις, -εως, ἡ, nature, natural disposition
ὡσαύτως, (adv.) likewise, similarly, in the
  same way
ὥστε, (conj.) so that, so as

---

1 κελεύει sc. αὐτούς as obj.

2 καὶ γάρ "for in fact" (cf. Smyth § 2814-15)

3 ἴδιον...εἶναι = νομίζουσιν τὸ ἀργύριον (παρὰ τῶν ἀνθρώπων) εἶναι ἴδιον

4 πεπονθέναι perf. act. inf. < πάσχω
  ἐπὶ τούτῳ...ἐφ' ᾧ "on this condition...on the condition that" (cf. BrDAG s.v. ἐπί
  II.H and Smyth § 2279)

5 τὸν θέμενον lit. "the one having made the deposit," i.e., the depositor

5-6 ὡσαύτως...ἔχειν another example of ἔχω + adv. = (at least in terms of their
  English equivalent) εἰμί + adj. (see note to ὡσαύτως...ἔχει on p. 21, lines 3-4); lit.,
  "to hold (oneself) in the same way," i.e., to be the same

6 κελεύει sc. αὐτούς, i.e., the ones entering life

7 ὥστε result cl. (+ inf. = potential result)

7-8 ἃ δέδωκεν ἀφελέσθαι...ἀφελέσθαι ἃ δέδωκεν note *chiasmus*, the crosswise
  arrangement of contrasted pairs to give alternate stress

8 οὐ μόνον δέ, sc. these things

1 ἀλλὰ καὶ τὰ προϋπάρχοντα. ἃ γοῦν δίδωσι, λαβεῖν κελεύει παρ' αὐτῆς καὶ

2 συντόμως ἀπελθεῖν βλέποντας πρὸς τὴν βεβαίαν καὶ ἀσφαλῆ δόσιν.

3 **[32] Ξένος:** Ποίαν ταύτην; ἔφην ἐγώ.

4 **Πρεσβύτης:** Ἣν λήψονται παρὰ τῆς Παιδείας, ἢν διασωθῶσιν ἐκεῖ.

5 **Ξένος:** Αὕτη οὖν τίς ἐστιν;

6 **Πρεσβύτης:** Ἡ ἀληθὴς ἐπιστήμη τῶν συμφερόντων, ἔφη, καὶ ἀσφαλὴς δόσις

7 καὶ βεβαία καὶ ἀμεταμέλητος. φεύγειν οὖν κελεύει συντόμως πρὸς ταύτην· καὶ

8 ὅταν ἔλθωσι πρὸς τὰς γυναῖκας ἐκείνας, ἃς καὶ πρότερον εἶπον ὅτι Ἀκρασία

9 καὶ Ἡδυπάθεια καλοῦνται, καὶ ἐντεῦθεν κελεύει συντόμως ἀπαλλάττεσθαι

ἀληθής, -ές, true
ἀμεταμέλητος, -ον, not to be regretted, never causing regret
ἀπαλλάττω, -άξω, set free; (mid./pass.) depart
ἀπέρχομαι, ἀπελεύσομαι, ἀπῆλθον, depart, go away
ἀσφαλής, -ές, safe, secure
βέβαιος, -αία, -ον, stable, constant, secure, certain
βλέπω, look; + πρός, look to, rely on, have regard for
γοῦν (γε οὖν), (particle) at all events, at any rate
διασῴζω, bring safely through; (pass.) arrive safely

δόσις, -εως, ἡ, gift
ἐκεῖ, (adv.) there
ἐντεῦθεν, (adv.) from here, from there
ἐπιστήμη, ἡ, knowledge
ἔρχομαι, ἐλεύσομαι, ἦλθον, come
ἡδυπάθεια, ἡ, luxury
ἤν (= ἐάν [εἰ ἄν]), if (ever) (+ subju.)
λαμβάνω, λήψομαι, ἔλαβον, take
προϋπάρχω, possess previously, exist before, be preexistent; τὰ προϋπάρχοντα, things in one's possession beforehand
συμφέρω, serve; (as impers.) it profits; τὰ συμφερόντα, things that are advantageous, advantages
συντόμως, (adv.) immediately, quickly
φεύγω, flee

---

1 δίδωσι sc. Τύχη as subj.
κελεύει sc. τὸ Δαιμόνιον/ὁ Δαίμων as subj. and αὐτούς as obj.

3 Ποίαν ταύτην; = Ποίαν ταύτην τὴν δόσιν;

4 ἣν sc. ἡ δόσις as antecedent
διασωθῶσιν 3rd pl. aor. pass. subju. < διασῴζω; subju. in the protasis of a FMV condit.

5 αὕτη i.e., αὕτη ἡ δόσις

6 δόσις sc. ἐστὶ.

7-2 κελεύει...κελεύει...κελεύει sc. τὸ Δαιμόνιον/ὁ Δαίμων as subj. and αὐτούς, i.e., the ones entering life, as obj.

καὶ μὴ πιστεύειν μηδὲ ταύταις μηδέν, ἕως ἂν πρὸς τὴν Ψευδοπαιδείαν   1
ἀφίκωνται. κελεύει οὖν αὐτοῦ χρόνον τινὰ ἐνδιατρῖψαι καὶ λαβεῖν ὅ τι ἂν   2
βούλωνται παρ᾽ αὐτῆς ὥσπερ ἐφόδιον· εἶτα ἐντεῦθεν ἀπιέναι πρὸς τὴν Ἀληθινὴν   3
Παιδείαν συντόμως. ταῦτά ἐστιν ἃ προστάττει τὸ Δαιμόνιον. ὅστις τοίνυν παρ᾽   4
αὐτά τι ποιεῖ ἢ παρακούει, ἀπόλλυται κακὸς κακῶς.   5

[33] **Πρεσβύτης:** Ὁ μὲν δὴ μῦθος, ὦ ξένοι, ὁ ἐν τῷ πίνακι τοιοῦτος ἡμῖν   6
ἐστίν. εἰ δὲ δεῖ τι προσπυθέσθαι περὶ ἑκάστου τούτων, οὐδεὶς φθόνος· ἐγὼ γὰρ   7
ὑμῖν φράσω.   8

ἄπειμι, go away, depart
ἀπόλλυμι, destroy; (mid.) perish, die
αὐτοῦ, (adv.) here, there
ἀφικνέομαι, ἀφίξομαι, ἀφικόμην, arrive
βούλομαι, wish, want
Δαιμόνιον, τό = Δαίμων, Δαίμονος, ὁ
δεῖ, (impers. vb.) it is necessary, one should (+ acc. and inf.)
εἰ, (conj.) if
ἕκαστος, -η, -ον, each, every
ἐνδιατρίβω, (w/ or w/out χρόνον) spend time (in a place)
ἐφόδιος, -ον, requisite for travelling; τὸ ἐφόδιον, travelling provisions, supplies for travelling (e.g., money and provisions)
ἕως, (conj.; + ἄν w/ subju. [most often aor.], of an event at an uncertain future time) until
ἤ, (conj.) or
μηδέ, (conj.) and not, nor yet, neither

μηδείς, μηδεμία, μηδέν, no one, nothing; μηδέν, (adv.) not at all, by no means
μῦθος, ὁ, fable, myth, allegory
ξένος, ὁ, stranger, foreigner; guest-friend
ὅστις, ἥτις, ὅ τι, who(ever), what(ever)
παρά (prep. + acc.) contrary to, in violation of
παρακούω, refuse to listen, pay no attention to
πίναξ, -ακος, ὁ, tablet
πιστεύω, put one's trust in X (dat.), believe (in) X (dat.)
προσπυνθάνομαι, προσπεύσομαι, προσεπυθόμην, inquire further
προστάττω, command
τοιοῦτος, -αύτη, -οῦτο, of that kind, of such character
φθόνος, ὁ, envy; grudging; ill-will; + οὐδείς, no refusal, no objection, no reluctance
φράζω, φράσω, say, explain
χρόνος, ὁ, time
Ψευδοπαιδεία, ἡ, False Education

---

1 μὴ...μηδὲ...μηδέν emphatic repetition of the neg. (Smyth § 2761): "not to trust in them at all." (cf. p. 39, line 2 and p. 53, line 6)

2 ἐνδιατρῖψαι Jerram (41) notes that: "The ἐν means 'in that place,' i.e. with False Learning (cf. XII.); the διὰ implies continuance for some time."
ὅ τι ἂν "whatever" (+ subju. = general rel. cl. [Smyth § 2567])

3 ἀπιέναι pres. act. inf. < ἄπειμι/ἀπέρχομαι

4 ταῦτά ἐστιν ἅ = ταῦτά ἐστιν ἐκεῖνα ἅ

5 κακὸς κακῶς Jerram (42) notes that this: "[is] not a redundant phrase..., but a forcible way of expressing a superlative, = κάκιστα, 'in *utter* miser.' Lit. 'a miserable man in a miserable way.'"

6 ἡμῖν dat. of interest expressing possession (Smyth § 1476): "Such is *our* fable" (Jerram, 42)

7 οὐδεὶς φθόνος sc. ἔστι μοι

1 **Ξένος:** Καλῶς λέγεις, ἔφην ἐγώ. ἀλλὰ τί κελεύει αὐτοὺς τὸ Δαιμόνιον

2 λαβεῖν παρὰ τῆς Ψευδοπαιδείας.

3 **Πρεσβύτης:** Ταῦτα ἃ δοκεῖ εὔχρηστα εἶναι.

4 **Ξένος:** Ταῦτ᾽ οὖν τίνα ἐστι;

5 **Πρεσβύτης:** Γράμματα, ἔφη, καὶ τῶν ἄλλων μαθημάτων ἃ καὶ Πλάτων

6 φησὶν ὡσανεὶ χαλινοῦ τινος δύναμιν ἔχειν τοῖς νέοις, ἵνα μὴ εἰς ἕτερα

7 περισπῶνται.

8 **Ξένος:** Πότερον δὲ ἀνάγκη ταῦτα λαβεῖν, εἰ μέλλει τις ἥξειν πρὸς τὴν

9 Ἀληθινὴν Παιδείαν, ἢ οὔ;

10 **Πρεσβύτης:** Ἀνάγκη μὲν οὐδεμία, ἔφη· χρήσιμα μέντοι ἐστὶ πρὸς τὸ

11 συντομώτερον ἐλθεῖν. πρὸς δὲ τὸ βελτίους γενέσθαι οὐδὲν συμβάλλεται ταῦτα.

ἀνάγκη, ἡ, necessity, compulsion; ἀνάγκη
  (w/ or w/out ἐστί), it is necessary to do a
  thing (inf.)
βελτίων, -ον, better
γράμμα, -τος, τό, letter; (pl.) literature
Δαιμόνιον, τό = Δαίμων, Δαίμονος, ὁ
δύναμις, -εως, ἡ, force
ἔρχομαι, ἐλεύσομαι, ἦλθον, go
εὔχρηστος, -ον, useful
ἥκω, ἥξω, come, have come
ἵνα, (conj. initiating a purp. cl.) in order that,
  that; ἵνα μή = neg. purp. cl.
καλῶς, (adv.) well
κελεύω, command, order, urge
λαμβάνω, λήψομαι, ἔλαβον, take

μάθημα, -ατος, τό, academic discipline,
  (field of) study
μέλλω, intend (+ inf., usu. fut.)
μέντοι, (particle) however
νεός, -α, -ον, young; ὁ νέος, οἱ νέοι, young
  person, youth
περισπάω, draw away, distract
Πλάτων, -ονος, ὁ, Plato
συμβάλλω, contribute; (mid. = act.) + πρός
  (+ acc.), contribute to/towards
συντομώτερον, (adv.) more quickly
χαλινός, ὁ, bridle
χρήσιμος, -ον, useful
ὡσανεί (adv.; = ὡς ἂν εἰ, lit., as [it] would
  [be] if), as if

----

5 τῶν ἄλλων μαθημάτων partitive gen.; sc. ἐκεῖνα

5-6 Πλάτων...τοῖς νέοις "Plato in the seventh book of the *Laws* says that a boy is
  the most unmanageable of wild animals, needing many an application of the bit."
  (Parsons, 73-4). τοῖς νέοις dat. of interest (Smyth § 1474)

6 εἰς ἕτερα "that is, to other pursuits, which are of themselves evil" (Parsons, 74)

7 περισπῶνται 3rd pl. pres. mid./pass. subju. < περισπάω; subju. in a neg. purp. cl. in
  primary sequence (Smyth § 2193, 2196)

8 μέλλει + pres., fut., or aor. inf. = periphrastic fut. construction (Smyth § 1959)

10 ἀνάγκη...οὐδεμία sc. ἐστι

10-11 πρὸς τὸ...ἐλθεῖν...πρὸς...τὸ...γενέσθαι prep. + acc. articular inf. (Smyth §
  2034b): "for going...", "to becoming...", respectively

11 βελτίους syncopated alternative form (which occurs more frequently in everyday
  speech than in literature; Smyth § 293b) of masc./fem. nom./acc. pl. βελτίονες, formed
  from βελτίο(σ)ες -> βελτίους, comp. of ἀγαθός

64

Ξένος: Οὐδὲν ἄρα, ἔφην, λέγεις ταῦτα χρήσιμα εἶναι πρὸς τὸ βελτίους 1
γενέσθαι ἄνδρας; 2

Πρεσβύτης: Ἔστι γὰρ καὶ ἄνευ τούτων βελτίους γενέσθαι. ὅμως δὲ οὐκ 3
ἄχρηστα κἀκεῖνά ἐστιν. ὡς γὰρ δι᾽ ἑρμηνέως συμβάλλομεν τὰ λεγόμενά ποτε, 4
ὅμως μέντοι γε οὐκ ἄχρηστον ἂν ἦν ἡμᾶς καὶ αὐτοὺς τὴν φωνὴν εἰδέναι, 5
ἀκριβέστερον γὰρ ἄν τι συνήκαμεν· οὕτω καὶ ἄνευ τούτων τῶν μαθημάτων 6
οὐδὲν κωλύει ⟨βελτίους⟩ γενέσθαι 7

[34] Ξένος: Πότερον οὖν οὐδὲ προέχουσιν οὗτοι οἱ μαθηματικοὶ πρὸς τὸ 8
βελτίους γενέσθαι τῶν ἄλλων ἀνθρώπων; 9

ἀκριβέστερον, (adv.) more accurately
ἄνευ, (prep. + gen.) without
ἄχρηστος, -ον, useless
ἑρμηνεύς, -έως, ὁ, interpreter
μαθηματικός, -ή, -όν, skilled in learning;
  ὁ μαθηματικός, scholar
οἶδα, (2nd perf. w/ pres. sense) know
ὅμως, (conj.) nevertheless
ποτέ, (particle) sometimes

προέχω, have a head start, have an
  advantage (over + gen.), surpass or excel
  (someone [gen.])
πρός, (prep. + acc.) for the purpose of, in
  order to (esp. of πρὸς τό w/ inf.)
συμβάλλω, infer, conjecture, surmise
συνίημι, understand
φωνή, ἡ, language

---

11 συμβάλλεται subj. is ταῦτα (neut. pl. subj. w/ sing. vb.; see note to ἔχοντα on p.
23, line 1)

3 Ἔστι "it is possible" (+ inf.; Smyth § 1985)

4 κἀκεῖνα = καὶ ἐκεῖνα

5 ἂν ἦν w/ the indic. mood of historical tenses (i.e., the "past potential"), ἄν signifies
past potentiality, probability, or necessity (Smyth § 1784): "would be" or "would have
been"; so too w/ συνήκαμεν
  καὶ αὐτούς "also ourselves." Some mss. have αὐτὴν or αὐτῶν for αὐτούς.

6 τι an adverbial acc. of measure and degree (Smyth § 1609), "somewhat," "a little," "a
bit," modifying ἀκριβέστερον, not the pronominal dir. obj. of συνήκαμεν
  συνήκαμεν 1st pl. aor. act. indic. < συνίημι

7 κωλύει sc. "one" as obj.
  ⟨βελτίους⟩ γενέσθαι . . . . "The ellipsis is probably resolved on the basis of 33.4
as follows: οὕτω καὶ ἄνευ τούτων τῶν μαθημάτων οὐδὲν κωλύει ⟨βελτίους⟩ γενέσθαι
ὅμως μέντοί γε χρήσιμα ἐστὶ πρὸς τὸ συντομώτερον ἐλθεῖν πρὸς τὴν ἀληθινὴν
Παιδείαν⟩. The point of the comparison is then as follows: Just as the knowledge of a
foreign language is useful for increasing the accuracy of one's understanding of what is
said, so also the knowledge of the general studies is useful for increasing rapidity of
one's journey to true Paideia. But just as one, without knowing the language, can
grasp the meaning of a statement with the help of an interpreter, so also one can arrive
at true Paideia without knowing the μαθήματα." (Fitzgerald and White, 164)

1 **Πρεσβύτης:** Πῶς [γὰρ] μέλλουσι προέχειν, ἐπειδὰν φαίνωνται
2 ἠπατημένοι περὶ ἀγαθῶν καὶ κακῶν, ὥσπερ καὶ οἱ ἄλλοι, καὶ ἔτι κατεχόμενοι
3 ὑπὸ πάσης κακίας; οὐδὲν γὰρ κωλύει εἰδέναι μὲν γράμματα καὶ κατέχειν τὰ
4 μαθήματα πάντα, ὁμοίως δὲ μέθυσον καὶ ἀκρατῆ εἶναι καὶ φιλάργυρον καὶ
5 ἄδικον καὶ προδότην καὶ τὸ πέρας ἄφρονα.

6 **Ξένος:** Ἀμέλει πολλοὺς τοιούτους ἔστιν ἰδεῖν.

7 **Πρεσβύτης:** Πῶς οὖν οὗτοι προέχουσιν, ἔφη, εἰς τὸ βελτίους ἄνδρας
8 γενέσθαι ἕνεκα τούτων τῶν μαθημάτων;

9 **[35] Ξένος:** Οὐδαμῶς φαίνεται ἐκ τούτου τοῦ λόγου. ἀλλὰ τί ἐστιν, ἔφην
10 ἐγώ, τὸ αἴτιον ὅτι ἐν τῷ δευτέρῳ περιβόλῳ διατρίβουσιν ὥσπερ ἐγγίζοντες
11 πρὸς τὴν Ἀληθινὴν Παιδείαν;

ἄδικος, -ον, unjust
αἴτιον, τό, cause, reason
ἀκρατής, -ές, intemperate, w/out command over oneself
ἀμέλει, (3rd sing. impersonal of ἀμελέω ["don't trouble yourself"] used as adv.) doubtless, of course
ἀνήρ, ἀνδρός, ὁ, man
ἀπατάω, deceive
ἄφρων, -ον, mindless, foolish
βελτίων, -ον, better
δεύτερος, -έρα, -ερον, second
διατρίβω, spend time
ἐγγίζω, approach, come or draw near
ἕνεκα, (prep. + gen., mostly after its case) because of; as a result of
ἐπειδάν [ἐπεί + δή + ἄν] whenever (+ subju.)

κατέχω, control, hold down; overpower, oppress, afflict; master, understand
κωλύω, prevent X (acc.) from doing Y (inf.)
λόγος, ὁ, argument
μάθημα, -ατος, τό, academic discipline, (field of) study
μέθυσος, -ον, drunken
μέλλω, be going to (+ inf., usu. fut.)
ὁμοίως, (adv.) likewise, at the same time
οὐδαμῶς, (adv.) in no way/manner
πέρας, -τος, τό, end; (acc. as adv.) in short
προδότης, -ου, ὁ, traitor, treacherous person
πῶς, (adv.) how?
φαίνω, bring to light; (pass.) be seen, seem, appear; (+ part.) be clearly doing X/X-ed
φιλάργυρος, -ον, greedy, avaricious

---

1 ἐπειδάν always has a temporal meaning, but here the simple causal ἐπειδή ("since") seems to fit the narrative better

2 ἠπατημένοι masc. nom. pl. perf. pass. part. < ἀπατάω

3 κωλύει sc. "one" as obj.

7 εἰς (+ articular inf.) "w/ regard to" (Smyth § 2034b)

6 ἔστιν "it is possible" (+ inf.)
     ἰδεῖν aor. act. inf. < ὁράω

8 τῶν ἀνθρώπων gen. of comp. (Smyth § 1431)

Πρεσβύτης: Καὶ τί τοῦτο ὠφελεῖ αὐτούς, ἔφη, ὅτε πολλάκις ἔστιν ἰδεῖν 1

παραγινομένους ἐκ τοῦ πρώτου περιβόλου ἀπὸ τῆς Ἀκρασίας καὶ τῆς ἄλλης 2

Κακίας εἰς τὸν τρίτον περίβολον πρὸς τὴν Παιδείαν τὴν Ἀληθινήν, οἳ τούτους 3

τοὺς μαθηματικοὺς παραλλάτουσιν; ὥστε, πῶς ἔτι προέχουσιν ἄρα, εἰ 4

ἀκινητότεροι ἢ δυσμαθέστεροί εἰσι; 5

Ξένος: Πῶς τοῦτο, ἔφην ἐγώ; 6

Πρεσβύτης: Ὅτι οἱ ἐν τῷ δευτέρῳ περιβόλῳ, εἰ μηδὲν ἄλλο, ὃ 7

προσποιοῦνταί γε ἐπίστασθαι οὐκ οἴδασιν. ἕως δ' ἂν ἔχωσι ταύτην τὴν δόξαν, 8

ἀκινήτους αὐτοὺς ἀνάγκη εἶναι πρὸς τὸ ὁρμᾶν πρὸς τὴν Ἀληθινὴν Παιδείαν. 9

ἀκίνητος, -ον, unmoved, inert, inflexible,
  intractable
ἄλλος, -η, -ο, other, any other; τὰ ἄλλα,
  (all) the other things, the rest
ἀνάγκη, ἡ, necessity; ἀνάγκη (w/ or w/out
  ἐστί), it is necessary/must be (that X [acc.]
  do or be Y [inf.])
ἄρα, (conj.) then
γέ, (particle) at least
δόξα, ἡ, opinion
δυσμαθής, -ές, slow at learning, slow-
  witted, dull, obtuse
εἰ, (conj.) if
ἐπίσταμαι, understand
ἕως, (conj.) until, as long as; (+ ἄν w/ subju.
  = gen. temporal cl.), until, as long as, while
ἤ, (conj.) than; or

μαθηματικός, -ή, -όν, skilled in learning;
  ὁ μαθηματικός, scholar
μηδείς, μηδεμία, μηδέν, no one, nothing
οἶδα, (2nd perf. w/ pres. sense) know
ὁρμάω/ὁρμῶ, move toward, set out for
ὅτε, (conj.) when
ὅτι, (conj.) because
παραλλάττω, pass by (in a race), overtake,
  surpass
πολλάκις, (adv.) often, many times
πρός, (prep. + acc.) in terms of, w/ regard to
  (esp. of πρὸς τό w/ inf.)
προσποιέω, make over to; (mid.) pretend to,
  lay claim to (+ inf.)
τρίτος, -η, -ον, third
ὥστε, (conj.) so, so then
ὠφελέω, help, benefit

---

1 ἔστιν "it is possible" (+ inf.)

2-3 τῆς ἄλλης Κακίας "the rest of Vice/Wickedness"

4-5 εἰ ἀκινητότεροι ἢ δυσμαθέστεροί εἰσι; two possible readings: (1) "if they are
  more intractable than they are more slow-witted"; (2) "if they are more intractable or
  (possibly = and) more slow-witted." Commentators add: "the conclusion is a sarcastic
  demonstration of the way that the μαθηματικοί surpass others" (Steadman, 47); "ἄρα
  seems ironical, and sharpens the exposure of the error; as if he said, "They are superior
  only in stolidity or obtuseness." (Parsons, 74)
  ἀκινητότεροι...δυσμαθέστεροί comps. of ἀκίνητος, -ον and δυσμαθής, -ές

8 μηδὲν ἄλλο "nothing else," "for no other (reason)"

10 ὁρμᾶν (α-contract; ὁρμάω + ειν) pres. act. inf. < ὁρμάω/ὁρμῶ
  τὸ ἕτερον "the other (reason)"; in addition to the εἰ μηδὲν ἄλλο of line 7

1   εἶτα τὸ ἕτερον οὐχ ὁρᾷς, ὅτι καὶ αἱ Δόξαι ἐκ τοῦ πρώτου περιβόλου

2   εἰσπορεύονται πρὸς αὐτοὺς ὁμοίως; ὥστε, οὐδὲν οὗτοι ἐκείνων βελτίους εἰσὶν,

3   ἐὰν μὴ καὶ τούτοις συνῇ ἡ Μεταμέλεια καὶ πεισθῶσιν ὅτι οὐ Παιδείαν ἔχουσιν,

4   ἀλλὰ Ψευδοπαιδείαν, δι' ἣν ἀπατῶνται. οὕτω δὲ διακείμενοι οὐκ ἄν ποτε

5   σωθεῖεν. καὶ ὑμεῖς τοίνυν, ὦ ξένοι, ἔφη, οὕτω ποιεῖτε καὶ ἐνδιατρίβετε τοῖς

6   λεγομένοις, μέχρις ἂν ἕξιν λάβητε. ἀλλὰ περὶ τῶν αὐτῶν πολλάκις δεῖ

7   ἐπισκοπεῖν, καὶ μὴ διαλείπειν· τὰ δὲ ἄλλα πάρεργα ἡγήσασθαι. εἰ δὲ μή, οὐδὲν

8   ὄφελος ὑμῖν ἔσται ὧν νῦν ἀκούετε.

ἀκούω, hear (+ gen.)

ἄλλος, -η, -ο, other, any other; τὰ ἄλλα, (all) the other things, the rest

ἀπατάω, deceive

δεῖ, (impers. vb.) it is necessary, one should (+ acc. and inf.)

διά, (prep. + acc.) through, by

διάκειμαι, be disposed, be in a certain state (+ adv.)

διαλείπω, cease, stop

δόξα, ἡ, opinion

ἐάν, (conj. =) εἰ ἄν, if (ever) (+ subju.); + μή, unless, if...not

εἰ, (conj.) if

ἐκ/ἐξ, (prep. + gen.) from

ἐνδιατρίβω, spend time w/, dwell w/, continue in the practice (of a thing) (+ dat.)

ἕξις, -εως, ἡ, habit

ἐπισκοπέω, watch over, reflect on

ἡγέομαι, consider X (acc.) to be/as Y (acc.)

μεταμέλεια, ἡ, repentance

μέχρι, (conj.; before a vowel = μέχρις) until; (w/ ἄν + subju. = a gen. templ. cl.) until

ξένος, -η, -ον, strange, foreign, unusual; (subst.) stranger

ὁμοίως, (adv.) likewise, in the same way, as well

οὐδείς, οὐδεμία, οὐδέν, no one, nothing; no; οὐδέν, (acc. of respect as adv.) not at all, in no way

ὄφελος, -ους, τό, advantage

πάρεργος, -ον, secondary

πείθω, persuade

ποιέω, act, do

πολλάκις, (adv.) often, many times

ποτέ, (particle) ever; (after negatives) never

σύνειμι, be w/ (+ dat.)

ὥστε, (conj.) so, so then

2-3 εἰσὶν, ἐὰν μή...συνῇ...πεισθῶσιν pres. gen. condit. (see note to ἐὰν...μὴ συνιῇ ἀπόλλυται on p. 22, line 1); συνῇ 3rd sing. pres. act. subju. < σύνειμι; πεισθῶσιν 3rd pl. aor. pass. subju. < πείθω; sc. by her

3 Μεταμέλεια Repentance (lit., "After-purpose"; synonymous w/ Μετάνοια, lit., "After-thought", in Chapters 10 and 11 [pp. 23-24])

5 σωθεῖεν 3rd pl. aor. pass. opt. < σῴζω/σώζω; w/ ἄν, a potential opt. (Smyth § 1824)

6 ἕξιν λάβητε English idiom prefers "*acquire* or *adopt* the habit"

6-7 δεῖ ἐπισκοπεῖν...μὴ διαλείπειν...ἡγήσασθαι sc. ὑμᾶς as the acc. subj. of the three infs.

7-8 εἰ δὲ μή,...ἔσται the so-called "emotional" fut. condit. (aka the fut. minatory), used when the protasis (i.e., the "if" cl.) expresses strong feeling (Smyth § 2328); sc. ποιήσετε (all the things I just told you to do) in the protasis

[36] Ξένος: Ποιήσομεν. τοῦτο δὲ ἐξήγησαι, πῶς οὐκ ἔστιν ἀγαθὰ, ὅσα **1**

λαμβάνουσιν οἱ ἄνθρωποι παρὰ τῆς Τύχης; οἷον τὸ ζῆν, τὸ ὑγιαίνειν, τὸ **2**

πλουτεῖν, τὸ εὐδοκιμεῖν, τὸ τέκνα ἔχειν, τὸ νικᾶν καὶ ὅσα τούτοις παραπλήσια; **3**

ἢ πάλιν, τὰ ἐναντία πῶς οὐκ ἔστι κακά; πάνυ γὰρ παράδοξον ἡμῖν καὶ ἄπιστον **4**

δοκεῖ τὸ λεγόμενον. **5**

Πρεσβύτης: Ἄγε τοίνυν, ἔφη, πειρῶ ἀποκρίνασθαι τὸ φαινόμενον περὶ ὧν **6**

ἄν σε ἐρωτῶ. **7**

Ξένος: Ἀλλὰ ποιήσω τοῦτο, ἔφην ἐγώ. **8**

Πρεσβύτης: Πότερον οὖν, ἐὰν κακῶς τις ζῇ, ἀγαθὸν ἐκείνῳ τὸ ζῆν; **9**

Ξένος: Οὔ μοι δοκεῖ, ἀλλὰ κακόν, ἔφην ἐγώ. **10**

ἄγε, (imper. of ἄγω used as adv. that introduces another impera.) come, come now, come on

ἄπιστος, -ον, incredible

ἀποκρίνω, choose; (mid.) answer

δοκέω, seem, think; δοκεῖ μοι, it seems (so) to me, I think so

ἐναντίος, -ία, -ίον, opposite

ἐξηγέομαι, explain

ἐρωτάω/ἐρωτῶ, ask

εὐδοκιμέω, be held in esteem, be honored, be famous, be popular, have a good reputation

ζάω/ζῶ, live

νικάω, win, be victorious

οἷος, οἵα, οἷον, of which kind or sort, such as; οἷον, (acc. of respect as adv.) such as, like, for example

παράδοξος, -ον, unexpected, strange, contradictory

παραπλήσιος, -ον, like (+ dat.)

πειράω, try (to + inf.); (mid./dep. = act.)

πλουτέω, be rich or wealthy

τέκνον, τό, child

ὑγιαίνω, be healthy

φαίνω, bring to light; (pass.) be seen, seem, appear; τὸ φαινόμενον, (lit., the thing appearing/what appears [to be the case]) one's opinion (LSJ s.v. φαίνω B.II.2.b.)

---

1 ἐξήγησαι 2nd sing. mid. aor. impera. < ἐξηγέομαι

2-3 τὸ ζῆν...τὸ νικᾶν six articular infs.

3 ὅσα τούτοις παραπλησια sc. ἐστί

6-7 A stylistic shift occurs at this point in the dialogue, as the narrative dynamic switches to the Socratic interrogative pattern found in many of Plato's *Dialogues*
πειρῶ (πειράσο -> πειράͱο -> πειρῶ) 2nd sing. mid./dep. pres. impera. < πειράω
περὶ ὧν ἄν...ἐρωτῶ in rel. cls., ἄν is more closely linked w/ the rel. pron. (making it indef., i.e., "whatever [things]") than w/ the subju. vb. (Smyth § 2328).
ἐρωτῶ 1st sing. pres. act. subju. < ἐρωτάω/ἐρωτῶ

8 Ἀλλὰ (in agreement, BrDAG s.v. ἀλλά 2D) "(but) yes," "(but) indeed"

9 ἐὰν...ζῇ protasis of a pres. gen. condit. (see note to ἐὰν...μὴ συνιῇ ἀπόλλυται on p. 22, line 1); for the apodosis, τὸ ζῆν ἀγαθὸν ἐκείνῳ τὸ ζῆν, sc. ἐστί
ἐκείνῳ dat. of interest (Smyth § 1474); so also τούτῳ two sentences later

1   **Πρεσβύτης:** Πῶς οὖν ἀγαθόν ἐστι τὸ ζῆν, ἔφη, εἴπερ τούτῳ ἐστὶ κακόν;

2   **Ξένος:** Ὅτι τοῖς μὲν κακῶς ζῶσι κακόν μοι δοκεῖ εἶναι, τοῖς δὲ καλῶς

3 ἀγαθόν.

4   **Πρεσβύτης:** Καὶ κακὸν ἄρα λέγεις τὸ ζῆν καὶ ἀγαθὸν εἶναι;

5   **Ξένος:** Ἔγωγε.

6   [37] **Πρεσβύτης:** Μὴ οὖν ἀπιθάνως λέγε. ἀδύνατον τὸ αὐτὸ πρᾶγμα

7 κακὸν καὶ ἀγαθὸν εἶναι. τοῦτο μὲν γὰρ καὶ ὠφέλιμον καὶ βλαβερὸν ἂν εἴη, καὶ

8 αἱρετὸν καὶ φευκτὸν τὸ αὐτὸ πρᾶγμα ἀεί.

9   **Ξένος:** Ἀπίθανον μέν. ἀλλὰ πῶς οὐχὶ τὸ κακῶς ζῆν, ᾧ ἂν ὑπάρχῃ, κακόν τι

10 αὐτῷ ὑπάρχει; οὐκοῦν εἰ κακόν τι ὑπάρχει αὐτῷ, κακὸν αὐτὸ τὸ ζῆν ἐστιν.

ἀδύνατος, -ον, impossible; ἀδύνατον, (w/ or w/out ἐστί) it is impossible (that X [acc.] be [inf.] Y [acc.])

ἀεί, (adv.) always

αἱρετός, -ή, -όν, (vb. adj.) be chosen, desirable

ἀπίθανος, -ον, incredible, implausible, not persuasive, unconvincing

ἀπιθάνως, (adv.) incredibly, implausibly, in a manner that is not persuasive, unconvincingly

ἄρα, (conj.) then

αὐτός, -ή, -όν, he, she, it; himself, herself, itself; ὁ αὐτός, the same

βλαβερός, -ά, -όν, harmful

δοκέω, seem, think; δοκεῖ μοι, it seems to me, I think

ἔγωγε, I, for my part, I myself; (frequently in answers, as an affirmative) I certainly do

εἴπερ, (conj.) if indeed, if in fact

ζάω/ζῶ, live

πρᾶγμα, -τος, τό, thing

ὑπάρχω, exist, be; belong

φευκτός, -ή, -όν, (vb. adj.) be shunned

ὠφέλιμος, -ον, useful

---

2 ζῶσι (α-contract; ἀναπηδά + ουσι) masc. dat. pl. pres. act. part. < ζάω

2-3 τοῖς...καλῶς ἀγαθόν = τοῖς...καλῶς ζῶσι ἀγαθόν ἐστί

7 εἴη 3rd sing. pres. act. opt. < εἰμί; w/ ἄν, a potential opt.

9 ἀπίθανον μέν sc. ἐστί; solitary μέν (i.e., w/out a corresponding δέ, is an asseverative, emphatic particle; Smyth § 2895-8) = "surely," "certainly," "indeed"

9-10 οὐχὶ τό κακῶς ζῆν...ὑπάρχει take οὐχὶ w/ ὑπάρχει; τὸ κακῶς ζῆν articular inf.

9 ᾧ ἂν ὑπάρχῃ "to whomever it belongs" (for ἄν in rel. cls., see note to περὶ ὧν ἄν...ἐρωτῶ on p. 71, lines 6-7); ὑπάρχῃ ""is", as often, but in philosophical discourse typically, though not always, in the sense of "to subsist as, to belong to, to be predicated of" rather than with an absolute existential force. It is a critical component in the vocabulary of Aristotelian syllogisms as they are categorized, e.g., in the *Prior Analytics.*" (Banchich, 44)

10 αὐτὸ τὸ ζῆν "living itself" (articular inf. [Smyth § 2025-30] + intensive adj. pron. [Smyth § 1204, 1206])

70

Πρεσβύτης: Ἀλλ' οὐ ταὐτό, ἔφη, ὑπάρχει τὸ ζῆν καὶ τὸ κακῶς ζῆν· ἢ οὐ   **1**

σοι φαίνεται;   **2**

Ξένος: Ἀμέλει οὐδ' ἐμοὶ δοκεῖ ταὐτὸ εἶναι.   **3**

Πρεσβύτης: Τὸ κακῶς τοίνυν ζῆν κακόν ἐστι· τὸ δὲ ζῆν οὐ κακόν. ἐπεί, εἰ   **4**

ἦν κακόν, καὶ τοῖς ζῶσι καλῶς κακὸν ἂν ὑπῆρχεν, ἐπεὶ τὸ ζῆν αὐτοῖς ὑπῆρχεν,   **5**

ὅπερ ἐστὶ κακόν.   **6**

Ξένος: Ἀληθῆ μοι δοκεῖς λέγειν.   **7**

[38] Πρεσβύτης: Ἐπεὶ τοίνυν ἀμφοτέροις συμβαίνει τὸ ζῆν, καὶ τοῖς   **8**

καλῶς ζῶσι καὶ τοῖς κακῶς, οὐκ ἂν εἴη οὔτε ἀγαθὸν εἶναι τὸ ζῆν οὔτε κακόν·   **9**

ὥσπερ οὐδὲ τὸ τέμνειν καὶ καίειν ἐν τοῖς ἀρρωστοῦσίν ἐστι νοσερὸν καὶ   **10**

ὑγιεινόν, ἀλλὰ τὸ πῶς τέμνειν· οὐκοῦν οὕτω καὶ ἐπὶ τοῦ ζῆν, οὐκ ἔστι κακὸν   **11**

αὐτὸ τὸ ζῆν, ἀλλὰ τὸ κακῶς ζῆν.   **12**

ἀληθής, -ές, true
ἀμέλει, (3rd sing. impersonal of ἀμελέω
  ["don't trouble yourself"] used as adv.)
  doubtless, of course
ἀμφότερος, -έρα, -ερον, both
ἀρρωστέω, -ήσω, be sick
ἐπεί, (conj.) since
ἐπί, (prep. + gen.) in the case of
καίω, burn, cauterize (a wound)
νοσερός, -ά, -όν, hurtful, harmful, causing
  sickness

ὅσπερ, ἥπερ, ὅπερ, (the very one) who,
  (the very thing) which
οὐκοῦν, (adv.) therefore, then
οὔτε, (conj.) and not; οὔτε...οὔτε, neither...
  nor; (after a neg. cl.) either...or
συμβαίνω, belong to (+ dat.)
τέμνω, cut, perform surgery
ὑγιεινός, -ή, -όν, healing, good for one's
  health
φαίνω, bring to light; (pass.) be seen, seem,
  appear

---

1 ταὐτό = τὸ αὐτό

4 τὸ δὲ ζῆν οὐ κακόν sc. ἐστί

4-5 εἰ ἦν κακόν...κακὸν ἂν ὑπῆρχεν pres. C-to-F condit., w/ ἄν also governing ἐπεὶ
  τὸ ζῆν αὐτοῖς ὑπῆρχεν

7 ἀληθῆ (syncopated form of ἀληθέα), neut. pl. acc. adj. ("true things") as subst. ("the truth")

9 οὐκ ἂν εἴη οὔτε ἀγαθὸν εἶναι τὸ ζῆν οὔτε κακόν w/ the text printed here
  (Praechter's), οὐκ...εἴη (3rd sing. pres. act. opt. < εἰμί; w/ ἄν, a potential opt.) translates
  as: "it would not be possible for living to be either good or bad"; others, however,
  delete εἶναι, thus translating the cl. as: "living would not be either good or bad."

10 ὥσπερ...ἐν τοῖς ἀρρωστοῦσίν, Jerram (45): "i.e. in *some cases* the operation
  does harm, in others it does good. This illustrates the argument that not life *per se* is
  good or bad, but only a certain *kind* of life."
  οὐδὲ take w/ ἐστι νοσερὸν καὶ ὑγιεινόν; i.e., is not even (both) νοσερὸν and ὑγιεινὸν
  τὸ τέμνειν καὶ καίειν articular infs., here understood in their medical sense

11 τὸ πῶς τέμνειν lit., "the how to cut/perform surgery," i.e., "the manner (or
  conditions) of surgery," "how the surgery is performed" (Fitzgerald and White)

1   Ξένος: Ἔστι ταῦτα.

2   Πρεσβύτης: Εἰ τοίνυν οὕτως ⟨ἔχει⟩, θεώρησον πότερον ἂν βούλοιο ζῆν

3   κακῶς ἢ ἀποθανεῖν καλῶς καὶ ἀνδρείως;

4   Ξένος: Ἀποθανεῖν ἔγωγε καλῶς.

5   Πρεσβύτης: Οὐκοῦν οὐδὲ τὸ ἀποθανεῖν κακόν ἐστιν, εἴπερ αἱρετώτερόν

6   ἐστι πολλάκις τὸ ἀποθανεῖν τοῦ ζῆν.

7   Ξένος: Ἔστι ταῦτα.

8   Πρεσβύτης: Οὐκοῦν ὁ αὐτὸς λόγος καὶ περὶ τοῦ ὑγιαίνειν καὶ νοσεῖν.

9   πολλάκις γὰρ οὐ συμφέρει ὑγιαίνειν, ἀλλὰ τοὐναντίον, ὅταν ᾖ περίστασις

10   τοιαύτη.

11   Ξένος: Ἀληθῆ λέγεις.

αἱρετός, -ή, -όν, be chosen, desirable
ἀληθής, -ές, true
ἀνδρείως, (adv.) bravely, courageously
ἀποθνήσκω, ἀποθανοῦμαι, ἀπέθανον, die
βούλομαι, wish, want (+ inf.)
ἔγωγε, I, for my part, I myself
εἴπερ, (conj.) if indeed, if in fact
ἐναντίος, -ία, -ίον, opposite
θεωρέω, consider

νοσέω, be sick
περίστασις, -εως, ἡ, circumstance, situation
πολλάκις, (adv.) often
συμφέρω, (as impers.) it is advantageous to X (dat.) to do or be Y (inf.)
τοιοῦτος, -αύτη, -οῦτο, of that kind, such as this
ὑγιαίνω, be healthy

---

1 Ἔστι ταῦτα "These things are (so)" (see note to οὐκ ἔστι on p. 37, line 9)

2 οὕτως [ἔχει] see note to ὡσαύτως...ἔχει on p. 21, lines 3-4 and note to ταῦθ’ (= ταῦτα) οὕτως ἔχει on p. 22, line 7
βούλοιο 2nd sing. pres. mid./pass. (dep.) opt. < βούλομαι; w/ ἄν, a potential opt.

4 Ἀποθανεῖν ἔγωγε καλῶς = Ἀποθανεῖν ἔγωγε ἂν βουλοίμην καλῶς

5 οὐδὲ τὸ ἀποθανεῖν..., Jerram (45): "This, about death, sickness, etc., not being evils, is an extreme Stoic doctrine... Zeno taught thus: 'Some things are *good*, some *bad*, others *neutral* (οὐδέτερα). Among the good are the virtues, Justice, Temperance and the like; the bad are their opposites, Injustice, Intermperance, etc. Neutral things are such as of themselves neither benefit nor harm men, as life, pleasure, health, wealth, etc., and their opposites death, pain, disease, or poverty.' (Diogenes Laertius vii. § 101.)"

6 τοῦ ζῆν gen. of comparison dependent on the comp. adj. αἱρετώτερόν < αἱρετός, -ή, -όν

8 τοῦ ὑγιαίνειν καὶ νοσεῖν περί articular infs., objs. of the prep. περί

9 τοὐναντίον = τὸ ἐναντίον
ᾖ 3rd sing. pres. act. subju. < εἰμί; subju. in a general temporal cl.

[39] Πρεσβύτης: Ἄγε δὴ σκεψώμεθα καὶ περὶ τοῦ πλουτεῖν οὕτως· εἴγε   1

θεωρεῖν ἔστιν — ὡς πολλάκις ἔστιν ἰδεῖν — ὑπάρχοντά τινι πλοῦτον, κακῶς δὲ   2

ζῶντα τοῦτον καὶ ἀθλίως.   3

Ξένος: Νὴ Δία, πολλούς γε.   4

Πρεσβύτης: Οὐκοῦν οὐδὲν τούτοις ὁ πλοῦτος βοηθεῖ εἰς τὸ ζῆν καλῶς;   5

Ξένος: Οὐ φαίνεται· αὐτοὶ γὰρ φαῦλοί εἰσιν.   6

Πρεσβύτης: Οὐκοῦν τὸ σπουδαίους εἶναι οὐχ ὁ πλοῦτος ποιεῖ, ἀλλὰ ἡ   7

Παιδεία.   8

Ξένος: Εἰκός γε.   9

Πρεσβύτης: Ἐκ τούτου ἄρα τοῦ λόγου οὐδὲ ὁ πλοῦτος ἀγαθόν ἐστιν, εἴπερ   10

οὐ βοηθεῖ τοῖς ἔχουσιν αὐτὸν εἰς τὸ βελτίους εἶναι.   11

ἄγε, (imper. of ἄγω used as adv. that introduces either another impera. or a hortatory subju.) come, come now, come on
ἀθλίως, (adv.) wretchedly
ἄρα, (conj.) then
βελτίων, -ον, better
βοηθέω, help (+ dat.)
γέ, (adv.) indeed
δή, (particle) now
εἴγε, (conj.) if indeed; whether in fact
εἰκός, -ότος, τό, likely, probable, reasonable
εἴπερ, (conj.) if indeed, if in fact
εἰς, (prep. + acc.) into, to; in regard to

Ζεύς, Διός, ὁ, Zeus
θεωρέω, see
λόγος, ὁ, argument
νή, (adv. of swearing) yes, by X! (acc.)
οὐκοῦν, (adv.) therefore, then
πλουτέω, be rich or wealthy
πλοῦτος, ὁ, wealth
πολλάκις, (adv.) often
σκέπτομαι, σκέψομαι, ἐσκεψάμην, examine, consider
σπουδαῖος, -α, -ον, good, excellent
ὑπάρχω, belong to; possess; exist, be
φαῦλος, -η, -ον, bad, worthless, base

---

1 σκεψώμεθα 1st pl. aor. mid./pass. (dep.) subju. < σκέπομαι; hortatory subju. (i.e., let us...)

2 ἔστιν...ἔστιν "it is possible" (+ inf.)

5 εἰς τὸ ζῆν καλῶς εἰς + acc. (here an articular inf.) can express purp. (see note to εἰς τὸ σῴζεσθαι...τὸ ἀπόλλυσθαι on p. 27, line 3)

6 Οὐ φαίνεται sc. οὕτως μοι; in dialogue, φαίνεται virtually = "yes" and οὐ φαίνεται virtually = "no" (LSJ s.v. φαίνω B.II.3)

7 τὸ σπουδαίους εἶναι articular inf. as obj. of ποιεῖ: "makes (them) to be..." σπουδαίους this adj. is often used "in reference to [an] exceptional sense of civic responsibility or ἀρετή" (BDAG s.v. σπουδαῖος, α, ον)

9 Εἰκός γε sc. ἐστί

10 ἐκ τούτου ἄρα τοῦ λόγου note emphatic position of ἄρα, which would normally follow λόγου; Jerram (46) translates ἄρα thus: "as we must conclude"

11 βελτίους for this syncopated alternative form, see note on p. 64, line 11

1   Ξένος: Φαίνεται οὕτως.

2   Πρεσβύτης: Οὐδὲ συμφέρει ἄρα ἐνίοις πλουτεῖν, ὅταν μὴ ἐπίστωνται τῷ

3 πλούτῳ χρῆσθαι.

4   Ξένος: Δοκεῖ μοι.

5   Πρεσβύτης: Πῶς οὖν τοῦτο ἄν τις κρίνοι ἀγαθὸν εἶναι, ὃ πολλάκις οὐ

6 συμφέρει ὑπάρχειν;

7   Ξένος: Οὐδαμῶς.

8   Πρεσβύτης: Οὐκοῦν εἰ μέν τις ἐπίσταται τῷ πλούτῳ χρῆσθαι καλῶς καὶ

9 ἐμπείρως, εὖ βιώσεται· εἰ δὲ μή, κακῶς.

10   Ξένος: Ἀληθέστατά μοι δοκεῖς τοῦτο λέγειν.

11   [40] Πρεσβύτης: Καὶ τὸ σύνολον δέ· ἔστι τὸ τιμᾶν ταῦτα ὡς ἀγαθὰ ὄντα

12 ἢ ἀτιμάζειν ὡς κακά, τοῦτο δέ ἐστι τὸ ταράττον τοὺς ἀνθρώπους καὶ βλάπτον·

13 ὅτι ἐὰν τιμῶσιν αὐτὰ καὶ οἴωνται διὰ τούτων μόνων εἶναι τὸ εὐδαιμονεῖν, [καὶ]

ἀτιμάζω, dishonor
βλάπτω, harm
διά, (prep. + gen.) through, by
ἐάν, (conj. =) εἰ ἄν (+ subju.)
ἐμπείρως, (adv.) expertly, skillfully, wisely
ἔνιοι, -αι, -α, some
ἐπίσταμαι, understand how (+ inf.)
εὖ, (adv.) well
εὐδαιμονέω, be happy
κρίνω, judge
οἴομαι, think

οὐδαμῶς, (adv.) in no way/manner
συμφέρω, (as impers.) it is advantageous [to X (dat.) to do or be Y (inf.)]
σύνολος, -η, -ον, all together; τὸ σύνολον, (acc. of respect used as an adv.) on the whole, to sum up, in short
ταράττω, trouble, disturb
τιμάω, honor
ὑπάρχω, belong to; possess; exist, be
χράομαι/χρῶμαι, use (+ dat.)
ὡς, (adv.) as, on the grounds of

---

2 ἐπίστωνται 3rd pl. pres. mid./pass. (dep.) subju. < ἐπίσταμαι; subju. in a gen. temp. cl.

5 κρίνοι 3rd sing. pres. act. opt. < κρίνω; w/ ἄν, a potential opt.

7 Οὐδαμῶς sc. τοῦτο ἄν τις κρίνοι ἀγαθὸν εἶναι

10 Ἀληθέστατά neut. acc. pl. superl. adj. as adv. < ἀληθής, -ές

11 καὶ τὸ σύνολον δέ w/ καὶ...δέ "...καὶ emphasizes the important intervening word or words, δέ connects" (Smyth § 2891): "So, it all comes down to this" (Fitzgerald and White), "So it boils down to this" (King)
    ἔστι w/ the articular infs. τὸ τιμᾶν...ἀτιμάζειν as its subjs., lit., "to honor...or to dishonor...is possible," i.e., "it is possible to honor...or to dishonor..."

12 τὸ ταράττον...καὶ βλάπτον "the thing disturbing...and harming"

13 ἐὰν τιμῶσιν...οἴωνται... protasis of a FMV condit. (τιμῶσιν and οἴωνται are 3rd pl. pres. subjus.); the condit. has no real apodosis, but transitions ([καὶ], included by Praechter) to two indic. statements (ὑπομένουσι, οὐ παραιτοῦνται)
    τὸ εὐδαιμονεῖν the articular inf. is the subj. of the indir. statement (οἴωνται...εἶναι)

πάνθ' ὑπομένουσι πράττειν ἕνεκα τούτων, καὶ τὰ ἀσεβέστατα καὶ τὰ   1
αἰσχρότατα δοκοῦντα εἶναι οὐ παραιτοῦνται. ταῦτα δὲ πάσχουσι διὰ τὴν τοῦ   2
ἀγαθοῦ ἄγνοιαν. ἀγνοοῦσι γὰρ ὅτι οὐ γίνεται ἐκ κακῶν ἀγαθόν. πλοῦτον δὲ ἔστι   3
πολλοὺς κτησαμένους ἰδεῖν ἐκ κακῶν καὶ αἰσχρῶν ἔργων· οἷον λέγω ἐκ τοῦ   4
προδιδόναι καὶ λῄζεσθαι καὶ ἀνδροφονεῖν καὶ συκοφαντεῖν καὶ ἀποστερεῖν καὶ   5
ἐξ ἄλλων πολλῶν καὶ μοχθηρῶν.   6

    Ξένος: Ἔστι ταῦτα.   7

ἀγνοέω, do not know, fail to understand
αἰσχρός, -ά, -όν, shameful
ἀνδροφονέω, -ήσω, commit homicide,
    murder
ἀποστερέω, defraud, rob, steal
ἀσεβής, -ές, impious, unholy, profane,
    sacrilegious
διά, (prep. + acc.) on account of, because of
ἕνεκα, (prep. + gen.) on account of, for the
    sake of
ἔργον, τό, deed
κτάομαι, κτήσομαι, ἐκτησάμην, get,
    acquire, obtain
λέγω, mean

λῄζομαι, pillage, plunder, get by force
μόνος, -η, -ον, alone
μοχθηρός, -ά, -όν, bad, wicked, vicious
οἷος, οἵα, οἷον, of which kind or sort, such
    as; οἷον, (acc. of respect as adv.) such as,
    like, for example, for instance
ὅτι, (conj.) that
παραιτέομαι, avoid
πράττω, do
προδίδωμι, betray, surrender, give up to the
    enemy
συκοφαντέω, accuse falsely; extort by false
    charges or threats
ὑπομένω, undertake, dare (+ inf.)

---

1 πάνθ' = πάντα

2-3 τὰ...δοκοῦντα εἶναι "things...seeming to be"

2 ἀσεβέστατα neut. pl. acc. superl. < ἀσεβής, -ές

3 αἰσχρότατα neut. pl. acc. superl. < αἰσχρός, -ά, -όν
    ἔστι "it is possible" (+ inf.)

4 οἷον λέγω lit., "w/ respect to which sort of thing I mean," i.e., I mean, for example,
    ἐκ governing five gen. articular infs.: τοῦ προδιδόναι ("betrayal," "treachery");
    λῄζεσθαι ("pillaging"); ἀνδροφονεῖν ("homicide"); συκοφαντεῖν ("false accusation,"
    "extortion"); ἀποστερεῖν ("fraud," "robbery," "theft")

6 ἐξ ἄλλων πολλῶν καὶ μοχθηρῶν in Gk., adjs. of quantity (e.g., πολύς, πολλή,
    πολύ) in the pl. are often joined to another adj. by καί in the same construction,
    whereas in English καί is not translated (Smyth § 2879)

7 Ἔστι ταῦτα "These things are (so)" (see note to οὐκ ἔστι on p. 37, line 9)

75

1   **[41] Πρεσβύτης:** Εἰ τοίνυν γίνεται ἐκ κακοῦ ἀγαθὸν μηδέν, ὥσπερ εἰκὸς,

2 πλοῦτος δὲ γίνεται ἐκ κακῶν ἔργων, ἀνάγκη μὴ εἶναι ἀγαθὸν τὸν πλοῦτον.

3   **Ξένος:** Συμβαίνει οὕτως ἐκ τούτου τοῦ λόγου.

4   **Πρεσβύτης:** Ἀλλ᾽ οὐδὲ τὸ φρονεῖν γε οὐδὲ δικαιοπραγεῖν οὐκ ἔστι

5 κτήσασθαι ἐκ κακῶν ἔργων· ὡσαύτως δὲ οὐδὲ τὸ ἀδικεῖν καὶ ἀφρονεῖν ἐκ

6 καλῶν ἔργων, οὐδὲ ὑπάρχειν ἅμα τῷ αὐτῷ δύναται. πλοῦτον δὲ καὶ δόξαν καὶ

7 τὸ νικᾶν καὶ τὰ λοιπὰ ὅσα τούτοις παραπλήσια, οὐδὲν κωλύει ὑπάρχειν τινὶ

8 ἅμα μετὰ κακίας πολλῆς. ὥστε οὐκ ἂν εἴη ταῦτα ἀγαθὰ οὔτε κακά, ἀλλὰ τὸ

9 φρονεῖν μόνον ἀγαθὸν, τὸ δὲ ἀφρονεῖν κακόν.

ἀδικέω, act unjustly, wrong; τὸ ἀδικεῖν, injustice, wrong-doing

ἅμα, (adv.) at the same time, together; (prep. + dat.) together w/

ἀνάγκη, ἡ, necessity; ἀνάγκη (w/ or w/out ἐστί), it is necessary that (+ inf.)

ἀφρονέω, be foolish or stupid; τὸ ἀφρονεῖν, foolishness, stupidity

δικαιοπραγέω, do right, act honestly or w/ justice; τὸ δικαιοπραγεῖν, just action

δόξα, ἡ, (good) reputation

εἰκός, -ότος, τό, likely, probable, reasonable

ἔργον, τό, deed

κτάομαι, κτήσομαι, ἐκτησάμην, get, acquire, obtain

κωλύω, prevent X (acc.) from doing Y (inf.)

λόγος, ὁ, argument

λοιπός, -ή, -όν, remaining; τὰ λοιπά, the rest

μηδείς, μηδεμία, μηδέν, no one, nothing; μηδέν, (adv.) not at all, by no means

μόνος, -η, -ον, alone; μόνον (adv.) alone, only

νικάω, win, be victorious; τὸ νικᾶν, victory

παραπλήσιος, -ον, like (+ dat.)

πλοῦτος, ὁ, wealth

συμβαίνω, result, follow (of consequences and of logical conclusions; often 3rd sing. is used impersonally)

ὑπάρχω, belong to; exist, be

φρονέω, have understanding, be wise or prudent; τὸ φρονεῖν, wisdom, understanding

ὡσαύτως, (adv.) in the same way, likewise, similarly

ὥστε, (conj.) and so, therefore, consequently

---

1 εἰκός sc. ἐστί

2 ἀνάγκη μὴ εἶναι ἀγαθὸν τὸν πλοῦτον "The article τόν with πλοῦτον shows that it, rather than ἀγαθόν, is the subject of μὴ εἶναι." (Banchich, 46)

4 Ἀλλ᾽ οὐδέ...οὐδέ "Moreover, not even...nor" (for ἀλλ᾽ οὐδέ, cf. BDF § 448.(6))
οὐκ strengthens οὐδέ, and so is not translated into English (Jerram, 46)
ἔστι "it is possible"
τὸ φρονεῖν...δικαιοπραγεῖν, the articular infs. are the acc. objs. of κτήσασθαι (aor. mid. inf. < κτάομαι)

6 δύναται subj. = τὸ φρονεῖν, δικαιοπραγεῖν, ἀδικεῖν and ἀφρονεῖν
τῷ αὐτῷ "the same person" (i.e., at the same time; Jerram, 46)

8 ὥστε at the beginning of a sentence marks a strong conclusion
ταῦτα neut. pl. subj. of sing. vb. (see note to ἔχοντα on p. 23, line 1)

8-9 τὸ φρονεῖν μόνον ἀγαθὸν, τὸ δὲ ἀφρονεῖν κακόν for both cls. sc. ἐστί

ἱκανῶς, (adv.) sufficiently, adequately

****

At this point, the Greek text breaks off. As Seddon (199) notes, "Although the narrative does seem to have reached a satisfactory conclusion, it is possible that there was once a longer ending in the original Greek to account for the existence of an Arabic paraphrase that extends the work.[21] The standard text of the *Tablet*, therefore, concludes with the following brief section, translated from Johannes Elichmann's Latin rendering of the Arabic, first published posthumously in 1640, printed by Karl Praechter in his 1893 edition, and included in the 1983 edition by Fitzgerald and White."[22]

The (mostly literal, and thus rather clunky) translation of Elichmann's Latin that follows is, except for a few phrases taken from previous translations (Fitzgerald and White, Seddon), my own.

"And we have given up this opinion in which those things [i.e., wealth, reputation, success, etc.] are believed to be from evil deeds."

[42] Old Man: "In any case, this conclusion is very important, and the same as that which we have said before, that such things are neither good nor bad. Moreover, if these things came from evil deeds alone, then they would be altogether bad. But all things derive from both kinds of actions. And for that reason, we said that these are neither good nor bad, just as being asleep and being awake are neither good nor bad. And my judgment, in fact, is similar in matters of walking and sitting and the rest, which happen to each and every one of these, both those who have understanding and those who are ignorant. Some things, however, are appropriate to one or the other, since some are good and others bad—such as tyranny and justice, two things which belong to one or the other

---

[21] R. Keen, in his review of J. T. Fitzergald and L. M. White (edd.), *The Tabula of Cebes* (Chico, CA, 1983) in *Apeiron: A Journal for Ancient Philosophy and Science*, Vol. 18, No. 1 (1984), 75, suggests that the Arabic paraphrase may, in fact, have been less of a paraphrase and more of a close translation of the original Greek text.

[22] There is also another ending in the Latin ms. *An* (*c.* 1475-*c.* 1525) that gives a conclusion which, C. E. Finch argues ("The Translation of *Cebes' Tabula* in Codex Vaticanus Latinus 4037," *Transactions and Proceedings of the American Philological Association* 85 [1954], 79-87), is similar in content to the longer one found in the Latin translation of the Arabic paraphrase. This conclusion follows the sentence in Chapter 40: ταῦτα δὲ πάσχουσι διὰ τὴν τοῦ ἀγαθοῦ ἄγνοιαν. (Ms. *An* is a member of the *CK(P)* family of the *Tablet* ms. tradition, which ends at that point and not where the other *Tablet* mss. end in Chapter 41.) The text of ms. *An* translates as: "And, my passionately devoted young men, so that *you* may obtain that thing at last, pursue it with all the strength of your heart and mind, and believe that nothing ever is greater, nothing is more excellent, nothing is more worthy of a free-born man, and nothing, in the end, is more fortunate than goodness. Farewell!"

type of individual. And that is because justice continually clings to those who possess understanding, and tyranny accompanies no one except the ignorant. In fact, it is not possible for that thing, which we mentioned above, to happen: that two things find themselves belonging to one and the same person at one and the same moment of time in such a way that a single man at the same moment of time is sleeping and awake, and that he is simultaneously wise and ignorant, or anything else of the things which we pair with their opposites.

Stranger: To these things I responded: "I believe," I said, "with this entire preceding discussion that you have now brought to an end all these matters."

[43] **Old Man:** "However," he said, "I say that all these things proceed from that truly divine principle."

Stranger: "But what is that thing," I said, "which you are hinting at?"

Old Man: "Life and death," he said, "health and sickness, wealth and poverty, and all the other things, which you have said are both good and bad, that happen to most people from no evil act."

Stranger: "Clearly we deduce," I said, "that it necessarily follows from this argument that such things are neither good nor bad. Nevertheless, the situation is such that I have not yet reached a firm judgment regarding these matters."

Old Man: "This happens, therefore," he said, "because that habit is far from you by which you can conceive of this way of thinking with your mind. And so follow the practice of these things, the one which a little earlier I pointed out to you, throughout the entire course of your life, so that these things which we have said to you might become implanted in your minds and by practicing these things you may develop a habit. If, however, you should have any doubts about anything, return to me so that I might provide you with explanations that may dispel your doubts concerning that matter.

Prodicus'

"Choice of Heracles"

(Xenophon, *Memorabilia* 2.1.21-34)

The Athenian-born Xenophon (*c.* 430-354 BCE) wore two authorial masks: (1) a writer of an historically important (if uninspiring) continuation of Thucydides' *History of the Peloponnesian War* as well as practical treatises on subjects ranging from horsemanship to dealing with Athens' economic crisis after the collapse of the Second Athenian Empire in 355 BCE; (2) a pioneer of literary genres, including the first-person military memoir (*Anabasis*, "The March Up-Country") and the proto-novel (*Cyropaidea*, "The Education of Cyrus"). But perhaps Xenophon's greatest legacy is the series of influential sketches depicting his mentor and friend Socrates (*c.* 470-399 BCE) in conversation with various interlocutors. Known by their Latin title *Memorabilia* ("Memorable Things [said by Socrates]"), these sketches, as well as a *Symposium* and an *Apology* which also feature Socrates, present a portrait of him that, in many ways, is quite different from the one that appears in the writings of his Athenian contemporary, the philosopher Plato (*c.* 427-347 BCE).[23]

THE CONTEXT OF *MEMORABILIA* 2.1.21-34

The central theme of the second book of the *Memorabilia*, which depicts Socrates dealing with his acquaintances' personal problems and affairs, is self-control/self-discipline (ἐγκράτεια), especially of bodily pleasures and pains involving desire (ἐπιθυμία) for food, drink, and sex, and with regard to sleep, cold, heat, and hard work (πόνος). In 2.1.1-20, Socrates initiates a dialogue with one of his associates, Aristippus of Cyrene (*c.* 435-*c.* 356 BCE), when he learned that the latter "was undisciplined in such matters as these [i.e., as to the importance ἐγκράτεια should play in one's life]" (ἀκολαστοτέρως ἔχοντα πρὸς τὰ τοιαῦτα, 2.1.1). Aristippus believes that there is a middle path (μέση ὁδός) between being a ruler or a slave, which he calls liberty/freedom (ἐλευθερία). And it is this path, not that of being a ruler (which requires ἐγκράτεια) or that of a slave (who suffers pain at the hands of his master) that "most of all leads to happiness (εὐδαιμονία)." (2.1.11) For Aristippus, then, the life of a private individual, with no ties to any state, is preferable to that of the onerous task of ruling (e.g., serving in some kind of civic office) or the painful life of being a slave. In response to this, Socrates tries to

---

[23] Xenophon remained a well-loved author throughout Antiquity and into the early 20th century. Through his texts (especially the *Memorabilia* and *Cyropaideia*) he exerted a strong influence on such individuals as, for example, Machiavelli, Benjamin Franklin and John Adams. For Machiavelli, see L. Strauss, *Thoughts on Machiavelli* (Seattle, 1969) and W. R. Newell, "Machiavelli and Xenophon on Princely Rule: A Double-Edged Encounter" (*The Journal of Politics* 50 [1988], 108-130); for Benjamin Franklin, see L. S. Pangle, "Ben Franklin and Socrates," in P. E. Kerry and M. S. Holland, *Benjamin Franklin's Intellectual World* (Madison/Teaneck [NJ], 2012, 137-151); for John Adams, see C. J. Richard, *The Founders and the Classics: Greece, Rome, and the American Enlightenment* (Cambridge [MA], 1994, 49, 57).

show that, while excellence/moral goodness/virtue (ἀρετή) is, at first, a difficult path that requires significant ἐγκράτεια, and wickedness/vice (κακία) is, at the beginning, the easier of the two paths, ultimately it is the former—after much hard work and delayed gratification—that pays off in terms of securing good friendships, defeating one's enemies, managing one's home well, helping one's friends, and benefiting one's country, while the latter ends in a physically weak body and an intellectually deficient mind (2.1.18-20). In support of these assertions, Socrates then quotes lines 287-292 from the poet Hesiod's *Works and Days* (see **Appendix A**) and two lines from the comic playwright Epicharmus (37 Diels-Kranz) (2.1.20) before presenting as his culminating argument (in some degree of paraphrase) the sophist Prodicus' performance piece (ἐπίδειξις), the "Choice of Heracles" (2.1.21-34). After this, the remainder of *Memorabilia* 2 (2-10) consists of a series of Socrates' conversations with other interlocutors (including his oldest son) on the topic of human relationships as components of the good life: parents give selflessly to their children (with the highlight being a moving passage describing the tireless work of mothers—2.2.5); friends being "the most productive possession of all" (2.4.7); the value of work being underscored by a lengthy discussion between Socrates and his friend Aristarchus (2.7), who has 14 female relatives living under his roof as war refugees. Socrates advises him to start a home textile business putting these women to work, since by doing so they will both be happier and their work will make them morally better. (The importance of work, even that of hard manual labor, to ἀρετή is a continuing theme throughout Xenophon's writings, and one on which his views run—to a very great extent—counter to the aristocratic mindset of his time.)

PRODICUS THE SOPHIST

Between *c.* 450-*c.* 375 BCE an intellectual revolution occurred in the Greek world that had a profound influence on society and its cultural, political, and philosophical movers and shakers. This movement came about through the activities of itinerant professional educators, known as sophists, who taught a variety of courses for (often extraordinary amounts of) money. Their students primarily consisted of young aristocratic elites, many of them Athenian, who had come to believe that they needed to gain some sort of additional advantage, especially in politics and in the courts (in which, in addition to legal issues, much political power now resided), over their fellow citizens of lesser socio-economic status. The reasons for this are complex, but in Athens they can probably be traced primarily to two interdependent developments that had a transformative impact on fifth-century Athenian society: (1) political reforms initiated by Pericles (*c.* 495-429 BCE) and Ephialtes (assassinated in 461 BCE) in 462 BCE that led (nominally, at first, but in many cases effectively as the century developed) to all male Athenian citizens possessing (more or less) equal political power (i.e., the so-called "radical" democracy); (2) the expanding economic, political, military, and cultural power of Athens and its imperial democracy at this time, which provided a greater influx of monetary resources into Athens from its tribute-paying "allies," thus allowing the Athenian *polis* to pay many of its citizens to participate in a wide variety of public affairs.

Although sophists taught a variety of subjects (including music, astronomy, mathematics, and linguistics), many specialized in teaching others how to deploy the tools of philosophy and rhetoric to better achieve one's goals in life by convincing other people of the validity of one's own point of view. Since the ultimate objective was winning the argument (and thus be in a better position to satisfy one's desires, even at the expense of others' well-being), sophists and their students came to be regarded with great suspicion both by non-elite citizens and by moral philosophers such as Plato. After all, the very first sophist, Protagoras of Abdera (*c.* 490-*c.* 420 BCE), had declared that "man is the measure of all things." This idea, his critics claimed, had provided the (intellectually suspect, in their eyes) basis for the grounding of one's moral outlook on life in terms of relativism: there is no absolute truth, only one's own "truths" that may or may not be in agreement with another person's "truths."

Prodicus (*c.* 465-*c.* 395 BCE) came to Athens frequently as a public official from his island state of Ceos (located about 19 miles/30 kilometers off the southeast coast of Attica) and quickly established himself there as a speaker and teacher. Contemporary Athenian reactions to him varied: the comic playwright Aristophanes considered him "a sophistic dabbler in cosmology at odds with the traditional Olympian outlook"[24]; Plato portrays him rather respectfully, at least in comparison with the other sophists who appear in the *Dialogues*, as a scholar interested in linguistics, especially those aspects involving lexicography and semantic domains;[25] Xenophon seems to treat him with the most respect, "as the author of a powerful and sincere defense of traditional virtue against a life of vice."[26] Almost nothing of Prodicus' own words survive, so scholars have to reconstruct his thought based on the (mostly meager) remnants of his words and ideas preserved by other writers, along with their occasional portrayals of him (especially that found in Plato's *Protagoras*). Later testimonia (which can often be problematic in terms of the value of its information) suggests that he was an atheist. Although not unusual for a fifth-century sophist, this would have put him at odds with the vast majority of the Greeks of his time.

---

[24] R. Mayhew, *Prodicus the Sophist: Texts, Translations, and Commentary*, Oxford, 2011, p. xiii.

[25] Plato, however, does suggest slightly more than a hint of mockery in Socrates' response to the (overfastidious) nature of some of Prodicus' fine lexical distinctions (cf., e.g., *Cratylus* 384b, *Protagoras* 337a-c and 339e-342a).

[26] Mayhew, p. xiii

XENOPHON'S PRODICUS' "CHOICE OF HERACLES"

Prodicus' allegorical fable, known as the "Choice of Heracles," has been called "the first true personification allegory in the West."[27] It was a written text that Prodicus performed orally as a sophistic display piece (ἐπίδειξις) in two flavors: (1) a presentation designed for a general audience (apparently given to very many people/ audiences, πλείστοις ἐπιδείκνυται, 2.1.21) for which Prodicus charged one drachma (the average daily pay of a Greek mercenary soldier in the fourth century BCE); (2) a more advanced seminar (set of lectures/classes?) which cost 50 drachmas.[28] According to an ancient scholar's note on Aristophanes' *Clouds*, the "Choice of Heracles" was also part of a book by Prodicus entitled Ὧραι ("Seasons" or "Hours").[29] This same ancient scholar also reports that in Prodicus' original text, Heracles "inclined toward Virtue and preferred the sweat of her [way of life] over the transitory pleasures of Vice."[30] Xenophon's paraphrase leaves out this rather explicit conclusion, though the ending he has Socrates deliver implicitly suggests that this indeed was the choice made by the young hero (see note to 2.1.34 [lines 2-3 on p. 104])

There are two essential questions scholars have asked with respect to the paraphrase Xenophon puts into the mouth of Socrates of Prodicus' "Choice of Heracles": (1) What is the degree to which Xenophon has faithfully represented

---

[27] J. Whitman, *Allegory: The Dynamics of an Ancient and Medieval Technique* (Cambridge [MA], 1983), 22.

[28] In Plato's *Cratylus* (384b), Socrates says that he attended one of Prodicus' one-drachma linguistic lectures, but not the same one costing 50 drachmas. For the relationship between an author's oral performance and written text of the same work, see R. Thomas, "Prose Performance Texts: *Epideixis* and Written Publication in the Late Fifth and Early Fourth Centuries," in H. Yunis (ed.), *Written Texts and the Rise of Literate Culture in Ancient Greece* (Cambridge, 2003), pp. 162-88, especially 180-5. Aristotle notes that Prodicus would inject a little something from his 50-drachma lecture whenever his audience began to nod off (*Rhetoric* 1415b15-17).

[29] For a (very) speculative reconstruction of the contents of this book, of which almost nothing except the "Choice of Heracles" (in Xenophon's paraphrase) survives, see Mayhew, pp. xxii-xxiii. Aristophanes' *Clouds* (first performed in 423 BCE; revised text with new material published sometime between 420-417), included (at least in its revised form) a very Prodicean-like verbal contest between two allegorical figures, "Just Argument" and "Unjust Argument", over which of the two can provide a better education (and therefore a more successful life) to a young man about to enroll in Socrates' "college." If, as seems likely, Aristophanes' allegorical scene is a parody of Prodicus' speech, than the latter was probably first performed before audiences in the mid-to-late 420s. For the relationship between *Clouds* and Prodicus' allegory, see Z. P. Ambrose, "Socrates and Prodicus in the *Clouds*," in J. P. Anton and A. Preus (edd.), *Essays in Ancient Greek Philosophy*, Vol. 2 (Albany, NY, 1983), 129-44.

[30] Scholium on Aristophanes' *Clouds* (Σ Aristophanes, *Nubes* 361a [Diels-Kranz B1]). The translation is Mayhew's (51).

Prodicus' language and thought; (2) What side, if any, does Xenophon/Prodicus ultimately come down on, that of Ἀρετή or that of Κακία?

With respect to the first question, although most recent scholarship has championed the view that the language and sentiments are thoroughly characteristic of Xenophon (see especially V. Gray, "The Linguistic Philosophies of Prodicus in Xenophon's 'Choice of Heracles'?" *Classical Quarterly* 56 [2006], 426-35), an interesting argument has been recently put forth by David Sansone that Xenophon's paraphrase is closer to Prodicus' original (now lost) piece than scholars had previously believed ("Heracles at the Y." *Journal of Hellenic Studies* 124 [2004], 125-42, and "Xenophon and Prodicus' 'Choice of Heracles'." *Classical Quarterly* 65 [2015], 371-77; also cf. R. Mayhew, *Prodicus the Sophist: Texts, Translations, and Commentary*, Oxford, 2011, pp. xviii-xx, 203-4).

With respect to the second question, the key here is the joint/ambiguous authorship I have noted with the forward slash: "Xenophon/Prodicus." If one believes that Xenophon's "voice" is dominant in the fable, and so may have "adjusted" it to accord better with his own preferences, then it seems more likely that the allegory supports Ἀρετή's viewpoint, which is basically identical with that of Xenophon as expressed throughout his oeuvre. This is not an unusual reading, since nearly all readers from antiquity to the twentieth century understood the allegory to be one that strongly affirms Ἀρετή's ideas.

If, however, one believes that the paraphrase essentially conveys Prodicus' ideas, then the waters become a bit muddier, for Prodicus was a sophist, (probably) an atheist, and a linguist interested in correct language usage, believing that "no one word should have more than one meaning or connotation."[31] As a sophist, he might have been expected to produce a work that argued both sides' positions (though before a general audience he may have played it a little more safe by leaning in the direction of "traditional morality"). As a (probable) atheist, it may seem strange that he has Ἀρετή alone mention the gods in the allegory. As Sansone provocatively asks: "Does this represent further evidence that what we have is an expression of Xenophon's conventional outlook rather than that of Prodicus? Or is it another indication that the views of the atheist Prodicus are in fact aligned with those of the voluptuous coquette in the sexy dress and heavy make-up?"[32] In fact, the ancient testimonia (limited as they are) paint a picture of Prodicus' own life that suggests he chose the path of Κακία at least as much as

---

[31] R. Mayhew, *Prodicus the Sophist: Texts, Translations, and Commentary* (Oxford, 2011) in *Classical Philology* 108 (2013), xv.

[32] Review of R. Mayhew, *Prodicus the Sophist: Texts, Translations, and Commentary* (Oxford, 2011) in *Classical Philology* 108 (2013), 163. See also Mayhew, 217-8.

that of Ἀρετή.[33] And as a linguist interested in correct language usage, he depicts Ἀρετή and Κακία as two individuals who, as Sansone points out, "both claim repeatedly that their followers attain pleasure; ἡδύς and words from the same root [ἥδομαι, ἡδονή] occur over a dozen times, most often in the mouth of Virtue [Ἀρετή]. It is their *definition* of pleasure that differs, so much so that the case can be made that they are not talking about the same thing when they refer to pleasure."[34]

If there is a truth that can be extracted from this debate, it is that the "Choice of Heracles" still retains its provocative power for eliciting from its readers at least two different ways of understanding its meaning and purpose: (1) as a sincere and compelling defense of Ἀρετή's way of life over that of Κακία's; (2) as a sophistic text in which "Prodicus makes a case for the life of Virtue and a case for the life of Vice," but makes no claim for "objective moral truths and/or moral absolutes."[35]

NACHLEBEN ("AFTERLIFE")

Xenophon's paraphrase of Prodicus' allegorical fable has had an extremely long-lived and varied *nachleben* (German, "afterlife").[36] Ancient authors such as Philo, Ovid, Lucian, Silius Italicus, Philostratus, Dio, Clement of Alexandria, and St. Basil imitated or adapted it. Beginning in the Renaissance, dozens of artists have depicted it visually in different media (see, e.g., **Appendix F** for Albrecht Dürer's fascinating take on it and **Appendix G** for Pompeo Girolamo Batoni's more traditional approach).[37] Musically, composers such as Handel, Bach, and Saint-Saëns have created works with it as their theme. Recently, the philosopher A. C. Grayling has explored its meaning in reponse to contemporary ethical and moral issues in elegant, non-technical language (see **Bibliography** below).

---

[33] See, e.g., R. Mayhew, *Prodicus the Sophist: Texts, Translations, and Commentary* (Oxford, 2011), 92.

[34] Review of R. Mayhew, *Prodicus the Sophist: Texts, Translations, and Commentary* (Oxford, 2011) in *Classical Philology* 108 (2013), 160.

[35] R. Mayhew, 205.

[36] For an extensive collection of bibliographies on the fable's *nachleben*, see M. Davies, "The Hero at the Crossroads: "Prodicus and the Choice of Heracles."" (*Prometheus* 29 [2013]), 3, n. 1.

[37] The classic study of Prodicus' allegory in western art is E. Panofsky, *Hercules am Scheidewege* (Lepizig, 1930; reprinted Ann Arbor, 1979).

LANGUAGE AND STYLE

As an Athenian born in the fifth century BCE, Xenophon of course writes in Attic Greek. However, because he was mostly away from Athens after the age of 30 (some of it by choice, much of it due to being exiled for an extended period), and because he associated throughout his life with Ionic-speaking and (especially) Doric-speaking Greeks, his works contains many Ionic, Doric, poetic, and even foreign words not used by other Attic authors. On the other hand, his prose style is relatively straightforward, something that won him the honor of being an author whose texts (especially the *Anabasis*, "The March Up-Country") were often read by intermediate students learning Ancient Greek from the 15th to the early 20th centuries.

THE TEXT

The text used in this edition is:

Marchant, E. C. *Xenophontis Opera Omnia*, vol. 2, 2nd ed. Oxford, 1921

The differences between my text and that of Marchant's are as follows:

24 ἀεὶ ἔσῃ **for** †διέσῃ
30 καὶ τὰς κλίνας **for** [καὶ τὰς κλίνας]

BIBLIOGRAPHY

A recent and well-written overview of Xenophon from multiple perspectives by several scholars is:

Flower, M. (ed.) *The Cambridge Companion to Xenophon*. Cambridge, 2017

The standard bibliography (though now somewhat dated) on the *Memorabilia* is:

Morrison, D. R. *Bibliography of Editions, Translations, and Commentary on Xenophon's Socratic Writings, 1600-Present*. Pittsburgh, 1988

For recent work in English on Xenophon's paraphrase of Prodicus' "Choice of Heracles," see:

Davies, M. "The Hero at the Crossroads: Prodicus and the "Choice of Heracles."" *Prometheus* 29 (2013), 3-17

Gray, V. "The Linguistic Philosophies of Prodicus in Xenophon's 'Choice of Heracles'?" *Classical Quarterly* 56 (2006), 426-35

Grayling, A. C. *The Choice of Hercules: Pleasure, Duty and the Good Life in the 21st Century*. London, 2007

Johnson, D. M. "Aristippus at the Crossroads: The Politics of Pleasure in Xenophon's *Memorabilia*." *Polis* 26 (2009), 204-22

Kuntz, M. "The Prodikean "Choice of Herakles": A Reshaping of Myth." *Classical Journal*, Vol. 89, No. 2 (1993-1994), 163-181.

Mayhew, R. *Prodicus the Sophist: Texts, Translations, and Commentary*, Oxford. 2011, 52-9, 201-221

Sansone, D. "Xenophon and Prodicus' 'Choice of Heracles'." *Classical Quarterly* 65 (2015), 371-77

Sansone, D. review of R. Mayhew, *Prodicus the Sophist: Texts, Translations, and Commentary* (Oxford, 2011) in *Classical Philology* 108 (2013), 159-63

Sansone, D. "Heracles at the Y." *Journal of Hellenic Studies* 124 (2004), 125-42

Whitman, J. *Allegory: The Dynamics of an Ancient and Medieval Technique*. Cambridge (MA), 1983, 22-5

Wolfsdorf, D. "Prodicus and the Correctness of Names: The Case of τέρψις, χαρά, and εὐφροσύνη." *Journal of Hellenic Studies* 131 (2011), 131-45

Wolfsdorf, D. "Hesiod, Prodicus, and the Socratics on Work and Pleasure." *Oxford Studies in Ancient Philosophy* 35 (2008), 1-18

ENGLISH TRANSLATIONS

Bonnette, A. L. *Xenophon, Memorabilia*. Ithaca (NY), 1994

Marchant, E. C. *Xenophon IV: Memorabilia, Oeconomicus, Symposium, Apology*. Cambridge (MA), 1923

Mayhew, R., *Prodicus the Sophist: Texts, Translations, and Commentary*, Oxford, 2011

Tredennick, H. and R. Waterfield. *Xenophon, Conversations of Socrates*. London, 1990

1   [21] καὶ Πρόδικος δὲ ὁ σοφὸς ἐν τῷ συγγράμματι τῷ περὶ Ἡρακλέους, ὅπερ δὴ

2   καὶ πλείστοις ἐπιδείκνυται, ὡσαύτως περὶ τῆς ἀρετῆς ἀποφαίνεται, ὧδέ πως

3   λέγων, ὅσα ἐγὼ μέμνημαι. φησὶ γὰρ Ἡρακλέα, ἐπεὶ ἐκ παίδων εἰς ἥβην ὡρμᾶτο,

---

ἀποφαίνω, show forth, display; (mid. = act.)

ἀρετή, ἡ, courage, manliness, virtue, excellence

δή, (particle) now, in fact

ἐπεί, (conj.) when, since

ἐπιδείκνυμι, exhibit as a specimen, show forth, display, exhibit; (mid. more freq. than act.) show off or display what is one's own, give a specimen of one's art

ἥβη, ἡ, youth, young adulthood

Ἡρακλῆς, -έους, ὁ, Heracles

μιμνήσκω, remind; (mid./pass.) remember

ὁρμάω, begin, get ready; (mid.) proceed, set out, move (from [ἐκ/ἀπό + gen.])

ὅσος, -η, -ον, as great as, as much as

ὅσπερ, ἥπερ, ὅπερ, [strengthened rel. pron.: ὅς + περ] that very one (which)

παῖς, παιδός, ὁ/ἡ, child, boy, girl; ἐκ παίδων, childhood

περί, (prep. + gen.) about, concerning

πλεῖστος, -η, -ον, [superl. of πολύς, πολλή, πολύ] most, very many, greatest, very great, largest, very large; (masc. sing. or pl. [the latter is more common]) very many (people)

Πρόδικος, ὁ, Prodicus

πως, (adv.) somehow, in some such manner; ὧδέ πως, somehow so

σοφός, -ή, -όν, wise, learned; ὁ σοφός almost = "the sophist"

σύγγραμμα, -ατος, τό, (written) work, composition, book

ὧδε, (adv.) thus, so

ὡσαύτως, (adv.) similarly

---

1 **Πρόδικος** Prodicus of Ceos (*c.* 465–*c.* 395 BCE) was one of the first Sophists (οἱ σοφισταί), a group of mostly itinerant professional educators who gave lectures on grammar, rhetoric, politics, ethics, mathematics, etc. in exchange for payment

   ὁ σοφὸς Xenophon's Socrates employs this title instead of ὁ σοφιστής, perhaps to remove the stain w/ which Plato and others had endowed the latter. Originally, ὁ σοφιστής meant "master of one's craft," "one who is wise or prudent," "philosopher." By the last quarter of the fifth century BCE, "sophist" came to have strongly negative connotations, including its current meaning of "one who uses plausible but fallacious reasoning," "one who is fallacious or deceptive in argument"

   τῷ συγγράμματι τῷ περὶ Ἡρακλέους the "Heracles" was part of a larger work entitled Ὧραι ("Hours" or "Seasons"), almost nothing of which survives

2 **ἐπιδείκνυται** Sophists often gave show-orations (αἱ ἐπιδείξεις), performance-oriented recitations that functioned as a demonstration of their wide range of learning and of their particular talents and interests

   ὡσαύτως the allegorical story of Heracles is the culminating "proof" in the opening sections of *Memorablia* 2 that Xenophon's Socrates employs against Aristippus's view that avoidance of trouble of any kind is pleasant and is the goal of life. Socrates's arguments include his own ideas (2.1.1-19) and the poetic evidence of Hesiod (*fl. c.* 700 BCE)—see **Appendix A**—and Epicharmus (*fl. c.* 500 BCE) (2.1.20)

3 **μέμνημαι** 1st sing. perf. (w/ pres. sense) mid./pass. indic. < μιμνήσκω

   φησὶ...Ἡρακλέα φησὶ sets up an indir. statement, w/ Ἡρακλέα as acc. subj. and the inf. καθῆσθαι as main vb. English, w/ its preference for vbs. over participles, would have used two indic. vbs. conjoined by "and." Gk., however, here as elsewhere, displays its special fondness for participles

ἐν ᾗ οἱ νέοι ἤδη αὐτοκράτορες γιγνόμενοι δηλοῦσιν εἴτε τὴν δι᾽ ἀρετῆς ὁδὸν   1

τρέψονται ἐπὶ τὸν βίον εἴτε τὴν διὰ κακίας, ἐξελθόντα εἰς ἡσυχίαν καθῆσθαι   2

ἀποροῦντα ποτέραν τῶν ὁδῶν τράπηται· [22] καὶ φανῆναι αὐτῷ δύο γυναῖκας   3

προσιέναι μεγάλας, τὴν μὲν ἑτέραν εὐπρεπῆ τε ἰδεῖν καὶ ἐλευθέριον φύσει,   4

κεκοσμημένην τὸ μὲν σῶμα καθαρότητι, τὰ δὲ ὄμματα αἰδοῖ, τὸ δὲ σχῆμα   5

αἰδώς, -όος/οῦς, ἡ, reverence, awe, respect (for the feeling or opinion of others or for one's own conscience); shame, self-respect

ἀπορέω, be perplexed or confused

αὐτοκράτωρ, -ορος, ὁ/ἡ, one's own master, free, independent

δηλόω, make plain or clear, assure

διά, (prep. + gen.) through,

δύο, (indecl.) two

εἶδον, [not used in act. pres.; ὁράω being used instead] saw; (inf.) ἰδεῖν, to see

εἴτε, (adv.) (generally doubled) εἴτε...εἴτε, either...or, whether...or

ἐλευθέριος, -ον, free; (of appearance) noble

ἐξέρχομαι, ἐξελεύσομαι, ἐξῆλθον, go out

εὐπρεπής, -ές, good-looking, attractive

ἤδη, (adv.) already, now

ἡσυχία, ἡ, quiet spot, deserted place

καθαρότης, -ητος, ἡ, (moral) purity; honesty

κάθημαι, sit

κακία, ἡ, evil, wickedness

κοσμέω, adorn, embellish

νεός, -α, -ον, young

ὄμμα, -ατος, τό, eye

πότερος, -έρα, -ερον, which of the two?

πρόσειμι/προσέρχομαι approach

σχῆμα, -ατος, τό, form, figure, appearance; (of a person) bearing, look, air, demeanor

σῶμα, -τος, τό, body

τρέπω, turn or direct X (acc.) (towards a thing); (pass. + ὁδόν) take the path or road

φαίνω, φανῶ, ἔφηνα, bring to light; (pass.) be seen, appear

φύσις, -εως, ἡ, nature, natural condition

---

2 ἐξελθόντα masc. acc. sing. aor. act. part. < ἐξέρχομαι
   καθῆσθαι perf. mid. inf. < κάθημαι

3 τράπηται 3rd sing. aor. mid./pass. subju. < τρέπω; deliberative subju. (Smyth § 1805, 2639) retained in indir. quest. (Smyth § 2662b)
   φανῆναι aor. pass. inf. < φαίνω

4 προσιέναι pres. act. inf. < πρόσειμι
   μεγάλας note emphatically delayed position of the attributive adj., i.e., "and they were (quite) tall"
   ἰδεῖν aor. act. inf. < εἶδον; epexegetic (i.e., "explanatory")/limiting inf. (Smyth § 2005)
   ἐλευθέριον φύσει i.e., she carried herself in the manner of a free-born citizen
   φύσει instrumental dat. (Smyth § 1507); so too καθαρότητι, αἰδοῖ, σωφροσύνῃ, and ἐσθῆτι...λευκῇ in the following cls.

5 κεκοσμημένην...καθαρότητι virtually an oxymoron, as the former implies adding embellishments, while the latter suggests purging, cleansing, and purifying
   κεκοσμημένην fem. acc. sing. perf. mid./pass. part. < κοσμέω
   τὸ...σῶμα acc. of respect (Smyth § 1600, 1601); so too τὰ...ὄμματα and τὸ...σχῆμα in the following cls.
   τὰ δὲ ὄμματα αἰδοῖ suggests that she averts her eyes/holds them downcast in a manner befitting a "proper" woman (according to the traditional ancient Greek view)

1 σωφροσύνη, ἐσθῆτι δὲ λευκῇ, τὴν δ' ἑτέραν τεθραμμένην μὲν εἰς πολυσαρκίαν τε

2 καὶ ἁπαλότητα, κεκαλλωπισμένην δὲ τὸ μὲν χρῶμα ὥστε λευκοτέραν τε καὶ

3 ἐρυθροτέραν τοῦ ὄντος δοκεῖν φαίνεσθαι, τὸ δὲ σχῆμα ὥστε δοκεῖν ὀρθοτέραν

4 τῆς φύσεως εἶναι, τὰ δὲ ὄμματα ἔχειν ἀναπεπταμένα, ἐσθῆτα δὲ ἐξ ἧς ἂν

5 μάλιστα ὥρα διαλάμποι· κατασκοπεῖσθαι δὲ θαμὰ ἑαυτήν, ἐπισκοπεῖν δὲ καὶ εἴ

ἀναπεπταμένος, -η, -ον, [perf. pass. part. < ἀναπετάννυμι, "spread out or unfold," used as an adj.] open

ἁπαλότης, -ητος, ἡ, softness, tenderness

διαλάμπω, shine through, be conspicuous

ἑαυτοῦ, -ῆς, -οῦ, himself, herself, itself; (pl.) themselves

εἰς, (prep. + acc.) as far as, to the point of

ἐπισκοπέω, look or examine carefully

ἐρυθρός, -ή, -όν, red

ἐσθής, -ῆτος, ἡ, clothing

θαμά, (adv.) often, frequently, many times

καλλωπίζω, paint or beautify one's face (w/ cosmetics)

κατασκοπέω, (mid. often = act. in Xenophon) view closely

λευκός, -ή, -όν, white, (of skin) fair or white (as a sign of youth and beauty)

μάλιστα, (adv.) most, most of all

ὄν, ὄντος, τό, [< neut. part. of εἰμί] that which (really) is, reality

ὀρθός, -ή, -όν, upright, erect, straight

πολυσαρκία, ἡ, fleshiness, plumpness

σωφροσύνη, ἡ, soundness of mind, common sense, wisdom, good sense, prudence; temperance, moderation, sense of proportion, sobriety, self-control

τρέφω, bring up, rear

φύσις, -εως, ἡ, nature, natural condition

χρῶμα, -ατος, τό, complexion; color

ὥρα, ἡ, springtime of life, flower of youth, youth, beauty

ὥστε, (conj.) so as to (+ inf.)

---

1 ἐσθῆτι...λευκῇ construe w/ κεκοσμημένην

τεθραμμένην fem. acc. sing. perf. mid./pass. part. < τρέφω

2 κεκαλλωπισμένην fem. acc. sing. perf. mid./pass. part. < καλλωπίζω

τὸ...χρῶμα acc. of respect (Smyth § 1600, 1601b)

2-3 λευκοτέραν...ἐρυθροτέραν...ὀρθοτέραν comp. adjs.

3 ὀρθοτέραν "*more erect*, in order to appear taller. Tallness was esteemed by the Greeks." (Smith, 81)

3-4 τοῦ ὄντος...τῆς φύσεως gens. of comparison (Smyth § 1431), equivalent to ἢ ἦν...ἢ ἐπεφύκει ("than she was...than was natural")

4 τὰ δὲ ὄμματα...ἀναπεπταμένα i.e., not cast down or looking away demurely

5 ὥρα "youthful beauty," a (modest) euphemism for her naked body; the pl. of this word (ὧραι, w/ the root meaning "hours" or "seasons") is the title of the work from which the "Choice of Heracles" comes

διαλάμποι 3rd sing. pres. act. opt. < διαλάμπω; potential opt. (Smyth § 1824) in a rel. cl. of purp. (Smyth § 2554). Her revealing clothing resembles that of several well-known contemporary sculptures displayed on the Athenian Acropolis (for images of which, see **Appendix E**)

κατασκοπεῖσθαι...ἐπισκοπεῖν...ἀποβλέπειν still part of the indir. statement governed by [ὁ Πρόδικος] φησὶ in 21; along w/ θεᾶται, four different terms for watching or looking in one cl.

δὲ καὶ "and also"

τις ἄλλος αὐτὴν θεᾶται, πολλάκις δὲ καὶ εἰς τὴν ἑαυτῆς σκιὰν ἀποβλέπειν. [23] 1

ὡς δ' ἐγένοντο πλησιαίτερον τοῦ Ἡρακλέους, τὴν μὲν πρόσθεν ῥηθεῖσαν ἰέναι 2

τὸν αὐτὸν τρόπον, τὴν δ' ἑτέραν φθάσαι βουλομένην προσδραμεῖν τῷ Ἡρακλεῖ 3

καὶ εἰπεῖν· ὁρῶ σε, ὦ Ἡράκλεις, ἀποροῦντα ποίαν ὁδὸν ἐπὶ τὸν βίον τράπῃ. ἐὰν 4

οὖν ἐμὲ φίλην ποιησάμενος, ἐπὶ τὴν ἡδίστην τε καὶ ῥᾴστην ὁδὸν ἄξω σε, καὶ 5

τῶν μὲν τερπνῶν οὐδενὸς ἄγευστος ἔσῃ, τῶν δὲ χαλεπῶν ἄπειρος διαβιώσῃ. 6

ἄγευστος, -ον, w/out taste of, not tasting or having tasted (+ gen.)

ἄπειρος, -ον, w/out experience of

ἀποβλέπω, look or gaze steadfastly at, look upon (w/ love or admiration) (+ εἰς)

ἀπορέω, be perplexed or confused

βούλομαι, wish, want (+ inf.)

διαβιόω, -ώσομαι, -εβίων, spend one's whole life

εἶμι [in Attic prose, εἶμι serves as the fut. of ἔρχομαι] will go, will come

εἶπον, [2nd aor.; pres. in use is φήμι, λέγω, and ἀγορεύω] said, spoke; (inf.) εἰπεῖν, to say or speak

ἐπί, (prep. + acc.) to, toward

ἐρῶ, [the place of the pres. is supplied by φημί, λέγω or ἀγορεύω; εἶπον serves as the aor.] will say or speak; (pass.) be mentioned

ἥδιστος, -η, -ον, [irreg. superl. adj. of ἡδύς, ἡδεῖα, ἡδύ] most or very pleasant, pleasing, or gratifying

θεάομαι, look on, gaze at, view, watch

πλησιαίτερον, (adv.) close(r) to, near(er) to (+ gen.)

πολλάκις, (adv.) often, many times

πρόσθεν, (adv.) first, before (some other specified thing)

προστρέχω, -δραμοῦμαι, -έδραμον, run to/towards (one), come to (one) (+ dat.)

ῥᾷστος, -η, -ον, [irregular superl. of ῥᾴδιος, -η, -ον] easiest, very easy

σκιά, ἡ, shadow

τερπνός, -ή, -όν, delightful, pleasant; τὰ τερπνά, delights, pleasures

τρέπω, turn or direct X (acc.) (towards a thing); (pass. + ὁδόν) take the path or road

τρόπος, ὁ, manner, way

φθάνω, φθήσομαι, ἔφθασα, get before, anticipate

φίλος, -η, -ον, loved, one's own; dear to one; ὁ φίλος, friend

χαλεπός, -ή, -όν, hard, grievous, difficult; τὰ χαλεπά, hardships, difficulties

ὡς, (conj.; + indic. past tense vb.) when

2-3 τὴν μὲν...τὴν δ' ἑτέραν... still part of the indir. statement governed by [ὁ Πρόδικος] φησὶ in 21, w/ these two accs. the subjs. of the infs. in their respective cls.

2 ῥηθεῖσαν fem. acc. sing. aor. pass. part. < ἐρῶ

3 τὸν αὐτὸν τρόπον i.e., w/out altering her pace; the entire phrase is an adverbial acc. of manner (Smyth § 1608); note αὐτὸν in the attributive position means "the same"

4 τράπῃ 2nd sing. pres. mid./pass. subju. < τρέπω; deliberative subju. (Smyth § 1805, 2639) retained in indir. quest. (Smyth § 2662b)

4-6 ἐὰν...ἄξω...ἔσῃ...διαβιώσῃ FMV condit., w/ ellipsis of τὴν ὁδὸν ἐπὶ τὸν βίον τράπῃ in the protasis (i.e., ἐὰν τὴν ὁδὸν ἐπὶ τὸν βίον τράπῃ...)

6 τῶν...τερπνῶν partitive gen. w/ οὐδενὸς (which is governed by ἄγευστος)
ἔσῃ 2nd sing. fut. mid. (dep.). indic. < εἰμί
διαβιώσῃ 2nd sing. fut. mid. (dep.). indic. < διαβιόω

1   [24] πρῶτον μὲν γὰρ οὐ πολέμων οὐδὲ πραγμάτων φροντιεῖς, ἀλλὰ

2   σκοπούμενος ἀεὶ ἔσῃ τί ἂν κεχαρισμένον ἢ σιτίον ἢ ποτὸν εὕροις, ἢ τί ἂν ἰδὼν ἢ

3   ἀκούσας τερφθείης ἢ τίνων ὀσφραινόμενος ἢ ἁπτόμενος, τίσι δὲ παιδικοῖς

4   ὁμιλῶν μάλιστ' ἂν εὐφρανθείης, καὶ πῶς ἂν μαλακώτατα καθεύδοις, καὶ πῶς

ἀεί, (adv.) always

ἀκούω, ἀκούσομαι, ἤκουσα, hear

ἅπτω, fasten, bind fast; (mid.) touch (+ gen.)

εἶδον, (not used in act. pres.; ὁράω being used instead) saw

εὑρίσκω, εὑρήσω, ηὗρον/εὗρον, find

εὐφραίνω, rejoice; (pass.) enjoy oneself, be happy

μαλακός, -ή, -όν, soft, gentle, comfortable

μάλιστα, (adv.) most, most of all, especially

ὁμιλέω, associate w/, be in company w/ (+ dat.)

ὀσφραίνομαι, smell (+ gen.)

παιδικός, -ή, -όν, of a child, boyish; τὰ παιδικά, [lit. boyish things] boys; (pl. often = sing.) boyfriend

πόλεμος, ὁ, war

ποτόν, τό, drink

πρᾶγμα, -τος, τό, anything of importance or consequence; (pl.) state affairs, politics, government; troublesome business, annoyances

πρῶτος, -η, -ον, first; πρῶτον, (adv.) first, first of all

σιτίον, τό, food

σκοπέω, (mid. = act.) consider

τέρπω, delight, give delight, gladden; (mid./pass.) enjoy

φροντίζω, φροντιῶ, ἐφρόντισα, think of, worry about, care about, be anxious about (+ gen.)

χαρίζομαι, gratify or indulge (a passion); (pass.) be pleasing or agreeable

---

1 πραγμάτων Athenian male citizens were expected to be regular and active members of their democratic form of government, an often onerous responsibility that the characters of Aristophanes' comedies are constantly bemoaning

2 ἔσῃ 2nd sing. fut. mid. (dep.). indic. < εἰμί

κεχαρισμένον neut. acc. sing. perf. mid./pass. part. < χαρίζομαι

εὕροις 2nd sing. aor. act. opt. < εὑρίσκω; potential opt. in indir. statement (so too τερφθείης, καθεύδοις, and τυγχάνοις)

3 τερφθείης 2nd sing. aor. pass. opt. < τέρπω

τίσι masc./neut. (here = neut.) dat. pl. < τίς, τί

παιδικοῖς a socially accepted (especially among the aristocratic elite) asymmetrical romantic and/or erotic relationship between an adult male citizen (the ἐραστής ["lover"]; usu. 19+ years of age) and a younger male citizen (the ἐρώμενος ["beloved"] or παιδικά; usu. 12-19 years of age), Greek pederasty was an important component in the ancient Greek social and educational system. The ἐρώμενος/ παιδικά, courted by the ἐραστής, traditionally played a more passive role, and was not expected to derive pleasure from the sexual act (normally intercrural)

4 εὐφρανθείης 2nd sing. aor. pass. opt. < εὐφραίνω

καθεύδοις 2nd sing. pres. act. opt. < καθεύδω

5-1 μαλακώτατα...ἀπονώτατα the superl. adv. has the same form as the neut. pl. of the superl. adj. (Smyth § 345)

92

ἂν ἀπονώτατα τούτων πάντων τυγχάνοις. [25] ἐὰν δέ ποτε γένηταί τις ὑποψία   1

σπάνεως ἀφ᾽ ὧν ἔσται ταῦτα, οὐ φόβος μή σε ἀγάγω ἐπὶ τὸ πονοῦντα καὶ   2

ταλαιπωροῦντα τῷ σώματι καὶ τῇ ψυχῇ ταῦτα πορίζεσθαι, ἀλλ᾽ οἷς ἂν οἱ ἄλλοι   3

ἐργάζωνται, τούτοις σὺ χρήσῃ, οὐδενὸς ἀπεχόμενος ὅθεν ἂν δυνατὸν ᾖ τι   4

κερδᾶναι. πανταχόθεν γὰρ ὠφελεῖσθαι τοῖς ἐμοὶ συνοῦσιν ἐξουσίαν ἐγὼ παρέχω.   5

ἀπέχω, keep off or away from; (mid.) abstain or refrain from (+ gen.)

ἄπονος, -ον, free from toil or trouble, w/out toil or trouble

δυνατός, -ή, -όν, possible; δυνατόν [w/ or w/out ἐστι], it is possible (+ inf.)

ἐξουσία, ἡ, power, authority

ἐργάζομαι, make, do, perform, accomplish

κερδαίνω, κερδήσω, ἐκέρδανα, gain, derive profit or advantage; (+ τι), gain something, derive any profit or advantage

ὅθεν, (adv.) from which

πανταχόθεν, (adv.) from everywhere, from all places, in every way

παρέχω, provide, furnish, give

πονέω, work hard, suffer

πορίζω, furnish, provide; (mid.) provide for oneself, furnish oneself w/, procure

ποτε, (enclitic particle) ever, at any time

σπάνις, -εως, ἡ, scarcity, lack, shortage

σύνειμι, be w/, associate w/ (+ dat.)

σῶμα, -τος, τό, body

ταλαιπωρέω, suffer hardship or distress

τυγχάνω, obtain (+ gen.)

ὑποψία, ἡ, suspicion

φόβος, ὁ, fear

χράομαι/χρῶμαι, χρήσομαι, use, make use of, enjoy (+ dat.; sometimes w/ a double dat. constr., i.e., use X [dat.] as Y [dat.])

ψυχή, ἡ, mind

ὠφελέω, aid, serve; (mid.) benefit oneself

-----

1 τυγχάνοις 2nd sing. pres. act. opt. < τυγχάνω

1-2 ἐὰν...γένηταί...οὐ φόβος pres. gen. condit. (Smyth § 2295), i.e., "if ever...should arise, (there is always) no fear"

2 οὐ φόβος sc. ἐστί
μή σε ἀγάγω in an obj. cl. after a vb. of fear, trans. μή as "that" (Smyth § 2221)
ἀγάγω 1st sing. aor. act. subju. < ἄγω; subju. in an obj. cl. after a vb. of fear (Smyth § 2220b, 2222)

2-3 τὸ...πορίζεσθαι articular inf. (Smyth § 2026) after a prep. (Smyth § 2034b); trans. as a simple inf. Note that the pres. act. parts. (πονοῦντα, ταλαιπωροῦντα), which modify σε, are imbedded in the articular inf. (which itself takes a dir. obj., ταῦτα)

3 τῷ σώματι καὶ τῇ ψυχῇ dats. of respect (Smyth § 1516)
οἷς neut. dat. pl. rel. pron. + ἂν = "whatever (things)"; ἐργάζωνται would regularly take an acc. dir. obj. (i.e., ἅ), but the rel. pron. is attracted into the case of its antecedent (Smyth § 2522; here τούτοις, a word that follows it in the sentence)

4 ἐργάζωνται 3rd pl. pres. mid./pass. (dep.) subju. < ἐργάζομαι; subju. in an indef. rel. cl. (Smyth § 2567), which here substitutes for the protasis w/ εἰ of a FMV condit. (Smyth § 2344, 2560)
χρήσῃ 2nd sing. fut. mid. < χράομαι/χρῶμαι (the apodosis of a FMV condit.)
ᾖ 3rd sing. pres. act. subju. < εἰμί; subju. in an indef. rel. cl. (ὅθεν = ἐξ οὗ)

5 πανταχόθεν...παρέχω note the emphatic position of πανταχόθεν; English word order would be: γὰρ ἐγὼ παρέχω τοῖς συνοῦσιν ἐμοὶ ἐξουσίαν ὠφελεῖσθαι πανταχόθεν

1   [26] καὶ ὁ Ἡρακλῆς ἀκούσας ταῦτα, ὦ γύναι, ἔφη, ὄνομα δέ σοι τί ἐστιν; ἡ δέ,

2   οἱ μὲν ἐμοὶ φίλοι, ἔφη, καλοῦσί με Εὐδαιμονίαν, οἱ δὲ μισοῦντές με

3   ὑποκοριζόμενοι ὀνομάζουσι Κακίαν. [27] καὶ ἐν τούτῳ ἡ ἑτέρα γυνὴ

4   προσελθοῦσα εἶπε· καὶ ἐγὼ ἥκω πρός σέ, ὦ Ἡράκλεις, εἰδυῖα τοὺς γεννήσαντάς

5   σε καὶ τὴν φύσιν τὴν σὴν ἐν τῇ παιδείᾳ καταμαθοῦσα, ἐξ ὧν ἐλπίζω, εἰ τὴν

6   πρὸς ἐμὲ ὁδὸν τράποιο, σφόδρ' ἄν σε τῶν καλῶν καὶ σεμνῶν ἀγαθὸν ἐργάτην

γεννάω, beget, engender

εἶπον, [2nd aor.; pres in use is φημί, λέγω, ἀγορεύω] said, spoke

ἐμός, -ή, -όν, my

ἐργάτης, -ου, ὁ, doer, performer

εὐδαιμονία, ἡ, good fortune, happiness

ἥκω, have come

κακία, ἡ, evil, wickedness

καταμανθάνω, καταμαθήσομαι, κατέμαθον, examine closely, observe well; learn thoroughly

μισέω, hate

ὄνομα, -ατος, τό, name

ὀνομάζω, name or call X (acc.) Y (acc.)

προσέρχομαι, πρόσειμι, προσῆλθον, go or come forward

σεμνός, -ή, -όν, holy, august

σός, -ή, -όν, your

σφόδρα, (adv.) very, very much

τρέπω, turn or direct X (acc.) (towards a thing); (pass. + ὁδόν) take the path or road

ὑποκορίζομαι, call by a petname/nickname; call by a euphemism; insult, call a good thing by a bad name

φύσις, -εως, ἡ, nature, natural disposition

---

1 σοι dat. of interest here expressing possession (Smyth § 1476), i.e., to you = your; ἐμοὶ in the following cl. could be either a dat. of interest (< ἐγώ) expressing possession or a nom. possessive adj.

ἡ δέ "And that one/she"; a demonstrative use of the article in Attic prose (Smyth § 1106)

3 ἐν τούτῳ sc. χρόνῳ, lit., "in this time," i.e., meanwhile, in the meantime

4 προσελθοῦσα fem. nom. sing. aor. act. part. < προσέρχομαι

καὶ ἐγώ "I too"

εἰδυῖα fem. nom. sing. perf. act. part. < οἶδα

4-5 οἱ γεννήσαντες σε i.e., your parents

5 τὴν φύσιν τὴν σὴν ἐν τῇ παιδείᾳ καταμαθοῦσα in Prodicus' allegory, Heracles' childhood and adolescence are a morally clean slate; in the mythological tradition (conveniently ignored by Prodicus/Xenophon's Socrates), however, Heracles infamously killed his music teacher Linus as a teenager (Apollodorus, 2.4.9; Diodorus 3.67.2; Pausanias 9.29.9)

καταμαθοῦσα fem. nom. sing. aor. act. part. < καταμανθάνω

6 τράποιο 2nd sing. aor. mid. opt. < τρέπω; opt. in the protasis of a FLV condit. (Smyth § 2329). Note that the FLV condit. is "less confident than the [FMV condit.] ἐάν [τραπῇ] of Κακία in 23." (Smith, 83)

6-1 ἄν σε...γενέσθαι καὶ ἐμὲ...φανῆναι the indir. statements are governed by ἐλπίζω, while the modal (ἄν) modifies both infs. (γενέσθαι, φανῆναι): "(I hope that) you may become...and that I may appear..." Note that ἄν...γενέσθαι...φανῆναι is equivalent to ἄν...γένοιο...φανείην in dir. discourse (Smyth § 1848a)

γενέσθαι καὶ ἐμὲ ἔτι πολὺ ἐντιμοτέραν καὶ ἐπ᾽ ἀγαθοῖς διαπρεπεστέραν φανῆναι.　1

οὐκ ἐξαπατήσω δέ σε προοιμίοις ἡδονῆς, ἀλλ᾽ ᾗπερ οἱ θεοὶ διέθεσαν τὰ ὄντα　2

διηγήσομαι μετ᾽ ἀληθείας. [28] τῶν γὰρ ὄντων ἀγαθῶν καὶ καλῶν οὐδὲν ἄνευ　3

πόνου καὶ ἐπιμελείας θεοὶ διδόασιν ἀνθρώποις, ἀλλ᾽ εἴτε τοὺς θεοὺς ἵλεως εἶναί　4

σοι βούλει, θεραπευτέον τοὺς θεούς, εἴτε ὑπὸ φίλων ἐθέλεις ἀγαπᾶσθαι, τοὺς　5

ἀγαπάω, love, treat w/ affection; (pass.) be loved, be regarded w/ affection

ἀλήθεια, ἡ, truth

ἄνευ, (prep. + gen.) without

διαπρεπής, -ές, eminent, distinguished, illustrious

διατίθημι, διαθήσω, διέθηκα, arrange

διηγέομαι, διηγήσομαι, narrate, explain in detail, describe

δυνατός, -ή, -όν, possible; powerful, capable

ἐθέλω, be willing, wish (+ inf.)

εἴτε, (adv.) [generally doubled] εἴτε...εἴτε, either...or, whether...or; [as a standalone in an indir. quest., can =] (and) if

ἐλπίζω, expect or hope that (+ fut./aor. inf.)

ἔντιμος, -ον, honored

ἐξαπατάω, ἐξαπατήσω, deceive or beguile (thoroughly)

ἐπί, (prep. + dat.) for

ἐπιμέλεια, ἡ, care (bestowed upon a thing), diligent attention paid (to it), concern

θεός, ὁ, god

θεραπευτέον, [vb. adj. of θεραπεύω, serve, tend to] one must do service to, one must tend (to) or take care of; (of gods) one must worship; (of land) one must cultivate

ἡδονή, ἡ, pleasure, sense-gratification

ᾗπερ, (conj.; ᾗ [fem. dat. sing. rel. pron. w/ adv. sense] + περ [intensive particle]) in the same way as, exactly as

ἵλεως, (indecl. adj.) (of gods) propitious, benign, benevolent, kind

ὄντα, τά [< neut. nom./acc. pl. part. of εἰμί] the things which actually exist, the facts, reality, truth

πολύ, (adv.; often joined with compar. adjs. and advs. to increase their compar. force) much, far

πόνος, ὁ, hard work; distress, suffering, pain

προοίμιον, τό, proem, preface, beginning

φαίνω, φανῶ, ἔφηνα, bring to light; (pass.) be seen, appear

---

1 ἀγαθοῖς "good deeds/actions" (that Heracles would perform under Arete's guidance)

2 προοιμίοις ἡδονῆς i.e., w/ the first part of my speech promising all kinds of pleasure (like my opponent Κακία did in 23-24). προοιμίοις instrumental dat. (Smyth § 1507) διέθεσαν 3rd pl. aor. act. indic. < διατίθημι

3 τῶν γὰρ ὄντων ἀγαθῶν καὶ καλῶν construe ἀγαθῶν καὶ καλῶν as predicates of ὄντων, which is partitive gen. w/ οὐδὲν

4 ἵλεως predicate adj. indecl. (here = masc. acc. pl.)

5-1 βούλει...ἐθέλεις...ἐπιθυμεῖς verbal variation, though here all three vbs. essentially have the same meaning (which may be intentionally ironic on the part of Xenophon, since Prodicus in his lectures on literary style was said to have laid stress on the right use of words and the accurate discrimination between synonyms) βούλει 2nd sing. pres. mid. (dep.) indic. < βούλομαι

5 θεραπευτέον impersonal construction of the verbal adj. (Smyth § 2149, 2152), i.e., the neut. nom. sing. (sometimes pl.) verbal adj. w/ ἐστί expressed or understood; it is active in sense. The impersonal verbal adj. expresses necessity, being the equivalent of δεῖ ("it is necessary") + the inf. of the vb. from which the verbal adj. is derived

1 φίλους εὐεργετητέον, εἴτε ὑπό τινος πόλεως ἐπιθυμεῖς τιμᾶσθαι τὴν πόλιν

2 ὠφελητέον, εἴτε ὑπὸ τῆς Ἑλλάδος πάσης ἀξιοῖς ἐπ' ἀρετῇ θαυμάζεσθαι, τὴν

3 Ἑλλάδα πειρατέον εὖ ποιεῖν, εἴτε γῆν βούλει σοι καρποὺς ἀφθόνους φέρειν, τὴν

4 γῆν θεραπευτέον, εἴτε ἀπὸ βοσκημάτων οἴει δεῖν πλουτίζεσθαι, τῶν

5 βοσκημάτων ἐπιμελητέον, εἴτε διὰ πολέμου ὁρμᾷς αὔξεσθαι καὶ βούλει

6 δύνασθαι τούς τε φίλους ἐλευθεροῦν καὶ τοὺς ἐχθροὺς χειροῦσθαι, τὰς

7 πολεμικὰς τέχνας αὐτάς τε παρὰ τῶν ἐπισταμένων μαθητέον καὶ ὅπως αὐταῖς

ἀξιόω, expect (+ inf.)

ἀπό, (prep. + gen.) from

αὐξάνω, increase X (acc.), make X (acc.) large; (pass.) grow or increase (in power, influence, etc.)

ἄφθονος, -ον, plentiful

βόσκημα, -τος, τό, herd of cattle

γῆ, ἡ, land

διά, (prep. + gen.) through, by (means of)

δύναμαι, be able (+ inf.)

ἐλευθερόω, set free

Ἑλλάς, Ἑλλάδος, ἡ, Greece

ἐπιθυμέω, desire (to + inf.)

ἐπιμελητέον, [vb. adj. of ἐπιμελέομαι, take care of] one must care for, take care of, or pay attention to (+ gen.)

ἐπίσταμαι, know, understand

εὖ, (adv.) well

εὐεργετητέον, [vb. adj. of εὐεργετέω, do well or good; show kindness] one must show kindness to

ἐχθρός, ὁ, one's (usu. non-military) enemy

θαυμάζω, admire

καρπός, ὁ, fruit, fruits of the earth, produce

μαθητέον, [vb. adj. of μανθάνω, learn] one must learn

οἴομαι, think

ὁρμάω, strive to, set out to, be eager to (+ inf.)

ὅπως, (conj.) how, in what manner

πειρατέον, [vb. adj. of πειράω, attempt, try to (+ inf.)] one must attempt or try to (+ inf.)

πλουτίζω, make wealthy, enrich; (pass.) gain one's wealth

ποιέω, make, do; + εὖ, do good to, treat well, benefit

πόλεμος, ὁ, war

πόλις, -εως, ἡ, city-state, state

τέχνη, ἡ, skill, art, technique

τιμάω, honor

φέρω, bear, carry; (of land) produce, bring forth

χειρόω, (mostly in mid.) subdue, bring into one's power, conquer

ὠφελητέον, [vb. adj. of ὠφελέω, help, aid, assist, serve] one must help, aid, assist or serve

---

1ff. Verbal adjs. in the following cls.: εὐεργετητέον, ὠφελητέον, πειρατέον, θεραπευτέον, ἐπιμελητέον, μαθητέον, ἀσκητέον, ἐθιστέον, and γυμναστέον

2 ἀξιοῖς 2nd sing. pres. act. indic. < ἀξιόω

4 Note the different meanings of θεραπεύω w/ θεούς (= "worship") on the previous page and w/ γῆν (= "cultivate") here

6 ἐλευθεροῦν pres. act. inf. [ἐλευθερό + ειν] < ἐλευθερόω

7 αὐτάς τε "the τέ is added, because the writer had in mind μαθητέον for both clauses, with some such obj. in the second as τὴν χρῆσιν αὐτῶν ["their use"], instead of which, by a slight change of construction we have ὅπως αὐταῖς δεί χρῆσθαι ἀσκητέον." (Smith, 84)

δεῖ χρῆσθαι ἀσκητέον· εἰ δὲ καὶ τῷ σώματι βούλει δυνατὸς εἶναι, τῇ γνώμῃ   1

ὑπηρετεῖν ἐθιστέον τὸ σῶμα καὶ γυμναστέον σὺν πόνοις καὶ ἱδρῶτι. [29] καὶ ἡ   2

Κακία ὑπολαβοῦσα εἶπεν, ὥς φησι Πρόδικος· ἐννοεῖς, ὦ Ἡράκλεις, ὡς χαλεπὴν   3

καὶ μακρὰν ὁδὸν ἐπὶ τὰς εὐφροσύνας ἡ γυνή σοι αὕτη διηγεῖται; ἐγὼ δὲ ῥᾳδίαν   4

καὶ βραχεῖαν ὁδὸν ἐπὶ τὴν εὐδαιμονίαν ἄξω σε. [30] καὶ ἡ Ἀρετὴ εἶπεν· ὦ   5

τλῆμον, τί δὲ σὺ ἀγαθὸν ἔχεις; ἢ τί ἡδὺ οἶσθα μηδὲν τούτων ἕνεκα πράττειν   6

ἀσκητέον, [vb. adj. of ἀσκέω, practice, train] one must practice
βραχύς, -εῖα, -ύ, short
γνώμη, ἡ, thought, judgment, opinion
γυμναστέον, [vb. adj. of γυμνάζω, train or exercise] one must train or exercise
δεῖ, [impersonal < δέω, lack, need] it is necessary, one must (+ inf.)
διηγέομαι, narrate, explain in detail, describe
δυνατός, -ή, -όν, powerful, capable
ἐθιστέον, [vb. adj. of ἐθίζω, accustom] one must accustom
εἶπον, [2nd aor.; pres. in use is φήμι, λέγω, and ἀγορεύω] said, spoke
ἕνεκα, (prep. + gen., mostly after its case) for, for the sake of
ἐννοέω, consider, understand
ἐπί, (prep. + acc.) to
εὐδαιμονία, ἡ, good fortune, happiness
εὐφροσύνη, ἡ, (pl. = sing.) joy, happiness

ἱδρώς, -ῶτος, ὁ, sweat
κακία, ἡ, evil, wickedness
μακρός, -ά, -όν, long
μηδείς, μηδεμία, μηδέν, no one, nothing
ὅστις, ἥτις, ὅ τι, whoever, someone who, anyone who, whichever, something which, anything which
πράττω, do
ῥᾴδιος, -η, -ον, easy
σῶμα, -τος, τό, body
τλήμων, -ονος, ὁ/ἡ, [voc. τλῆμον], wretched or miserable creature
ὑπηρετέω, [lit., ὑπό, under + ἐρέττω, row, i.e., do service on a ship as a rower, hence =] serve (+ dat.); submit, yield, obey (+ dat.)
ὑπολαμβάνω, ὑπολήψομαι, ὑπέλαβον, respond, reply
χαλεπός, -ή, -όν, hard, grievous, difficult
χράομαι/χρῶμαι, [pres. inf. χρῆσθαι < χρά + εσθαι] use (+ dat.)
ὡς, (adv.) as; how

---

1 εἰ δὲ emphatic after seven εἴτε's
  τῷ σώματι dat. of respect (Smyth § 1516)

4 ἡ γυνή σοι αὕτη note word order, w/ the 2nd pers. pron. trapped within the noun and its demonstrative adj. (the latter can be used emphatically to indicate scorn, i.e., *this* woman). Contrast this with the following cl., where the separation of the pronouns is extreme (ἐγὼ...σε), thus putting the emphasis on σε

5 ἡ Ἀρετή "that Virtue has not been previously mentioned by name is a refinement of the allegory, which has left it to the hearer or reader to identify her by her description at entrance, and by her words." (Smith, 85)

6 τί...σὺ ἀγαθὸν note interlocked word order, w/ emphatic σὺ (responding to the αὕτη of 29?)
  οἶσθα 2nd sing. perf. (w/ force of pres.) act. indic. < οἶδα

1 ἐθέλουσα; ἥτις οὐδὲ τὴν τῶν ἡδέων ἐπιθυμίαν ἀναμένεις, ἀλλὰ πρὶν ἐπιθυμῆσαι

2 πάντων ἐμπίμπλασαι, πρὶν μὲν πεινῆν ἐσθίουσα, πρὶν δὲ διψῆν πίνουσα, ἵνα μὲν

3 ἡδέως φάγῃς, ὀψοποιοὺς μηχανωμένη, ἵνα δὲ ἡδέως πίῃς, οἴνους τε πολυτελεῖς

4 παρασκευάζῃ καὶ τοῦ θέρους χιόνα περιθέουσα ζητεῖς, ἵνα δὲ καθυπνώσῃς

5 ἡδέως, οὐ μόνον τὰς στρωμνὰς μαλακάς, ἀλλὰ καὶ τὰς κλίνας καὶ τὰ ὑπόβαθρα

ἀναμένω, wait for
διψάω, be thirsty; [διψα + ειν = inf. διψῆν
  not διψᾶν; Smyth § 394, 641]
ἐθέλω, be willing, wish (+ inf.)
ἐμπίπλημι, fill quite full of X (gen.); (pass.)
  be filled full of X (gen.), sate oneself w/ X
  (gen.)
ἐπιθυμέω, desire, feel desire ([for] + gen. of
  obj.)
ἐπιθυμία, ἡ, desire, longing
ἐσθίω, ἔδομαι, ἔφαγον, eat
ζητέω, seek, search out
ἡδέως, (adv.) pleasantly, sweetly, w/
  pleasure
ἡδύς, ἡδεῖα, ἡδύ, pleasant
θέρος, -εος/ους, τό, summer
ἵνα, (conj.) in order that, that (+ subju.)
καθυπνόω, fall asleep
κλίνη, ἡ, bed, couch
μαλακός, -ή, -όν, soft

μηχανάομαι/μηχανῶμαι, procure for
  oneself; devise (by art or cunning)
μόνος, -η, -ον, alone; μόνον, (adv.) only;
  [often in the expression] οὐ μόνον...ἀλλὰ
  καὶ, not only...but also
οἶνος, ὁ, wine
ὀψοποιός, ὁ, cook, chef
παρασκευάζω, prepare; (mid.) provide
  oneself w/, or procure for oneself
πεινάω, be hungry; [πεινά + ειν = inf.
  πεινῆν not πεινᾶν; Smyth § 394, 641]
περιθέω, run around
πίνω, πίομαι, ἔπιον, drink
πολυτελής, -ές, very expensive, costly
πρίν, (conj.) before (+ inf. = before X-ing)
στρωμνή, ἡ, mattress, bedding
ὑπόβαθρον, τό, wooden frame (to support
  a couch or bed)
χιών, -όνος, ἡ, ice-cold water (used to
  chill wine)

----

1 ἐθέλουσα the part. here has causal force (Smyth § 2064), i.e., "since you are willing"
ἥτις note the force of the indef. rel. pron., which, unlike the def. rel. pron. (ὅς, ἥ, ὅ),
"denote(s) a person or thing in general, or mark(s) the *class*, *character*, *quality*, or
capacity of a person..." (Smyth § 2496). Trans. as "you (are the sort of person) who"

2 ἐμπίμπλασαι 2nd sing. pres. mid./pass. indic. < ἐμπίπλημι

3 φάγῃς 2nd sing. aor. act. subju. < ἐσθίω; subju. in a final/purp. cl. introduced by ἵνα
(Smyth § 2193, 2196); so too πίῃς, παρασκευάζῃ, καθυπνώσῃς, and παρασκευάζῃ in
the the following cls.

4 τοῦ θέρους gen. of time within which (Smyth § 1444)

5 καὶ τὰς κλίνας thought by some editors to be an interpolation, "as the possession of
couches could not be a subject for reproach." (Smith, 85). But the Spartans, a culture
deeply admired by Socrates and Xenophon (and Prodicus?), clearly engaged (esp. their
youths) in lifestyle choices similar to those promoted by Ἀρετή in 28 and 30. Cf., e.g.,
the education of young Spartan males in Plutarch's *Life of Lycurgus* 16: "They trained
children to eat up their food and not to be fussy about it.... The boys learned to read and
write no more than was necessary. Otherwise their whole education was aimed at
developing smart obedience, perseverance under stress, and victory in battle. So as they

ταῖς κλίναις παρασκευάζῃ· οὐ γὰρ διὰ τὸ πονεῖν, ἀλλὰ διὰ τὸ μηδὲν ἔχειν ὅ τι **1**

ποιῇς ὕπνου ἐπιθυμεῖς· τὰ δ᾽ ἀφροδίσια πρὸ τοῦ δεῖσθαι ἀναγκάζεις, πάντα **2**

μηχανωμένη καὶ γυναιξὶ τοῖς ἀνδράσι χρωμένη· οὕτω γὰρ παιδεύεις τοὺς **3**

σεαυτῆς φίλους, τῆς μὲν νυκτὸς ὑβρίζουσα, τῆς δ᾽ ἡμέρας τὸ χρησιμώτατον **4**

κατακοιμίζουσα. [31] ἀθάνατος δὲ οὖσα ἐκ θεῶν μὲν ἀπέρριψαι, ὑπὸ δὲ **5**

ἀθάνατος, -ον, immortal
ἀναγκάζω, force
ἀπορρίπτω, throw out, cast forth, reject, disown
ἀφροδίσια, τά, [lit., "the things of Aphrodite"] sexual pleasures, sex
δέομαι, be in want or need
ἡμέρα, ἡ, day
κατακοιμίζω, sleep through
μηδείς, μηδεμία, μηδέν, no one, nothing
νύξ, νυκτός, ἡ, night

παιδεύω, teach, train, educate
πονέω, work hard, suffer
πρό, (prep. + gen.) before
σεαυτοῦ, σεαυτῆς, of yourself
ὑβρίζω, behave in a dissolute manner, be given over to (sensual/sexual) pleasures
ὕπνος, ὁ, sleep
χράομαι/χρῶμαι, use (+ dat.; sometimes with a double dat. constr., i.e., use X [dat.] as Y [dat.])
χρήσιμος, -ον, useful

---

grew older they intensified their physical training, and got into the habit of cropping their hair, going barefoot, and exercising naked. From the age of twelve they never wore a tunic, and were given only one cloak a year. Their bodies were rough (αὐχμηροὶ; cf. 31 below and vocab.), and knew nothing of baths or oiling: only on a few days in the year did they experience such delights. They slept together by Squadron and Troop on mattresses which they made up for themselves from the tips of reeds growing along the River Eurotas, broken off by hand without the help of any iron blade." (R. Talbert, *On Sparta* [Penguin Classics, rev. ed., 2005], 21-22)

1 τὸ πονεῖν articular inf. w/ prep., translate here as "work"; so too τὸ μηδὲν ἔχειν ("having nothing") and τοῦ δεῖσθαι ("being in want or need") in the following cls.

1-2 τὸ μηδὲν ἔχειν ὅ τι ποιῇς lit., "having nothing whatever that you might do," i.e., being bored

2 ποιῇς 2nd sing. pres. act. subju.; deliberative subju. (Smyth § 1805, 2639) retained in indir. quest. (Smyth § 2662b)

3 γυναιξὶ τοῖς ἀνδράσι χρωμένη note that the condemnation is of adult (ἀνδράσι) same-sex physical relationships, not of the generally accepted (esp. in aristocratic elite circles) pedophilic relations (see note to παιδικοῖς, on p. 96, line 3)

4 τῆς...νυκτὸς gen. of time within which (Smyth § 1444)
τῆς...ἡμέρας τὸ χρησιμώτατον lit., "the most useful (part) of the day," i.e., when it is daylight

5 οὖσα the part. here has concessive force (Smyth § 2066), i.e, although...
ἐκ θεῶν ἐκ here expresses either place ("from [the company of] the gods") or agent ("by the gods"), though ἐκ + gen. w/ this meaning is mostly found in verse and in Herodotus. More commonly, agency is expressed by ὑπό + gen. (as seen, e.g., in the following cl.)
ἀπέρριψαι 2nd sing. perf. mid./pass. indic. < ἀπορρίπτω

1 ἀνθρώπων ἀγαθῶν ἀτιμάζῃ· τοῦ δὲ πάντων ἡδίστου ἀκούσματος, ἐπαίνου

2 σεαυτῆς, ἀνήκοος εἶ, καὶ τοῦ πάντων ἡδίστου θεάματος ἀθέατος· οὐδὲν γὰρ

3 πώποτε σεαυτῆς ἔργον καλὸν τεθέασαι. τίς δ' ἄν σοι λεγούσῃ τι πιστεύσειε; τίς

4 δ' ἄν δεομένῃ τινὸς ἐπαρκέσειεν; ἢ τίς ἄν εὖ φρονῶν τοῦ σοῦ θιάσου τολμήσειεν

5 εἶναι; οἳ νέοι μὲν ὄντες τοῖς σώμασιν ἀδύνατοί εἰσι, πρεσβύτεροι δὲ γενόμενοι

6 ταῖς ψυχαῖς ἀνόητοι, ἀπόνως μὲν λιπαροὶ διὰ νεότητος τρεφόμενοι, ἐπιπόνως δὲ

ἀδύνατος, -ον, w/out strength, powerless
ἀθέατος, -ον, not seeing, blind to (+ gen.)
ἀκούσματος, -ατος, τό, thing heard
ἀνήκοος, -ον, deaf to (+ gen.), ignorant of (+ gen.)
ἀνόητος, -ον, foolish, senseless, unintelligent
ἀπόνως, (adv.) free from toil or trouble, w/out toil or trouble, in an effortless manner
ἀτιμάζω, dishonor
δέομαι, be in want or need of (+ gen.)
ἔπαινος, ὁ, praise
ἐπαρκέω, help, aid, or assist X (dat.)
ἐπιπόνως, (adv.), painfully, w/ suffering, w/ difficulty, w/ hard work, laboriously
ἔργον, τό, work, deed, accomplishment
ἡδύς, ἡδεῖα, ἡδύ, pleasant, gratifying
θέαμα, θεάματος, τό, that which is seen, sight, spectacle

θεάομαι, look on, gaze at, view
θίασος, ὁ, band or company marching through the streets w/ song and dance (esp. in honor of Dionysus), band or company of revelers; company, troop
λιπαρός, -ά, -όν, [root meaning (of persons): anointed, covered w/ ointment, perfumed, shiny, smooth, w/out wrinkles], (figuratively of condition) rich, comfortable, easy
νεός, -α, -ον, young
νεότης, -ητος, ἡ, youth
πιστεύω, trust, believe (in) (+ dat.)
πρεσβύτερος, -α, -ον, older
πώποτε, (adv.) ever yet
σός, -ή, -όν, your
τολμάω, dare (to + inf.)
φρονέω, think, reflect
ψυχή, ἡ, mind

---

2 ἀθέατος sc. εἶ

3 τεθέασαι 2nd sing. perf. mid./pass. indic. < θεάομαι
πιστεύσειε 3rd sing. aor. act. opt. < πιστεύω; w/ ἄν, a potential opt. (so too ἐπαρκέσειεν and τολμήσειεν in the following cls.)

4 εὖ φρονῶν cf. the English idiom "in one's right mind"

5 οἳ νέοι...ὄντες lit., "who, being young," i.e., when they are young. οἳ νέοι refers to the members of Κακία's θίασος; the pl. is used "as if preceded by θιασωτῶν, instead of θιάσου, a const. κατὰ σύνεσιν ["according to sense"; more commonly known by its Latin phrase, *constructio ad sensum*]." (Smith, 86)

5-6 τοῖς σώμασιν...ταῖς ψυχαῖς dats. of respect

6 ἀνόητοι sc. εἰσί

6-1 λιπαροὶ...αὐχμηροὶ the pred. adj. is sometimes used in Gk. where English regularly employs an adv. (Smyth § 1043); thus λιπαροὶ here = "comfortably," "richly"; αὐχμηροὶ = "in squalor," "wretchedly," "miserably"

αὐχμηροὶ διὰ γήρως περῶντες, τοῖς μὲν πεπραγμένοις αἰσχυνόμενοι, τοῖς δὲ   1
πραττομένοις βαρυνόμενοι, τὰ μὲν ἡδέα ἐν τῇ νεότητι διαδραμόντες, τὰ δὲ   2
χαλεπὰ εἰς τὸ γῆρας ἀποθέμενοι. [32] ἐγὼ δὲ σύνειμι μὲν θεοῖς, σύνειμι δὲ   3
ἀνθρώποις τοῖς ἀγαθοῖς· ἔργον δὲ καλὸν οὔτε θεῖον οὔτ' ἀνθρώπειον χωρὶς ἐμοῦ   4
γίγνεται. τιμῶμαι δὲ μάλιστα πάντων καὶ παρὰ θεοῖς καὶ παρὰ ἀνθρώποις οἷς   5
προσήκω, ἀγαπητὴ μὲν συνεργὸς τεχνίταις, πιστὴ δὲ φύλαξ οἴκων δεσπόταις,   6
εὐμενὴς δὲ παραστάτις οἰκέταις, ἀγαθὴ δὲ συλλήπτρια τῶν ἐν εἰρήνῃ πόνων,   7

ἀγαπητός, -ή, -όν, beloved

αἰσχύνω, dishonor; (pass.) be ashamed

ἀνθρώπειος, -α, -ον, human

ἀποτίθημι, ἀποθήσω, ἀπέθηκα, put away; (mid.) lay up, put away, deposit, leave off

αὐχμηρός, -ά, -όν, [root meaning: arid, dry, devoid of moisture, dusty, rough, parched], (figuratively) squalid, bleak, wretched, miserable, unfortunate

βαρύνω, weigh down, oppress, weary, cause distress

γῆρας, -αος/ως, τό, old age

δεσπότης, -ου, ὁ, master

διά, (prep. + gen.) (of time) throughout, during

διατρέχω, διαθρέξομαι, διέδραμον, run through

εἰρήνη, ἡ, peace

εὐμενής, -ές, well-disposed, favorable, gracious, kind

θεῖος, -α, -ον, divine

θεός, ὁ, god

μάλιστα, (adv.) most

οἰκέτης, -ου, ὁ, household slave; οἱ οἰκέται, one's household, the women and children of the household

οἶκος, -ου, ὁ, house

πάρα, (prep. + dat.) in the estimation of

παραστάτις, -ιδος, ἡ, assistant, helper

περάω, (often + διά) pass (through)

πιστός, -ή, -όν, trusted or believed, faithful, trusty

πόνος, ὁ, hard work; distress, suffering, pain

πράττω, do

προσήκω, belong to, be related to (+ dat.)

συλλήπτρια, ἡ, partner, accomplice, assistant

σύνειμι, be w/, associate w/ (+ dat.)

συνεργός, ὁ, helpmate, fellow worker, accomplice

τεχνίτης, -ου, ὁ, artist, craftsman, skilled worker

τιμάω/τιμῶ, honor, prize

φύλαξ, φύλακος, ὁ/ἡ, guardian

χαλεπός, -ή, -όν, hard, grievous, difficult; τὰ χαλεπά, hardships, difficulties

χωρίς, (adv./prep. + gen.) apart from, without

1-2 τοῖς...πεπραγμένοις...τοῖς...πραττομένοις instrumental dats. (Smyth § 1507) πεπραγμένοις neut. dat. pl. perf. mid./pass. part. < πράττω

3 σύνειμι μέν, σύνειμι δέ an example of the rhetorical trope known as *anaphora* (ἀναφορά, "carrying or bringing back"), the repetition, with emphasis, of the same word or phrase at the beginning of several successive cls.

4 καλὸν οὔτε θεῖον οὔτ' ἀνθρώπειον "acc[ording]. to Greek usage, we should expect an οὐδέν before καλόν." (Smith, 87)

6 ἀγαπητὴ μὲν συνεργὸς τεχνίταις sc. οὖσα in this and the following cls.

101

1 βεβαία δὲ τῶν ἐν πολέμῳ σύμμαχος ἔργων, ἀρίστη δὲ φιλίας κοινωνός. [33]
2 ἔστι δὲ τοῖς μὲν ἐμοῖς φίλοις ἡδεῖα μὲν καὶ ἀπράγμων σίτων καὶ ποτῶν
3 ἀπόλαυσις· ἀνέχονται γὰρ ἕως ἂν ἐπιθυμήσωσιν αὐτῶν· ὕπνος δ' αὐτοῖς
4 πάρεστιν ἡδίων ἢ τοῖς ἀμόχθοις, καὶ οὔτε ἀπολείποντες αὐτὸν ἄχθονται οὔτε
5 διὰ τοῦτον μεθιᾶσι τὰ δέοντα πράττειν. καὶ οἱ μὲν νέοι τοῖς τῶν πρεσβυτέρων
6 ἐπαίνοις χαίρουσιν, οἱ δὲ γεραίτεροι ταῖς τῶν νέων τιμαῖς ἀγάλλονται· καὶ

ἀγάλλω, glorify; (pass.) take delight in (+ dat.)

ἄμοχθος, -ον, exempt from pain or effort; not tired

ἀνέχω, hold up; (mid.) hold out

ἀπόλαυσις, -εως, ἡ, enjoyment; advantage got from X (gen.)

ἀπολείπω, leave, abandon

ἀπράγμων, -ον, (lit., "free from business or involvement in public affairs") not troublesome or painful, easy-going, carefree

ἄριστος, -η, -ον, best

ἄχθομαι, be vexed, annoyed, or grieved

βέβαιος, -αία, -ον, steadfast, firm

γεραίτερος, -α, -ον, older; (subst.) elder (w/ notion of dignity and respect)

δέον, -οντος, τό, [lit., "that which is necessary (to do)"; < neut. pres. part. of δεῖ, "it is necessary," "one must"] one's duty, what is expected of one

διά, (prep. + acc.) (causal, of persons) through, by, by means of, because of

ἔπαινος, ὁ, praise

ἐπιθυμέω, desire, feel desire ([for] + gen. of obj.)

ἕως, (conj.) until; [w/ ἄν + subju. (usu. aor.) = indef. temporal cl. of an event at an uncertain fut. time]

ἡδίων, -ον, [comp. of ἡδύς, ἡδεῖα, ἡδύ] more pleasant, sweeter

κοινωνός, ὁ, companion, partner (in X [gen.])

μεθίημι, neglect (+ inf.)

νέος, -α, -ον, young

πάρειμι, be present

πόλεμος, ὁ, war

ποτόν, τό, drink

πράττω, do, accomplish; be in a certain state or condition; + εὖ, do or fare well, be successful

πρεσβύτερος, -α, -ον, older

σιτίον, τό, food

σύμμαχος, ὁ, ally

τιμή, ἡ, honor

ὕπνος, ὁ, sleep

φιλία, ἡ, friendship

χαίρω, rejoice at, be delighted w/, take delight in (+ dat.)

---

2 ἔστι note accent; this is the existential use of εἰμί, i.e., "there is"
ἀπράγμων σίτων καὶ ποτῶν "foods and drink that are not painful/trouble-free (to procure)"; contrast this w/ Ἀρετή's earlier assertion (30) that Κακία can promise the ability to eat and drink pleasantly only after one has procured chefs to cook gourmet meals, and only after one has provided oneself w/ expensive wines, replete w/ ice-water that one has gone to great lengths (περιθέουσα, 30) to obtain in order to chill such drinks. Arete's disciples, in contrast, partake of simple fare that costs them little to no effort to procure

3 ἐπιθυμήσωσιν 3rd pl. aor. act. subju. < ἐπιθυμέω

5 διὰ τοῦτον lit., "on account of this thing," i.e., sleep

ἡδέως μὲν τῶν παλαιῶν πράξεων μέμνηνται, εὖ δὲ τὰς παρούσας ἥδονται **1**

πράττοντες, δι᾽ ἐμὲ φίλοι μὲν θεοῖς ὄντες, ἀγαπητοὶ δὲ φίλοις, τίμιοι δὲ **2**

πατρίσιν· ὅταν δ᾽ ἔλθῃ τὸ πεπρωμένον τέλος, οὐ μετὰ λήθης ἄτιμοι κεῖνται, **3**

ἀλλὰ μετὰ μνήμης τὸν ἀεὶ χρόνον ὑμνούμενοι θάλλουσι. τοιαῦτά σοι, ὦ παῖ **4**

ἀγαπητός, -ή, -όν, beloved
ἀεί, (adv.) always, for ever; ὁ ἀεὶ χρόνος, eternity, all time
ἄτιμος, -ον, dishonored
γεραίτερος, -α, -ον, older; (subst.) elder (w/ notion of dignity and respect)
ἐμός, -ή, -όν, my
ἔπαινος, ὁ, praise
ἡδέως, (adv.) pleasantly, sweetly, w/ pleasure
ἥδομαι, rejoice, enjoy, be delighted, be happy ([to be] X-ing/[to have/having X-ed [part.])
ἡδύς, ἡδεῖα, ἡδύ, pleasant, pleasing
θάλλω, flourish, be in full bloom
κεῖμαι, lie
λήθη, ἡ, oblivion
μιμνήσκω, remind; (mid./pass.) remember
μνήμη, ἡ, remembrance, being remembered

παῖς, παιδός, ὁ/ἡ, child, boy, girl
παλαιός, -ή, -όν, old, long ago, past
πάρειμι, be present
πατρίς, -ίδος, ἡ, country, fatherland
πεπρωμένος, -η, -ον, [perf. pass. part. of πόρω, "offer," "present," "give," used as an adj.] allotted, fated, destined
πρᾶξις, -εως, ἡ, achievement
τέλος, -εος/ους, τό, end, death
τίμιος, -η, -ον, honored, held in honor (by + dat.)
τοιοῦτος, -αύτη, -οῦτο, of that kind, of such character, such (a person or thing)
ὑμνέω, sing of, commemorate, celebrate, praise
φίλος, -η, -ον, loved, one's own; dear to one; ὁ φίλος, friend
χρόνος, -ου, ὁ, time

---

1 μέμνηνται 3rd pl. perf. (w/ pres. sense) mid./pass. indic. < μιμνήσκω

1-2 εὖ δὲ τὰς παρούσας ἥδονται πράττοντες lit., either "and doing well/being successful, they are happy in their present accomplishments (sc. πράξεις)" or "and they are happy to be doing well w/ respect to their present accomplishments"
τὰς παρούσας acc. of respect (Smyth § 1600, 1601c; cf. 1611)

3 ἔλθῃ 3rd sing. aor. act. subju. < ἔρχομαι; subju. in an indef. temporal cl. (ὅταν, [conj. adv.] whenever [+ subju.]) (Smyth § 2399a)
μετὰ λήθης lit., "with oblivion," i.e., being forgotten

4 τοιαῦτά σοι an example of asyndeton (ἀσύνδετον, "not bound together"), which occurs when two or more sentences (or words) independent in form and thought, are juxtaposed, i.e., coordinated, without any connective. The absence of connectives in a language so rich in means of coordination as is Greek is more striking than in other languages. Rhetorical asyndeton generally expresses emotion of some sort, and is the mark of liveliness, rapidity, passion, or impressiveness of thought, each idea being set forth separately and distinctly

1 τοκέων ἀγαθῶν Ἡράκλεις, ἔξεστι διαπονησαμένῳ τὴν μακαριστοτάτην

2 εὐδαιμονίαν κεκτῆσθαι. [34] οὕτω πως διώκει Πρόδικος τὴν ὑπ᾽ Ἀρετῆς

3 Ἡρακλέους παίδευσιν· ἐκόσμησε μέντοι τὰς γνώμας ἔτι μεγαλειοτέροις ῥήμασιν

4 ἢ ἐγὼ νῦν. σοὶ δ᾽ οὖν ἄξιον, ὦ Ἀρίστιππε, τούτων ἐνθυμουμένῳ πειρᾶσθαί τι καὶ

5 τῶν εἰς τὸν μέλλοντα χρόνον τοῦ βίου φροντίζειν.

ἄξιον, [sc. ἐστι] it is worthwhile, it is
  appropriate for X (dat.) to do Y (inf.)
Ἀρίστιππος, ὁ, Aristippus
γνώμη, ἡ, thought
διαπονέω, (mid. w/ same meaning as act.)
  work hard, toil constantly
διώκω, pursue (an an argument or topic),
  treat
ἐνθυμέομαι, ponder, consider well, reflect
  on, think deeply about (+ gen.)
ἔξεστι, it is possible (+ inf.)
εὐδαιμονία, ἡ, good fortune, happiness
ἤ, (conj.) than
κοσμέω, adorn, embellish, dress up
κτάομαι, get, gain, acquire; (perf.) possess,
  have

μακάριος, -ία, -ον, blessed
μέλλω, intend, be about to, be likely to
  (+ inf.); (pres. part. as adj.) future
μέντοι, (adv. conj.) moreover
νῦν, (adv.) now
οὖν, (conj.) so, therefore
πειράω, (mid. = act. in meaning) attempt to,
  try to (+ inf.)
παίδευσις, -εως, ἡ, education
πως, (adv.) somehow, in some such manner;
  οὕτω πως, somehow thus or so, in some
  such way or manner
ῥῆμα, -ατος, τό, word, phrase
τοκεύς, -έως, ὁ, one who begets, father;
  (mostly in pl.) parents
φροντίζω, think of, care about, take thought
  for (+ gen.)

1-2 τοιαῦτά σοι...κεκτῆσθαι = ὦ Ἡράκλεις, παῖ τοκέων ἀγαθῶν, ἔξεστι σοι, διαπονησαμένῳ τοιαῦτά, κεκτῆσθαι τὴν μακαριστοτάτην εὐδαιμονίαν

2 εὐδαιμονίαν note how Ἀρετή has wrested εὐδαιμονία away from Κακία, who earlier had laid claim to it both as her name (26) and as her reward (29)
κεκτῆσθαι perf. mid./pass. inf. < κτάομαι; the Gk. perf. "denotes a completed action the effects of which still continue in the present" (Smyth § 1945), and is thus often best translated into English as a pres. (Smyth § 1946): "to have acquired" thus = "to possess," "to have"

2-3 τὴν ὑπ᾽ Ἀρετῆς Ἡρακλέους παίδευσιν "the education of Heracles (carried out) by or under (the guidance of) Arete"; ὑπό and the gen. w/ a vb. noun = "under the agency of" (Smyth § 1698b). "Though Xenophon does not state explicitly or underscore which path Heracles chose, it is implied by the expression 'the education of Heracles by Virtue.'" (Mayhew, 221)

3 μεγαλειοτέροις ῥήμασιν instrumental dats. (Smyth § 1507)

4 ἐγὼ sc. I have used or employed
σοὶ...ἄξιον sc. ἐστι
Ἀρίστιππε Aristippus of Cyrene (c. 435-c. 356 BCE) was the founder of the Cyrenaic school of philosophy, a short-lived sect that believed the goal of life was to seek pleasure. Although a follower of Socrates (470-399 BCE), he deviated from the latter's teachings as found in the writings of two other followers of Socrates, Plato (427-

347 BCE) and Xenophon (*c.* 430-354 BCE), that seeking pleasure was not the goal of life

4-5 πειρᾶσθαί τι...φροντίζειν τι ("a little," "some," "somewhat"), is an adverbial acc. of measure and degree (Smyth § 1609), modifying either πειρᾶσθαί or φροντίζειν (though, due to its position, the former is more likely), while τῶν εἰς τὸν μέλλοντα χρόνον is the obj. of φροντίζειν

APPENDIX A

Allegorical Forerunners: Hesiod, *Works and Days* 286-292 and Simonides fr. 37 Diehl (74 Page, 579 Campbell)

The ancestors of Prodicus' Ἀρετή and Κακία can be traced back to one of the earliest works of Greek literature, Hesiod's *Works and Days* (*c.* 700 BCE), a didactic poem that consists of 800 or so dactylic hexameters.

In *Works and Days*, Hesiod describes how his brother Perses had bribed their community's rulers to judge in his favor concerning a legal dispute between them over the inheritance of the family farm. Hesiod spends much of the poem giving his brother moralizing advice, describing how the world actually works and how one must live in order to secure for oneself a stable, successful existence.

Works and Days consists of a somewhat eclectic collection of different narrative genres, including folktales and myths (e.g., Prometheus, Pandora), an animal fable (the hawk and the nightingale), and a "historical" account of successive human generations (the so-called Five Ages of Man). Also included, in lines 286-292, is one of the first allegorical tales (or, at the very least, an embryonic form of such tales) in Greek literature, in which Hesiod describes how easy it is for humans to procure κακότης ("badness," "wickedness," "vice"), whereas the attainment of ἀρετή ("excellence," "moral virtue") is, at least initially, far more sweat-inducing.[38]

A century or so after Hesiod's (proto) allegory appeared, it was closely imitated by Simonides of Ceos (*c.* 556-468 BCE), a celebrated lyric poet whom Protagoras (*c.* 490-*c.* 420 BCE), the first sophist, believed was, along with Homer and Hesiod, one of his sophistic precursors (Plato, *Protagoras* 316d; see also *Protagoras* 339a-346d for Socrates, Protagoras, and Prodicus' "literary-linguistic-philosophical" analysis of one of Simonides' poems).

THE TEXTS

Hesiod: Evelyn-White, H. G., *Hesiod. The Homeric Hymns and Homerica.* Cambridge (MA); London,1914

Simonides: Campbell, D. *Greek Lyric III: Stesichorus, Ibycus, Simonides, and Others.* Cambridge (MA), 1991
[Reading ἐγγὺς δέ μιν θεῶν **for** †νῦν δέ μιν θοαν† in line 3]

---

[38] Another candidate for one of the first (proto) allegorical tales in Greek literature is the story Achilles tells Priam of Zeus' two jars—one of blessings, the other of evils—in *Iliad* 24.522-551.

Hesiod, *Works and Days* 286-292

1   σοὶ δ' ἐγὼ ἐσθλὰ νοέων ἐρέω, μέγα νήπιε Πέρση.

2   τὴν μέντοι κακότητα καὶ ἰλαδὸν ἔστιν ἑλέσθαι

3   ῥηιδίως· λείη μὲν ὁδός, μάλα δ' ἐγγύθι ναίει·

4   τῆς δ' ἀρετῆς ἱδρῶτα θεοὶ προπάροιθεν ἔθηκαν

5   ἀθάνατοι· μακρὸς δὲ καὶ ὄρθιος οἶμος ἐς αὐτὴν   **290**

6   καὶ τρηχὺς τὸ πρῶτον· ἐπὴν δ' εἰς ἄκρον ἵκηται,

7   ῥηιδίη δὴ ἔπειτα πέλει, χαλεπή περ ἐοῦσα.

ἀθάνατος, -ον, immortal, undying

αἱρέω, αἱρήσω, εἷλον, take; (mid.) take to or for oneself, choose

ἄκρον, τό, peak

ἐγγύθι, (adv.) near, close by

ἐπεί, (conj.) when

ἔπειτα, (adv.) then

ἐσθλός, -ή, -όν, good

ἱδρώς, -ῶτος, ὁ, sweat

ἱκνέομαι, come to, reach, arrive at (often + εἰς)

ἰλαδόν, (adv.) in abundance, in great numbers

κακότης, -ητος, ἡ, badness, wickedness, vice

λεῖος, -η, -ον, smooth

μακρός, -ά, -όν, long

μέντοι, (particle) indeed, of course, certainly

ναίω, dwell

νήπιος, -η, -ον, infantile, childish, foolish, ignorant, w/out foresight

νοέω, think, intend (often w/ neut. pl. adj.)

οἶμος, ὁ/ἡ, way, road, path

ὄρθιος, -η, -ον, steep

πέλω, become, be

περ, (enclitic particle, giving emphasis to an idea, usu. to what immediately precedes it)

Πέρσης, -ου, ὁ, Perses

προπάροιθε(ν), (prep. + gen.) before, in front of

πρῶτον, τό, (adv.) at first, in the beginning

ῥᾴδιος/ῥηιδίη (epic/Ionic), -η, -ον, easy

ῥαδίως/ῥηιδίως (epic/Ionic), easily

τίθημι, put, place

τραχύς/τρηχύς (epic/Ionic), -εῖα, -ύ, rough

χαλεπός, -ή, -όν, difficult, hard

---

1 σοὶ...μέγα νήπιε Πέρση note how the line is framed by "Perses"

ἐρέω 1st sing. fut. act. indic. < εἴρω (rare in epic and never in Attic; ἐρέω/ἐρῶ's pres. is supplied by φημί, λέγω or ἀγορεύω, while εἶπον serves as the aor.)

μέγα νήπιε Πέρση vocs.

2 ἔστιν "it is possible" (+ inf.)

ἑλέσθαι aor. mid. inf. < αἱρέω

3 λείη μὲν ὁδός sc. ἐστί ; i.e., the road *that leads to her* is...

4-5 τῆς δ'...ἀθάνατοι = δ' ἀθάνατοι θεοὶ ἔθηκαν ἱδρῶτα προπάροιθεν τῆς ἀρετῆς

4 ἔθηκαν 3rd pl. aor. act. indic. < τίθημι

5 μακρὸς δὲ καὶ ὄρθιος sc. ἐστί

6 τρηχὺς τὸ πρῶτον sc. ἐστί

ἐπὴν = ἐπεὶ ἄν (+ subju. = indef. temporal cl.)

ἵκηται 3rd sing. aor. mid. (dep.). subju. < ἱκνέομαι

7 ἐοῦσα = (Epic/Ionic form of) οὖσα; the part. is concessive ("though..."); sc. previously

Simonides, fr. 579 (Campbell)

ἐστί τις λόγος	1
τὰν Ἀρετὰν ναίειν δυσαμβάτοισ' ἐπὶ πέτραις,	2
ἐγγὺς δέ μιν θεῶν χῶρον ἁγνὸν ἀμφέπειν·	3
οὐδὲ πάντων βλεφάροισι θνατῶν	4
ἔσοπτος, ᾧ μὴ δακέθυμος ἱδρὼς	5
ἔνδοθεν μόλῃ,	6
ἵκῃ τ' ἐς ἄκρον ἀνδρείας.	7

ἁγνός, -ή, -όν, holy, hallowed
ἄκρον, τό, peak
ἀμφιέπω, tend; look after
ἀνδρεία, ἡ, courage, manliness
βλέφαρον, τό, eyelid; (mostly in pl.) eyes
βλώσκω, μολοῦμαι, ἔμολον, come
δακέθυμος, -ον, heart-eating, heart-vexing, distressing
δυσανάβατος, -ον, hard or difficult to climb, inaccessible
ἐγγύς, (adv./prep. + gen.) near to
εἴσοπτος/ἔσοπτος, -ον, visible

ἔνδοθεν, (adv.) from within
θνητός, -ή, -όν, mortal; (as substantive) θνητοί, mortals
ἱδρώς, -ῶτος, ὁ, sweat
ἱκνέομαι, come to, reach (often + εἰς/ἐς)
ἵκω, come to, reach (often + εἰς/ἐς)
λόγος, ὁ, story, tale
μιν, (Ionic acc. sing. pron. = αὐτόν, αὐτήν, αὐτο) him, her, it
ναίω, dwell
πέτρα, ἡ, rock; rocky peak or ridge
χῶρος, ὁ, place

---

1 ἐστί τις λόγος initiates an indir. statement w/ τὰν Ἀρετὰν as subj. of the inf. ναίειν and its pron. μιν the subj. of ἀμφέπειν
λόγος can occupy the semantic domain between fable (μῦθος) and history (ἱστορία)

2 τὰν Ἀρετὰν = (Doric form of) τὴν Ἀρετὴν
δυσαμβάτοισ' = (poetic form of) δυσαναβάτοισ'

4 θνατῶν = (Doric form of) θνητῶν

5 ἔσοπτος sc. ἐστί
ᾧ μὴ... sc. ἄν; lit., "(anyone) to whom δακέθυμος ἱδρὼς... does not μόλῃ ἔνδοθεν"; this is a particularization of the general statement in line 4. The implication of this cl. is that Ἀρετὴν is visible *only* to the person to whom δακέθυμος ἱδρὼς ἔνδοθεν μόλῃ

6 μόλῃ 3rd sing. aor. act. subju. < βλώσκω; subju. in an indef. rel. cl.

7 ἵκῃ τ' ἐς ἄκρον ἀνδρείας sc. ἄν; the last line seems only loosely connected syntactically w/ the preceding cls.—note, for example, that the subj. has now switched to the person to whom δακέθυμος ἱδρὼς ἔνδοθεν μόλῃ
ἵκῃ 3rd sing. aor. act. subju. < ἱκνέομαι or 3rd sing. pres. act. subju. < ἵκω;

APPENDIX B

Kenneth Sylvan Guthrie, *The Greek Pilgrim's Progress, Generally Known as the Picture of Kebes, a Disciple of Socrates?*

The popularity of *Cebes' Tablet*—both in translation and as a "bridge-text" employed to make the transition from the study of grammar and morphology to reading complete literary works as effective (and painless) as possible—came to an abrupt halt in the first decade or so of the 20th century. One of the last translations published in English before the current revival of interest in the *Tablet* began in earnest in the 1980s was that by Kenneth Sylvan Guthrie, a Ph.D., MD, and ordained priest in the Protestant Episcopal Church. Unable to find full-time academic work, Guthrie supplemented his meager income by self-publishing a significant number of books, the majority being on ancient philosophical and mystical authors, especially the Neoplatonists.[39]

Unlike many of his other titles, Guthrie's translation of *Cebes' Tablet* (56 pages, 5 ½ × 8 ½ in. [14 cm × 22 cm]), was not cheaply produced and mimeographed, but printed to higher standards. Its title page clearly announces the *Gesamtkunstwerk* nature of the book in terms of its author's multiple contributions to its creation: "Translated from the Greek Text published by B. G. Teubner of Leipzig / Set in Type, Illustrated, and Ornamented by Kenneth Sylvan Guthrie, Ph. D." Indeed, it is the typesetting, illustrations, and ornamentation that make Guthrie's translation rather special. The imitation gothic typeface (somewhere between *textura* and *rotunda*) and large initial letters that begin each chapter mimic those of medieval and Renaissance manuscripts and early printed books. In addition, its illustrations and ornamentation combine in a seemingly eclectic manner elements of the Art Noveau (especially that movement's American flavor, dominated by the innovations of Louis Comfort Tiffany) with classical and orientalist architectural elements in vogue at the time. Finally, Guthrie has stirred in hints of Pre-Raphaelite and Symbolist stylings to this mix, with the result being a visually fascinating book that is unique among English translations of the *Tablet*.

---

[39] His *The Pythagorean Sourcebook and Library* (1919) is still in print. Other works are listed on the final pages of *The Greek Pilgrim's Progress*. In addition to these titles, he also published a wide range of different kinds of texts (a small selection of which follows): *Popol Vuh* (1906-7; the first English translation of the Mayan Book of the People), *The Spiritual Message of Literature: A Manual of Comparative Literature with Topical Outlines and Lists of Useful Books for School, College, and Private Use* (1913), *Teachers' Problems, and How to Solve Them* (1917), *Stories for Young Folks and Their Parents and Teachers* (1918), *A Romance of Two Centuries: A Tale of the Year 2025* (1919; a work of science fiction).

Kenneth Sylvan Launfal Guthrie

A. M. (*Harvard and Sewanee*) ; *Ph. D. (Columbia and Tulane) ; M. D. (Pennsylvania).*
Professor in Extension, University of the South, Sewanee.
Address: Teocalli, 1177 Warburton Avenue, North Yonkers, N. Y.

If desirous of keeping informed of his latest achievements, send him one dollar
for a yearly subscription to his inspirational bi-monthly Magazine
GOOD NEWS FOR ALL.

Wisdom of the Ancients Library
Volume First.

The Greek PILGRIM'S PROGRESS

Generally known as the Picture

by

KEBES, a disciple of Sokrates?

Translated from the Greek Text
published by B. G. Teubner of Leipzig
Set in Type, Illustrated, and Ornamented by

Kenneth Sylvan Guthrie, Ph. D.

London: Luzac and Company
46 Great Russell Street W.
Philadelphia: Monsalvat Press
1501 North Marshall Street.

Introduction.

The author of *The Picture* was probably the Kebes who was a disciple of Sokrates, and one of the few witnesses of the latter's last words and moments, and who wrote three dialogues, of which the present one is the sole survivor, the *Phrynichos* and the *Hebdome* being lost. This our *Picture* seems genuine enough, the spirit being Sokratic, and the diction Boeotian. But even the casual reader will notice that the last discussion, on *Good and Evil*, is unnecessary, different, and probably Stoical. The use of the term *Scientific Recognition* may suggest another interpolation. Other similar conclusions may be reached by students who get the text from *B. G. Teubner* in *Leipzig,* or who study the German translation in *Langenscheidt's Bibliothek.*

But we are here interested only in the moral value of the work as we find it — the *Pilgrim's Progress* of Humanity, ignoring all limitations of sect, creed, age and race. Hence it is for all time that it will teach that neither sense-gratification, nor wealth, power, or honor can yield true contentment or happiness, which can come only from **True Culture** — not necessarily valuable scientific training, but rather *Virtue* and *Righteousness* — but if possible, **all.**

First:
The Gate of Life
and its Delusions.

HAPPENING

oneday to be meditatively

visiting a Temple of Saturn, we reverently contemplated its votive inscriptions. Prominently affixed to the front of the Temple, loomed up large a strange pictorial Tablet, containing certain peculiar words, whose significance we were not able to fathom.

It seemed to represent, not some city or military camp, but a triple ring, formed by three concentric walled enclosures.

Within the outer circular wall might be seen a crowd of women; while outside, around the outer Gate, surged a large mob, to whose entering streams a certain old man seemed, by his gestures, to be uttering some command.

E stood a long while, questioning with each other about the symbology of the Picture. Then an Old Man who chanced to pass by stopped, and addressed us, in the following words:

'O Strangers! Not exceptional is this your experience of uncertainty about this Picture: for it is a puzzle even to many of the local inhabitants. This votive symbol does not originate from this locality. A Stranger, full of understanding, and impressive with wisdom, arrived here long since, following with zeal the rule of life of Pythagoras or Parmenides in word and deed. ❖ It was he who dedicated to Saturn both Temple and Picture.' ❖

'So you yourself saw and knew this Man, did you?' asked I. ❖   ❖   ❖

'Yes, indeed! ❖ And what is more, I admired him for a long time during my youth.

'It was his way to indulge in many serious conversations. ❖ Many is the time that I have heard him expound this symbolic Picture!' ❖   ❖   ❖   ❖

Second
The Maker of
the Tablet.

‘Y Jupiter!’ cried I, ‘unless you happen to have a most pressing engagement elsewhere, do please explain the Picture to us also! I assure you that we are most anxious to understand the meaning of this symbol!’

‘With pleasure, Strangers!’ said he. ‘But first you must hear that such an explanation is not without its very real dangers.’

‘How so?’ cried we all.

‘Should you,’ said he, ‘understand and assimilate what I should say, you shall become wise and happy; but if not, you will live badly, having become foolish, unfortunate, bitter, and ignorant.

‘For the explanation is not unlike the Sphinx’s Riddle, that he propounded to all men. Whoever solved it was saved; but destruction by the Sphinx overtook those who could not. And this was the Sphinx’s question: Within our life, What is a good? What is an evil? What is neither?

‘If anyone does not solve this, the Sphinx destroys him; not all at once, as in ancient times, but gradually, in his whole life, he perishes away, just like victims tortured to death.

‘But if he understands, he is saved, and attains felicity.

‘Attention, therefore! and make sure you understand!’

THIRD
The Riddle of
the Sphinx.

OW, by Hercules!

What fires hast thou lit in us, if what thou saidst is true!'

'Why, surely!' said he.

'Start in to explain immediately, then! For we shall attend to some purpose, especially in view of the nature of the retribution.'

'Well,' said the Old Man, pointing with a wand, 'do you see that outer circular wall?'

'Yes, indeed!' ✢ ✢ ✢

'First, you must know that the name of this whole place is the Life. ✢ This innumerable multitude surging in front of the Gate, are they who are about to enter into Life. ✢ ✢ ✢ ✢

'The Old Man who holds in one hand a scroll, and with the other is pointing out something is ᵗʰᵉ Good Genius

'To those who are entering is he setting forth what they should do when they shall have entered; ✢ and he is pointing out to them which WAY they shall have to walk in if they propose to be saved
✢   in 'the Life.'   ✢

⟡ FOURTH, the Gate of Life, the Good Genius, and the Way. ⟡

'WHICH way does he command them to go? ✣ And why?' said I. ✣ ✣ ✣ ✣ ✣ ✣

'You see,' said he, 'by the side of the Gate by which the Multitude are to

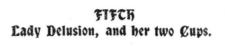

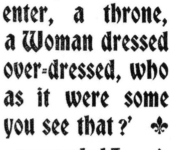

enter, a throne, a Woman dressed over=dressed, who as it were some you see that?' ✣

on which is seated stylishly—indeed, holds in her hands sort of cups — do

'Indeed I do,' responded I; ✣ but who is She?' ✣ ✣ ✣

'DELUSION is her name,' answered he, 'for the reason that She deludes and misleads e v e r y human being.' ✣ ✣ ✣

'But what is her office?' ✣

'She quenches the thirst of every soul that proceeds into Life, by making it drink of Her very own essence.' ✣

'And what might Her drink be, I wonder?' ✣ ✣

'ERROR and IGNORANCE' said he. ✣ ✣ ✣

'Why so?' ✣ ✣

'Because they would not en= ter into the Life, unless they were under that influence.' ✣

'I wonder whether this Del= usion is drunk by all, or only by some?' ✣ ✣ ✣

'All drink,' said he; 'al= though there are degrees, some drinking more, others less.' ✣

Error

Ignorance

False Opinion   **Desire**   **Pleasure**   **False Opinion**

HEN, do you not see within the Gate a crowd of Women wearing the motley garb of Courtesans?'

'Indeed do I see them!'

'Well, their names are FALSE OPINION, DESIRES, and PLEASURES. ✣ Upon the entering souls fall these, each of them embracing and leading away a soul.'

'And whither? would I like to know!'

'Some to be saved, indeed; but others, ✣ alas! ✣ to be destroyed by DELUSION.'

'O Good Genius of ours, how fateful is that Drink!'

'Surely, for each of those Courtesans promises to the soul that she has embraced that she will lead it to the best things and to a life happy and profitable; and she succeeds, for

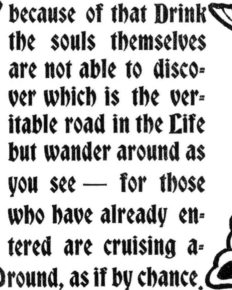because of that Drink the souls themselves are not able to discover which is the veritable road in the Life but wander around as you see — for those who have already entered are cruising around, as if by chance.

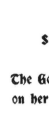

SEVENTH

The Goddess of Luck
on her Rolling Stone.

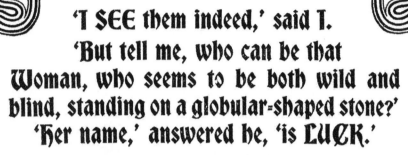

'I SEE them indeed,' said I.
'But tell me, who can be that
Woman, who seems to be both wild and
blind, standing on a globular=shaped stone?'
'Her name,' answered he, 'is LUCK.'

'Not only blind and wild is she, but deaf.'
'And what might her business be?'   ✤   ✤   ✤
'She circulates everywhere,' said he.   ✤   From some
she takes their substance, and freely gives it away to others.
Then, again, she suddenly withdraws what she has given,
and gives it to others without
any plan or steadfastness. ✤ So
you see that her symbol fits her
perfectly.'   ✤   ✤

'Which symbol,' asked I.

'Why, the Globular Stone on
which she stands.' ✤   ✤

'And what does that betoken,
I wonder?'   ✤   ✤

'That Globular Stone signi=
fies that no gift of hers is safe
or lasting; ✤ for whosoever
reposes any confidence in Her,
is sure to suffer great and right
grievous misfortune.' ✤   ✤

UT what is the wish and the name of that great Multitude standing around her?' ✤

'Oh! They are known as the UNREFLECTING ✤ they who desire whatever Luck might throw them.'

'But then, how is it that they do not be=have in the same manner? ✤ For some seem to rejoice, while others are agonizing, with hands outstretched?' ❀ ✤ ✤

'Well, those who seem to rejoice and laugh are they who have received somewhat from Her—and you may be sure that they call Her FORTUNE! ✤ On the contrary, those who seem to weep and stretch out their hands are they from whom She has taken back what She had given—they call Her MISFORTUNE!

'And what sort of things does She deal in, that they who receive them laugh, while they who lose them, weep?' ✤ ✤ ✤

'Why, what to the great Multitudes seems Good—of course Wealth; then Glory, Good Birth, Children, Power, Palaces, and the like.'

'But such things, are they not really good?'

'That question, let us postpone!'✤ ✤

'Willingly,' said I. ✤ ✤ ✤

OW, as you enter within the Gate, do you see the second circular enclosure, and without it, certain Women clad like courtesans?'

'Clearly!'

'Well, their names are INCONTINENCE, INDULGENCE, INSATIABLENESS, and FLATTERY.'

'And why do they stand there?'

'They are watching for those who may have received anything from the Luck-Goddess.'

'And then, what happens?'

'The Courtesans spring on those souls, embrace them, flatter them, and coax them not to go away, but to stay for a life of comfort, without effort or misadventure. Should, however, any soul be by them persuaded to enter into Enjoyment, this seems a pleasant pastime until he is satiated, but no longer. For whenever he sobers up, he notices that he has not eaten, but that he has, by Her, been devoured, and maltreated. Wherefore, when he has consumed all the goods he received from Fortune, he is forced to slave to those Women, to suffer all things, to be dishonored, and on their account to do many pitiable deeds—such as to steal, to profane Temples, to perjure himself, to betray, to plunder.

However, whenever he has degraded himself to the point of utter destitution, then is he handed over to PUNISHMENT.

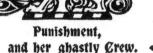

TENTH

Sorrow

Grief.

Punishment,
and her ghastly Crew.

BUT who is she?'

'Do you not see behind them,' said he, 'something that looks like a small door, and a narrow, dank place?'

'Yes, indeed!'

'And you notice therein Women—shameful, bedraggled, and ragged?'

'Why yes!'

'Well, among them, the one who holds the whip is called PUNISHMENT; while the one who holds her head bent over to her knees is SORROW; and the one who is pulling her own hair, is GRIEF.'

'But what about that THING standing by them,—so repulsive, thin, and naked; and near to it that other similarly shameful female,—who is she?'

'Ah,' said he, that is LAMENTATION, and his sister is DESPAIR. To these therefore is the soul handed over, and is punished by association with them. Hence, however, he is cast into another dwelling, into Unhappiness, where he ekes out his existence in every misery unless, indeed, to him unexpectedly, REPENTANCE, having planned it, should meet him.

Lamentation.

Despair.

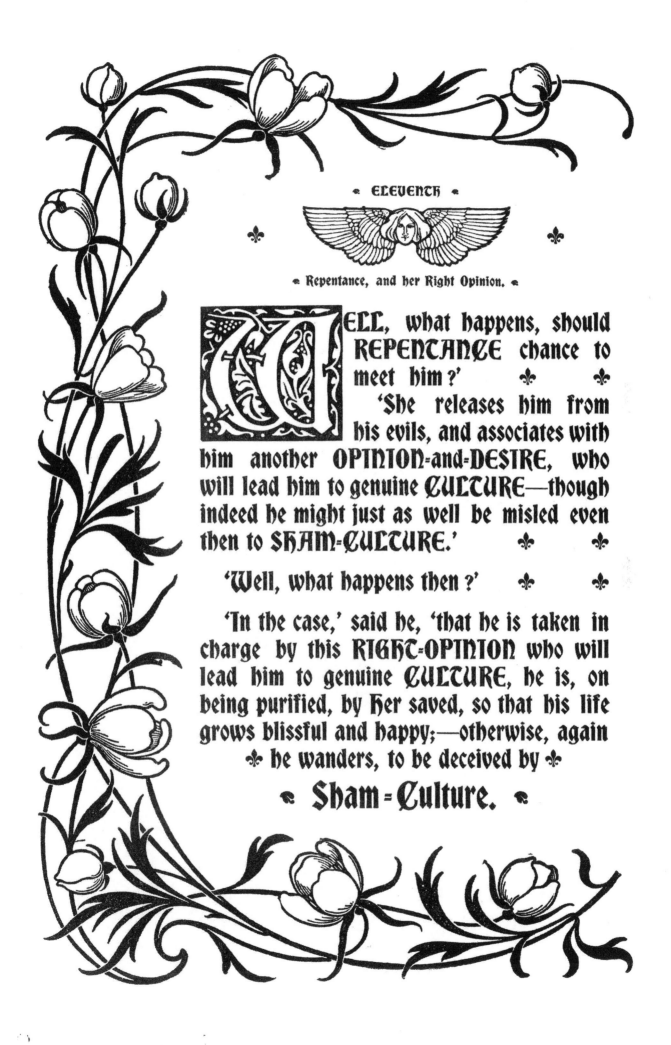

ELEVENTH

Repentance, and her Right Opinion.

WELL, what happens, should REPENTANCE chance to meet him?'

'She releases him from his evils, and associates with him another OPINION-and-DESIRE, who will lead him to genuine CULTURE—though indeed he might just as well be misled even then to SHAM-CULTURE.'

'Well, what happens then?'

'In the case,' said he, 'that he is taken in charge by this RIGHT-OPINION who will lead him to genuine CULTURE, he is, on being purified, by Her saved, so that his life grows blissful and happy;—otherwise, again he wanders, to be deceived by

Sham-Culture.

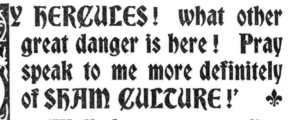

'Y HERCULES! what other great danger is here! Pray speak to me more definitely of SHAM CULTURE!'

'Well, do you see standing by the Gate of the inner enclosure a Woman seeming neat and well-groomed?'

'Well, she is, by the unreflecting Majority called CULTURE,—but that is an error, for she is no more than a SHAM.

XII. Sham Culture.

'Nevertheless, those who are being saved must, in order to reach genuine CULTURE, first pass here.'

'So there is no other way?'

'No, there is not.'

ND can you tell me who are those men, perambulating within the second enclosure?'

'Those,' said he, 'are the deluded Votaries of SHAM-CULTURE—honestly, they labor under the impression that they are, right now, associating with genuine CULTURE!'

'And what might they be called?'

'Some,' answered he, 'are Poets; some, so-called Orators. Some are Reasoners; others are Musicians Mathematicians, Geometricians, Astronomers, Critics, Aristippian Pleasure seekers, or Aristotelian Peripatetic scientists!

THIRTEENTH

The Scientists Who Profess Sham-Culture.

UT those Women who seem to circulate among them—indeed, they resemble the first, among whom was Pleasure, and her companions— who are they ?' ✤ ✤ ✤ ✤

'They are the very same,' said he. ✤

'But how did they get in ?' ✤ ✤

'By altering their looks; for here they are needy-looking, and not as before.' ✤ ✤

'And have those False-Opinions remained unchanged ?' asked I. ✤ ✤ ✤

'That potion which they received from De= lusion remains active in them; so also Ignor= ance, Senselessness, Prejudice and other Bad= ness. ✤ None of this fades out from them till they leave SHAM=CULTURE, enter on the right road, and drink the purifying medica= ments. ✤ Through this purification having sloughed off all their evils such as Prejudice and Ignorance, then, and not before, shall they be saved. ✤ ✤ ✤ ✤

'Should they, however, elect to remain with ✤ SHAM=CULTURE, they shall ✤

❧ **never be released;** ❧ nor shall they be released from a single evil **merely because of any Science.'**

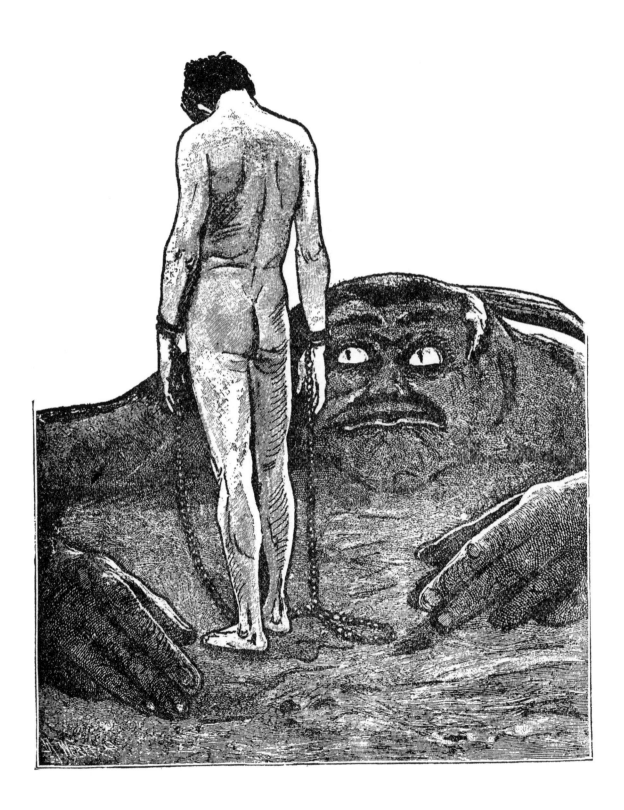

Second :
The Road Upwards
to Happiness.

WHAT then is the Road that leads to genuine CULTURE' asked I. ❧ ❧

'Do you see up there,' said he, 'a place where no one dwells, and which seems to be desert? ❧

'I do.' ❧ ❧ ❧ ❧

'Do you not see a small door, a path not much frequented,—only a few are ascending on it, for it is almost impassable, rough and rocky?' ❧ ❧ ❧ ❧

'Yes indeed,' said I. ❧ ❧ ❧

'And do you not see something like a steep hill, whose only access is a narrow ascent between precipices? ❧ ❧ ❧

'That then is the Road to Culture.'

'And difficult enough it seems!'❧ ❧

'But it leads up Culture's Rock, ❧ which is large, high, and inaccessible.' ❧

Self-
con-
trol.

En-
dur-
ance.

OW do you not further see, standing on the Rock, two healthy and well-formed Women who stretch out their hands invitingly?' ❧

'Yes; but who are they?' ❧ ❧

'SELF-CONTROL and ENDURANCE— two sisters.' ❧ ❧ ❧ ❧ ❧

'But why are they extending their arms so invitingly?' ❧

'They are exhorting the Pilgrims who reach that place not to despair, but to be of good courage, inasmuch as they will reach a fair road if only they will be brave for but a little while longer.' ❧ ❧ ❧ ❧ ❧

'Encouragement is good; but what is the use of it? as I see, way up on the Road, a gap, where there is no road.' ❧

'Those Women will themselves descend from the Cliff, draw the Pilgrims up to their present position. ❧ Then only will the Women bid the Pilgrims rest; and after a little while give them Strength and Courage, and promise to introduce them into the presence of genuine CULTURE. ❧ ❧ ❧

'Then the Women point out to the refreshed Pilgrims the further road which, there, is fair, level, passable, and free from all evils, as you see.' ❧ ❧ ❧ 'Clearly, by Jupiter!'

'DO YOU not behold, in front of that grove, a place which seems to be fair, grassy, and illuminated by a white light?'

'Yes, indeed!'

'Now do you perceive in the midst of the meadow another Enclosure, with its gate?'

'It is so, — but what is the name of that place?'

'It is the Dwelling of the Blessed,' said he. ✤ Here abide all the Virtues, and Happiness.'

'Is it possible? ✤ How beautiful must that Place be! ✤

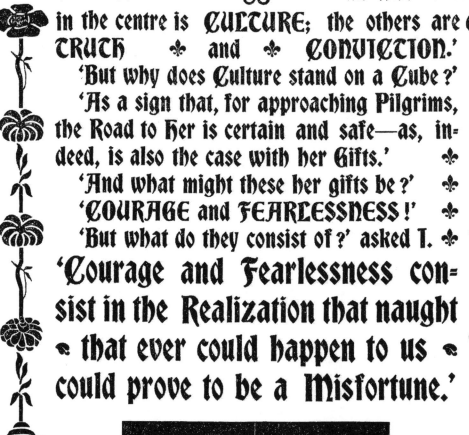

'NOW, do you see by the Gate, a Woman, fair and composed, of middle, or rather of advanced age, clad in a simple, unadorned robe? She stands, not on a globe, but on a solidly founded cube. With her are standing two other but younger Women who seem to be her daughters.' ❧ ❧ 'So it looks.' ❧

'Well, the Woman who is standing in the centre is CULTURE; the others are TRUTH ❧ and ❧ CONVICTION.'

'But why does Culture stand on a Cube?'

'As a sign that, for approaching Pilgrims, the Road to Her is certain and safe—as, indeed, is also the case with her Gifts.' ❧

'And what might these her gifts be?' ❧

'COURAGE and FEARLESSNESS!' ❧

'But what do they consist of?' asked T. ❧

'Courage and Fearlessness consist in the Realization that naught ❧ that ever could happen to us ❧ could prove to be a Misfortune.'

Y HERKULES !' said I, ✤ 'what fine gifts ! But why does She thus stand outside of the Circle?' ✤   ✤   ✤   ✤

'In order to heal the new arrivals,' said he. 'She furnishes them the cleansing medicament; ✤ and whenever they have been purified, She introduces them unto the Virtues.' ✤   ✤   ✤   ✤

'But how does this happen ? I do not understand that.' ✤

'But you will,' said he. ✤ 'It is as if an ambitious man should, on becoming sick, go to a physician, who first removes the cause of the sickness, thereby paving the way through convalescence to health. ✤ Should the sick man, however, not carry out the prescription, it is no more than fair that he should be abandoned to the ravages of the disease.' ✤   ✤   ✤   ✤   ✤   ✤

'Oh, I understand that,' said I.   ✤   ✤   ✤

'Just so acts Culture,' resumed our Guide. ✤ 'Whenever

any Pilgrim reaches
and doses him with
as first to purify
evils which lodged
and Error, with
infected the Pilgrim;
temperance, Anger,
all the rest of those
Pilgrim was affected

✤ XIX. Purification. ✤

Her, She heals him
Her own power, so
him from all the
in him — Ignorance
which Delusion had
Arrogance, Lust, In-
Love-of-Money, and
Evils with which the
in the first Enclosure.

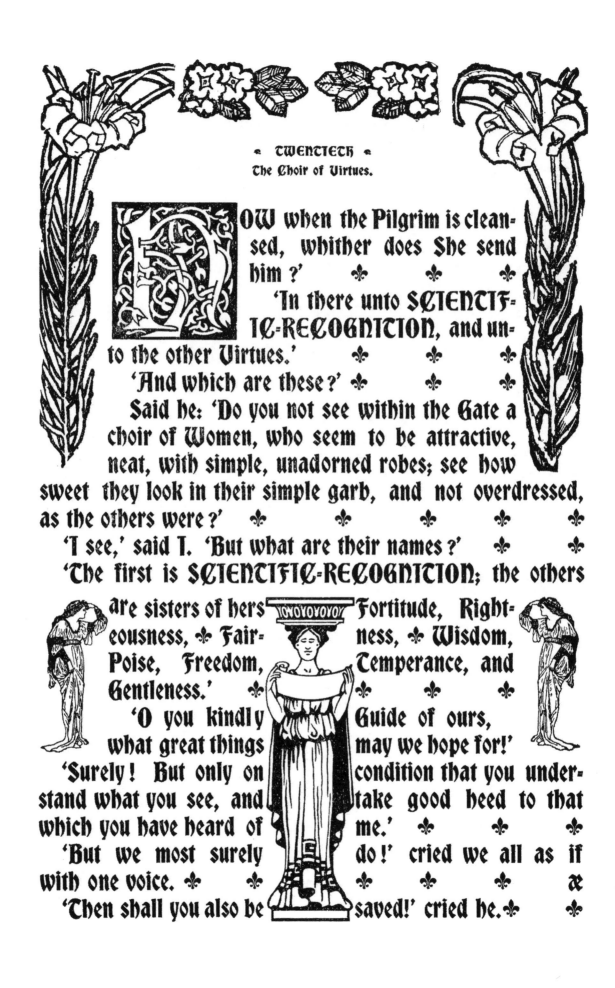

NOW when the Pilgrim is cleansed, whither does She send him ?' ❖ ❖ ❖

'In there unto SCIENTIF-IC-RECOGNITION, and unto the other Virtues.' ❖ ❖ ❖

'And which are these?' ❖ ❖ ❖

Said he: 'Do you not see within the Gate a choir of Women, who seem to be attractive, neat, with simple, unadorned robes; see how sweet they look in their simple garb, and not overdressed, as the others were?' ❖ ❖ ❖ ❖

'I see,' said I. 'But what are their names?' ❖ ❖

'The first is SCIENTIFIC-RECOGNITION; the others are sisters of hers Fortitude, Right-eousness, ❖ Fair-ness, ❖ Wisdom, Poise, Freedom, Temperance, and Gentleness.' ❖ ❖ ❖

'O you kindly Guide of ours, what great things may we hope for!'

'Surely! But only on condition that you under-stand what you see, and take good heed to that which you have heard of me.' ❖ ❖ ❖

'But we most surely do!' cried we all as if with one voice. ❖ ❖ ❖ ❖ ❖ 𝔛

'Then shall you also be saved!' cried he. ❖ ❖

'Now, when they have received the Pilgrim, whither do they lead him?'
To their mother HAPPINESS, said he.—'But who and where is she?'
Following the Road up yon Mountain which forms the heart of the
Enclosures, you come to the Temple=porch by which sits on a high throne
a glorious Woman, decked nobly, but artlessly, and crowned
with a splendid wreath of flowers. Well, she is HAPPINESS.

OW, whenever any one reaches hither, what does She do?'

'Happiness, ✤ with all the other Virtues, crown him as Victor in the greatest struggles, — namely, against the most terrible

Beasts, who before, enslaved, tormented, and devoured him. ✤ All these now has he overcome and repelled from himself, holding himself well in hand, ✤ so that they, to whom he formerly slaved, now must serve him.' ✤

'I am anxious to know the identity of the wild Beasts you mentioned!' ✤ ✤ ✤ ✤ ✤

'IGNORANCE, said he, and ERROR Or don't you consider them wild beasts? 'And pretty savage, too!' agreed I.

Then Sorrow, ✤ Despair, ✤ Love-of-Money, ✤ Intemperance and all other Badness. ✤ All these he now rules, instead of, as before, being ruled by them.'

'O glorious deeds,' cried I, 'and splendid victory! ✤ But what is the virtue of the   Victor's crown?' ✤

'It beatifies with   Felicity unspeakable. He who with this   Virtue is crowned, becomes very happy   reposing his hopes of getting Happiness   and of retaining it

not on others,   but on himself.'

Third :
Those Who Fail
and Why.

LORIOUS the Victory you wot of! ✠ But after the the Pilgrim is crowned, what does he do, and whither does he proceed?'

'The Virtues who had welcomed him lead him to that place whence he came out, and point out to him how badly fare they who there exist so wretchedly, as it were enduring ship-wreck of their lives, erring and wandering, as if dragged around by Enemies such as Incontinence, Arrogance, Love-of-Money, Fancies, and other such Evils. ✠ ✠

'By these Misfortunes they are unable to rescue themselves from this perpetual tossing by reaching the Mountain of Security.

'This they suffer only because they are not able to discover the road hither — for they have forgotten the Instructions they received from the Good Genius.' ✠ ✠ ✠

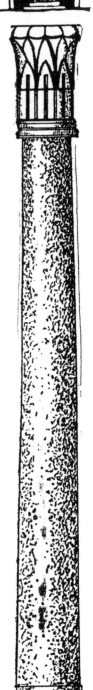

HEN said I: ❧ 'You seem to speak rightly. But I am not yet quite clear on this point: namely, Why to the Pilgrim the Virtues point out that Place from which he came originally.' ❧ ❧ ❧ ❧

Said our Guide: ❧ None of these things could the Pilgrim accurately understand or realize, himself being in doubt because of the Ignorance and Error which he had imbibed, so that he considered Good That-which-was-not-good, and Evil That-which-was-not-Evil. ❧ Wherefore, like those who remained there, the Pilgrim eked out a miserable existence. ❧

'Now, however, since he has attained to Scientific-Recognition of what really is advantageous, he lives pleasantly, realizing how badly off those others are.' ❧ ❧ ❧

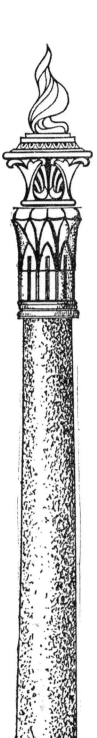

ELL, now that he contemplates all these things, what will he do, and whither will he wend his way?'

'Whithersoever he may fancy; for now is he as safe anywhere as if in a Korykian Cave; fairly and safely will he dwell, whithersoever he may arrive. For just as the sick welcome the physician, so will all receive him with pleasure and gratitude.' ⚜ ⚜

'And he fears no more that he shall suffer something from those Women, who, you say, are really wild Beasts?'

'No indeed! ⚜ No more can he be troubled by Grief or Sorrow, by Incontinence or Love-of-Money, by Need or any other evil—for now he lords it over all those by whom he formerly was grieved. ⚜ ⚜

'Just like a serpent-charmer, whose snakes, though they do to death all others but him, yet him they do not injure, because of an antidote against them which he possesses;—just like this immune snake-charmer, is the crowned Pilgrim no more grieved by any of them, being immune because of the antidote which he possesses.' ⚜

 XXVI. Heaven exists Best in Hell:
Like an immune Snake-charmer,
The Crowned Pilgrim flourishes among Passions.

O ME it seems that you have spoken well. ✢ But tell me further this: ✢ Who are they who seem to be descending from the Mountain? ✢ For while some of them are crowned and are making gestures of joy, ✢ others are uncrowned, grieved and distressed; they seem to be so weary in head and limb as to be in real need of that their support by certain Women!' ✢ ✢ ✢ ✢ ✢

'The crowned are those who were saved by Culture, and they are rejoicing at having reached Her. ✢ The uncrowned, however, are those who were by Culture rejected, and are returning to an existence miserable and wretched; or are such as, while ascending to Endurance, became timorous and turned back, wandering around without a path.' ✢ ✢

'And who are the Women supporting them?' ✢ ✢

'Griefs, Sorrows, Faint-heartedness, Obscure-Contempt, and Ignorances.' ✢ ✢ ✢ ✢ ✢

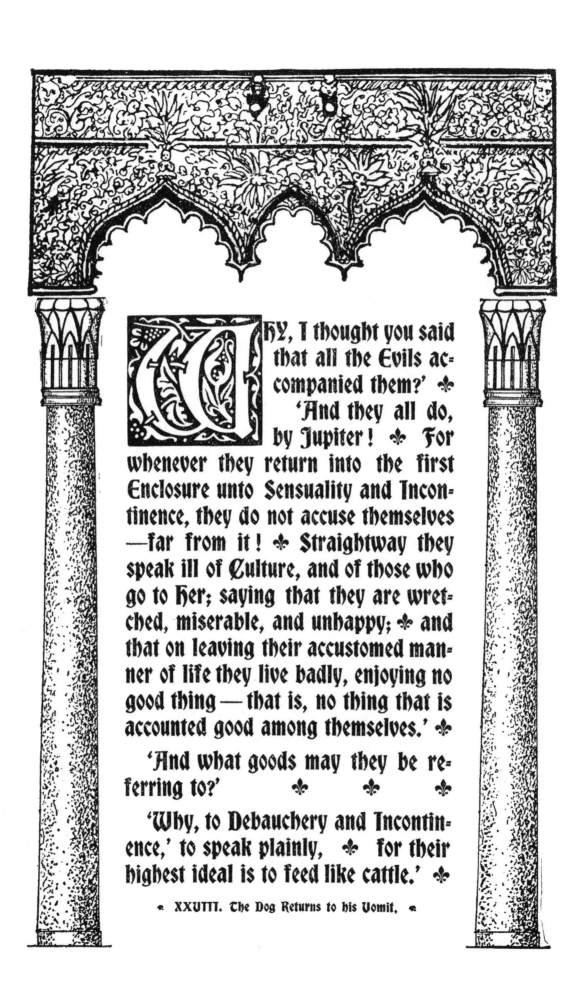

HY, I thought you said that all the Evils accompanied them?' ❧ 'And they all do, by Jupiter! ❧ For whenever they return into the first Enclosure unto Sensuality and Incontinence, they do not accuse themselves —far from it! ❧ Straightway they speak ill of Culture, and of those who go to Her; saying that they are wretched, miserable, and unhappy; ❧ and that on leaving their accustomed manner of life they live badly, enjoying no good thing — that is, no thing that is accounted good among themselves.' ❧

'And what goods may they be referring to?' ❧   ❧   ❧

'Why, to Debauchery and Incontinence,' to speak plainly, ❧ for their highest ideal is to feed like cattle.' ❧

❧ XXVIII. The Dog Returns to his Vomit, ❧

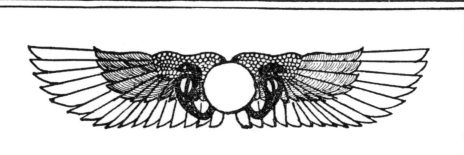

ND what about those other Women ✠ who descend thence cheerful in mien, ✠ and all wreathed in smiles?'

'They are OPINIONS; and whenever they have successfully conducted any Pilgrim to Culture, and introduced him to the Virtues, they return to lead up others, to whom they announce the beatification of those they had led up before.' ✠ ✠ ✠ ✠

'But why do not they themselves enter in among the Virtues, and stay?'

'Because it is not fitting for mere Opinions to enter in unto Scientific Recognition; their utmost capacity is to introduce a Pilgrim unto Culture. All that they then can do is to return and bring up others, — just as ships, when unloaded, return to be loaded again.' ✠ ✠ ✠ ✠

⚜ Twenty-Ninth ⚜ Opinion and Knowledge. ⚜

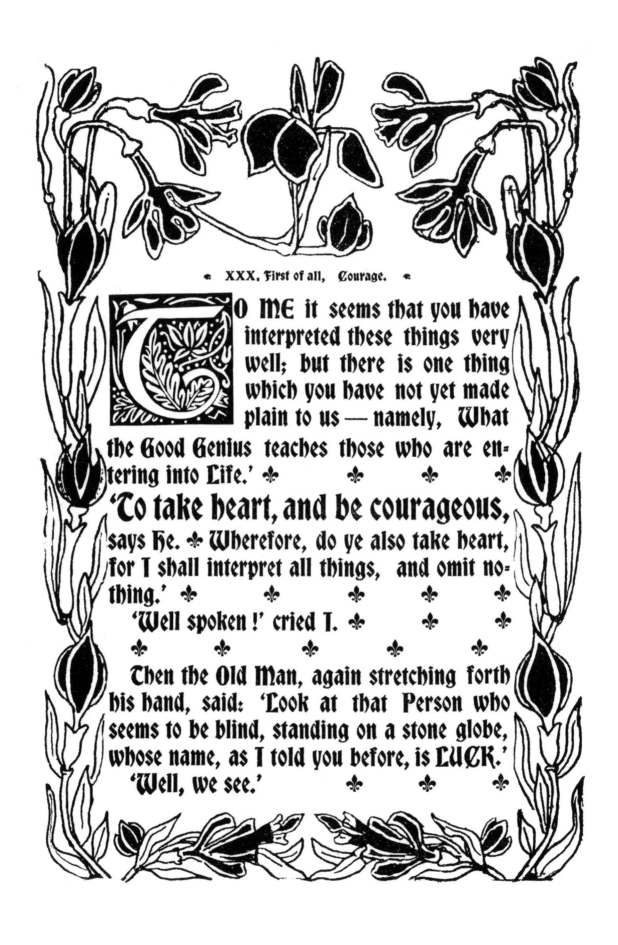

XXX. First of all, Courage.

TO ME it seems that you have interpreted these things very well; but there is one thing which you have not yet made plain to us — namely, What the Good Genius teaches those who are entering into Life.'

'To take heart, and be courageous, says he. Wherefore, do ye also take heart, for I shall interpret all things, and omit nothing.'

'Well spoken!' cried I.

Then the Old Man, again stretching forth his hand, said: 'Look at that Person who seems to be blind, standing on a stone globe, whose name, as I told you before, is LUCK.'

'Well, we see.'

WELL, He admonishes the souls not to trust Her; nothing received from Her should be considered reliable or safe : nor consider them his own, inasmuch as nothing hinders Her from taking them back, and again giving them away to somebody else—why, that is a common occurrence. ✤ Wherefore, he admonishes, no man should let himself be moved by Her gifts — neither to joy on receiving them, nor to sorrow on losing them; neither to praise, nor to blame them. ✤ For nothing done by Her proceeds from Reflexion; only by chance, and just as things come, as I told you before. ✤ ✤ ✤ ✤ ✤ ✤

'Wherefore the Good Genius admonishes men to take no notice of anything She does, and not to become like wicked bankers, who rejoice whenever they receive money from some man, and consider it their own; but, as soon as they receive notice of withdrawal, they become offended, and consider themselves grievously wronged, not remembering that they received the deposits on this very condition, that the depositor may withdraw it without difficulty. ✤ ✤ ✤

'The Good Genius advises a similar attitude towards the gifts of the Goddess of Luck; and to remember that it is no more than Her nature to take back what She gave, and again soon to give manifold other gifts, then again to withdraw not only this that She gave, but also whatever a man may have possessed before. ✤ Wherefore, he admonishes, accept whatever She may give; and as soon as you have possession of it, with it immediately depart to the blessings reliable and enduring.' ✤ ✤ ✤ ✤ ✤ ✤

BUT what may these be?'
asked I.   ❧   ❧
'That which is re-
ceived from Culture.'
'And what may it be?'
'The veritable SCIENTIFIC RE-
COGNITION of what is advantageous
and is a safe, reliable, enduring gift'
said he. 'To flee to Her incontinently
is His monition; and whenever the Pilgrim arrives to those Women who, as
I said before, are called Incontinence
and Sensuality, he is not to trust them
but to depart from them, and proceed
to Sham=Culture. ❧ Here he should
remain some little time, collecting from
Her Sham=Accomplishments whatever
may be suitable for a traveling-ration
to support him until he reach Genuine
Culture.   ❧   ❧   ❧
'Whosoever disobeys this monition,
or even only ❧ misunderstands it, ❧
perishes away miserably.'

❧ XXXII. The Best Gift Is Good Judgment. ❧

FOURTH:
The Value of
Science.

OW, Strangers, this is the meaning of the Picture. ✠ Do not hesitate to ask any additional questions about It; ✠ I shall be pleased to answer.'

'Well, then I will ask you what sort of accomplishments the Good Genius advises the Pilgrim to take from Sham=CULTURE?' ⚜

'Whatever a man may think might be of use to him.' ⚜ ⚜ ⚜ ⚜

'And what is your advice in the matter?'

'The knowledge of languages, first; and then, sufficient of other Sciences to act, in the words of Plato, as a check=rein from eccentricities—misunderstand me not: ✠ they are **not necessary, but advantageous** to proceed more efficiently — but, of course, they are not helpful MORALLY.' ⚜ ⚜

'So then you declare formally that these Accomplishments do not aid Moralization?'

'By no means; for although a man must improve without them, still they have their place. ✠ For although we may catch the meaning by means of an interpreter, yet might it not be useless to understand the words themselves, if we care at all for accuracy. Yet **Nothing hinders our becoming better without those accomplishments.**

ELL, then, according to what you say, the scientists have no advantage over other men in becoming holier?' ⚜

'What advantage could they have, inasmuch as they are involved in the same delusion about the nature of Goods, just as the Unscientific, and are yet dominated by their vices? ✠ For nothing hinders a man from knowing languages, and being an expert in every scientific field, and still being intoxicated and incontinent, fond of money, unjust, traitorous, and even a fool.' ⚜ ⚜

'Yes indeed!—one can see many such!' ⚜

'What advantage, then, could these, merely because of their scientific accomplishments, have in the matter of moralization?' ⚜

ERTAINLY not, according to what you say. But why then do they remain within the Second Enclosure, as if they still wished to approach unto Genuine=Culture?' ❧ ❧

'And of what use to them is that proximity? ❧ For how often do you see later Pilgrims arriving from the First Enclosure with its Incontinence and other evils, and before them entering in unto Genuine=Culture in the Third Enclosure, leaving those Scientists behind! ❧ Hence, what advantages have they? ❧ Are they not rather at the disadvantage of being less impressionable, and more incorrigible?' ❧ ❧ ❧ ❧ ❧ ❧

'How so?' asked I. ❧ ❧ ❧ ❧ ❧

'Why, because what is known by those who are in the Second Enclosure is never realized. ❧ As long as they hold to the speculative side of Opinion, they cannot possibly take any practical steps towards Genuine=Culture. ❧ Do you not see that, just as much as the more practical Pilgrim, they have the opportunity of making use of the Opinions who lead out from the First Enclosure. ❧ But are not Opinions useless without a meeting with Repentance, and without the resulting conviction that the Culture which they do possess is a sham, and a trap? ❧ Being satisfied with their abode, they never progress to Salvation. ❧ ❧ ❧ ❧

'And you also, O Strangers, you must practice what I said until you have attained unto its significance. ❧ Often, indeed, will you have to study afresh my instructions, nor relinquish the sacred Quest, relegating all other matters to secondary rank. ❧ If not, all you hear will remain useless.'

FIFTH :
What is
Good and Evil?

• Thirty-Sixth •
Good and Evil
Lie in the
Manner of one's Life.

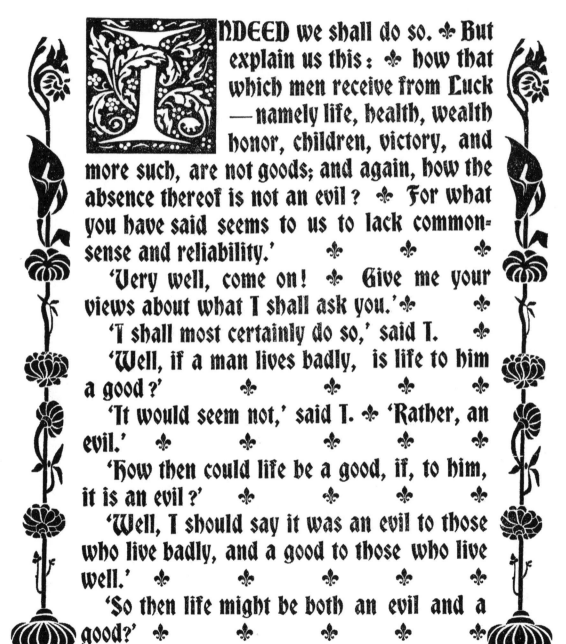

INDEED we shall do so. ✤ But explain us this: ✤ how that which men receive from Luck—namely life, health, wealth honor, children, victory, and more such, are not goods; and again, how the absence thereof is not an evil? ✤ For what you have said seems to us to lack common-sense and reliability.'

'Very well, come on! ✤ Give me your views about what I shall ask you.'✤

'I shall most certainly do so,' said I. ✤

'Well, if a man lives badly, is life to him a good?'

'It would seem not,' said I. ✤ 'Rather, an evil.'

'How then could life be a good, if, to him, it is an evil?'

'Well, I should say it was an evil to those who live badly, and a good to those who live well.'

'So then life might be both an evil and a good?'

'So I said.'

OME, do not express opinions so unlikely, for how could aught be at the same time good and evil? ✣ Did you ever hear of anything simultaneously useful and harmful, desired and scorned?' ✣ ✣ ✣

'That, really, is unlikely; but if living badly is an evil for the living man, why, for such a man is not life itself not an evil?' ✣ ✣ ✣

'Yes; but life and living badly are not identical;—or do you think so?' ✣

Our Guide answered, 'Neither do I. **The evil lies in living badly,** not in life itself. ✣ For were it an evil, it would be evil even to such as live righteously, in the degree that they are alive, if this was an absolute evil.' ✣ ✣ ✣ ✣

'I agree with you.' ✣ ✣

AS, THEREFORE, life belongs to both those who live badly, and to those who live rightly, might it not then be possible that life is neither a Good nor an Evil; just as cutting and burning in themselves are neither harmful nor sanatory for the sick—it all depends on the time and manner the patient is cut or burned. ❧ Is it not thus also with life?

'Yes, indeed, so it is.'

'Now consider the matter thus: ❧ What would you prefer, to live shamefully, or to die honorably, like a man?'

'I had rather die honorably.'

'So then even dying can be no evil, as it is often more desirable than living?'

'So it is.'

'Should we not also think likewise of health and sickness? ❧ For there are circumstances when health is unbearable.'

'You speak the truth,' said I.

GOOD! ✤ Let us consider wealth, in the same manner. Apparently, as is often seen, there are persons who possess wealth who live badly and shamefully.' ✤ ✤ ✤ ✤

'By Jupiter, there are many such! ✤ So then wealth does not help them to a righteous life?' ✤ ✤ ✤ ✤ ✤

'Evidently not, for they themselves are evil.

Culture, not wealth, gives virtue.

'Very probably so—at least, according to your argument,' grudgingly assented I. ✤

'Surely!' asseverated he. ✤ 'How could Wealth be an absolute good since it does not always make for the improvement of its possessors?' ✤ ✤ ✤ ✤

'Clearly not.' ✤ ✤ ✤ ✤

'Acknowledge then that Wealth is not at all advisable for such as do not know how to use it!' ✤ ✤ ✤ ✤ ✤

'I must say I think so!' ✤ ✤

'How then should that whose possession is often unbearable be considered an absolute good?' ✤ ✤ ✤ ✤

'By no means!' ✤ ✤ ✤

'Will not then a man live well as far as he knows how to employ wealth well and understandingly—and if not, badly?' ✤ ✤

'What you say seems to be entirely true.'

WELL, it seems to me that this is the cause of the restlessness and of the harm of men : ✤ they err in honoring Things as Goods, or scorning THINGS as evils; to lay values on THINGS, and to suppose that through THINGS one can improve, or for the sake of THINGS commit any, even godless actions. ⚜ This however is the result of ignorance of what is the real Good, they ignore that no real Goods result from Evil Means. Hence many are those who have amassed Wealth through evil and shameful deeds—such as treason, robbery, murder, eaves-dropping, theft, and other crimes.' ⚜ ⚜ ⚜

'So it is.' ⚜ ⚜ ⚜ ⚜ ⚜ ⚜

F THEN out of evil means can arise no good end, as is evident; and if out of evil deeds can arise wealth, then can Wealth never be an absolutely good end.' ❧ ❧ ❧

'An evident consequence!' ❧ ❧

'But, then, none can attain unto Righteousness thro any evil action; as little as one can attain Injustice or Foolishness thro good deeds. ❧ Besides, both oppo-sites cannot well coexist in one and the same thing. Wealth, ❧ Fame, Victory and other such external goods do not exclude bad-ness. Consequently these things are neither ❧ Goods nor ❧ even ❧ evils they are no more than external ap-plications of the internal principle

Wisdom alone is a Good, while Foolishness is the only Evil.

'It seems to me that you have proved your point.' ❧

❧ Forty-First and Last. ❧

COMPARATIVE RELIGION LIBRARY

I. Aspirations, Prayers, and Visions

Gathered during a Period of Retirement from the World.

is a compilation of articles having originally appeared in
the *Prophet* magazine,
and grouped into the following volumes of
The Comparative Religion Library:

II. Spiritual Unfoldment in Comparative Outline.
III. Systematic Spiritual Effort.
IV. Practical Efforts for Spiritual Advancement.
V. Spiritual Suggestions for the Higher Life.
VI. Allegories and Currents of the Spiritual Life.
VII. Suggestions for Mental Training.
VIII. Living in Touch with the Divine.

Price, separately, 75 cents each. The whole Volume, $2.50.

IX. Of Communion with God,

A Manual of Intimate Devotion,   50 cents; bound, $1.00.

X. Of the Presence of God,

Unpartisan Devotional Instructions for its Practice, $1.00

XI. The Ladder of God, and other Sermons, $1.00

XII. The Second Book of Acts,

Reincarnation in form of a scriptural story.   Ornamental, $1.00

XIII. The Song of Mysticism,

An attempt, in verse, at Sanity in Religion. Ornamental, 50 cts.
Also the Songs of *the Spirit,* of *the Resurrection,* and others.

XIV. The Mysteries of Mithra,

A reconstruction, in verse, of its XII Degrees.   Each. $1.00

XV. Voices of Prayer and Praise,

Poems; Hymns with original Music, $1.50

The Comparative Literature Press,
PHILADELPHIA: MONSALVAT, N. 71 st Avenue.
LONDON: LUZAC & Co, 46 Gt Russell St, W.

APPENDIX C

Matham and Goltzius, *TABVLA CEBETIS*

Latin translations of the *Tablet* (*Tabula Cebetis* is Latin for *Tablet of Cebes*) were very popular in the sixteenth and seventeenth centuries. Some of these editions were accompanied by woodcut illustrations, usually as a frontispiece or incorporated into the title page, though occasionally a larger fold-out illustrated page was included. Most illustrations of the *Tablet* from this period, however, were broadsides (i.e., large sheets of paper printed on one side only).

The print of *Cebes' Tablet* on the following pages was made by Jacob Matham (1571-1631) after a drawing by Hendrick Goltzius (1558-1617), the latter being the leading Dutch engraver of the early Baroque, the former being Goltzius' stepson and pupil. Goltzius and Matham employed a sophisticated engraving technique unsurpassed in their day. The usual mannerist tendencies of Goltzius' drawings (e.g., artificial poses and exaggerated musculature) have been toned down in this image of the *Tablet*, engraved and printed by Matham in 1592 on three separate sheets of paper glued together. The print measures 26 × 49 in. (66.5 × 124.8 cm), and was the largest ever to come out of Matham and Goltzius' studio.

A technical tour-de-force, Matham and Goltzius' print attempts to convey in its entirety the old exegete's description of the *Tablet* in a single image. To assist the viewer in deciphering the various allegorical figures, identifying labels proliferate: smaller ones for (a) important allegorical figures (e.g., *Genius* [= ὁ Δαίμων/τὸ Δαιμόνιον], *Seductio* [= ἡ Ἀπάτη]; *Fortuna* [= ἡ Τύχη], *Opiniones* [= αἱ Δόξαι]; *Cupiditates* [= αἱ Ἐπιθυμίαι], *Voluptates* [= αἱ Ἡδοναί], *Appetentia* [= ἡ Ἀπληστία], *Fucata Eruditio* [ἡ Ψευδοπαιδεία], *Assentatio* [= ἡ Κολακεία]), *Avaritia* [= ἡ Φιλαργυρία], *P[a]enitudo* [= ἡ Μετάνοια]), (b) categories of people (e.g., *Astrologi, Geometrae, Peripatetici, Dialectici, Critici, Epicurei, Poet[a]e, Oratores*—all transliterations of the Greek except for *Oratores* [= οἱ Ῥήτορες]; *Epicurei* ["Epicureans"], members of the ancient philosophical school, are the only named figures in this group that do not appear in the *Tablet*), and (c) general concepts, many of which do not appear in the *Tablet* (e.g., *Nemesis* ["Retribution"], *Pusillanimitas* ["Faintheartedness/Timidity," i.e., the vice of being timid and cowardly, and thus not living up to one's full potential], *Rebellio* ["Renewal of War/Rebellion/Revolt"). Larger labels are used for places: the entrance arch has engraved on it VITAE INTROITVS ("Beginning of/Entrance to Life"), the clouds that flank the temple-like structure of the third enclosure contain a calligraphic DOMICILIVM SALVTIS ("Abode/Dwelling of Salvation/Well-Being").

Moving up through the enclosures, the moderate chiaroscuro employed on the lower levels becomes progressively flatter, until one reaches the third, central enclosure that is dominated by a squat, mountain-like outcropping crowned by a large temple-like structure, in the center of which sits the figure of *Salus* ("Salvation," "Well-Being"), who is placing her hand on the head of a kneeling individual. This final level appears almost "washed out" on account of it being above (and within?) the celestial clouds, whose light source appears to be the figure of *Salus* herself. Two allegorical figures in trompe l'oeil recesses at top on either side frame the illustration: the left is a figure representing "light/life," the right a symbol of "death/destruction." A simple square-framed cartouche in the lower left corner contains the dedication by Goltzius to Peter Boom of Amsterdam and notes that Matham (*Goltzii privignus*, "the stepson of Goltzius") made the engraving (*sculp.*[*sit*]) in the year 1592. Finally, in the lower margin of the print are nine columns (with four lines each) of Latin verse by Franco Estius (*fl.* 1580s-1594), a Neo-Latinist poet who wrote verses for many prints by Goltzius and Matham. Estius' lines enlarge the allegory of the *Tablet* by referencing, among other things, the "barking Scyllas" (*latrantes Scyllas*), "swift Charybdases" (*rapidasque Charybdes*), "sweet-sounding Sirens" (*dulcisonas Syrenes*), and "Circes' cup" (*pocula Circes*)—all allusions to Homer's *Odyssey*, a work that was often interpreted from an allegorical perspective, especially the so-called "fairy-tale" adventures narrated by Odysseus himself in books 9-12.

The five images of Matham and Goltzius' print that follow include the entire work spread over two pages as well as a page devoted to each of the three separate sheets from which the complete print was assembled.[40] Opposite this page is a detail of *Fortuna* (= ἡ Τύχη), appearing to be blind and mad and standing on a round rock (*Cebes' Tablet* 7: ἡ ὥσπερ τυφλή καὶ μαινομένη τις εἶναι δοκοῦσα, καὶ ἑστηκυῖα ἐπὶ λίθου τινὸς στρογγύλου), she holds a large Dutch money bag[41] in her right hand, while her outstretched left hand is randomly tossing to the crowd below coins, a smaller Dutch money bag, jewelry, a crown, scepters, a laurel wreath, a vase/covered goblet, a crosier (i.e., a bishop's pastoral staff), a baby, and what appears to be a (partially occluded by *Fortuna*'s fluttering garment) escutcheon (i.e., a shield or emblem bearing a coat of arms, which is symbolic of noble birth), on which are depicted a eyes and ears (which symbolize fame, glory, and reputation). In front of the escutcheon is what looks to be a trumpet (symbolic of authority, social standing, and warfare). Compare *Cebes' Tablet* 8: Πλοῦτος δηλονότι καὶ δόξα καὶ εὐγένεια καὶ τέκνα καὶ τυραννίδες καὶ βασιλεῖαι καὶ τᾶλλα ὅσα τούτοις παραπλήσια.

---

[40] A high-definition image of Matham and Goltzius' print, in which its remarkable details can be truly appreciated, is available on the Rijksmuseum website: https://www.rijksmuseum.nl/en

[41] These money bags consisted of soft leather pouches joined together at the top beneath a wrapped leather handle.

169

SALVTIS

Sed quos illa procax in deuia duxit, et orbem
Inftabilem celeri vertigine vafra rotauit,
Iam cædes meditantur, et atra incendia fraude,
Spurcantes casta gemitha fædera lecti.

Hos Nemesis contriftat atrox, Metanæa laceffit
Atq; ardens Phlegethon flammante minatur ab vnda
Styx hos atra manet diræ, fluenta Cocyti.
O miseri mentes deplorandæ cateruæ.

Felices animæ, quas, ô quas inclyta virtus
Terras despicere, et cæli connexa tueri
Edocuit, vos templa vocant vestita Orichalco,
Chrysolito, ac flammas fulgore æquante Pyropo.

Fransc Effius

APPENDIX D

West, "Allegorical Sketch"

The allegorical sketch (10 1/16 × 8 in. [25.56 × 20.32 cm]) on the facing page, made in 1814 by the American-born artist Benjamin West (1738-1820), is an ink drawing known as a "holograph," that is, a document whose words (and, where present, also images) are written (and drawn) entirely by the hand of the person whose signature it bears.[42]

West's allegorical sketch is both an extensive abridgment and an "Americanization" of the *Tablet*'s ideas and images, with a noticeable emphasis on positivity. In fact, not a single negative personification that is found in the original work is referenced either in West's drawing or in his text.

The seated female figure, with her (Indian-themed?) plumed headband, flag-like cape and "halo of stars," is an allegorical representation of "American Virtue."[43] Structurally, this figure replaces Τύχη/*Fortuna* (note her *cornucopia* ["horn of plenty"], which is often part of *Fortuna*'s iconography) and Ἀπάτη ("Deceit"), who sits in front of the entrance to "Life" (*Cebes' Tablet* 5). In addition, "American Virtue" also serves as a stand-in for Ἀληθινή Παιδεία ("True Education," *Cebes' Tablet* 18-20; note the scrolls in two of the students' hands who are leaving her).

The large male figure on the right is West's version of the *Tablet*'s Δαίμων (called *Genius* in Latin translations and illustrations), depicted in the original as "an old man...gesturing to the entering crowd" (*Cebes' Tablet* 1), which is also his usual portrayal in art (cf., e.g., Matham and Goltzius' image). West's "Genius," however, is a far younger man—he is virtually a heroic nude—who energetically gestures *and* leads four youths away from the terrestrial world in their "cloud ascent" to the more spiritual world above in which temples bearing the labels of "Honor" and "Virtue" are located (Matham and Goltzius' image has a similar visual progression, though West's figures literally walk on clouds in their journey upwards, not travel through them as the figures do in the Dutch engraving).

---

[42] Greek ὁλόγραφος, -ον, "written or drawn entirely (by the same hand)."

[43] The circular star configuration of the "Betsy Ross Flag" is very similar to the circular star halo that crowns the head of the Virgin Mary in Giovanni Battista Tiepolo's painting *The Immaculate Conception* (1767-1768). There is strong evidence that West studied this painting in Italy. Francis Hopkinson, who was probably involved in the design of the "Besty Ross Flag" in some capacity, happened to be a friend of West.

Benjamin West, "Allegorical Sketch"

Text:

Dear Sir,

May the youths of the United States of America, who are endowed with Mental talents, be led on by Virtue and Genius while cultivating them; by which they will know that Virtue is the road to Honours, and the basis on which every refinement has been raised. Those men who have improved on Arts and Sciences will then be appreciated by them, as the greatest ornaments of nations throughout the civilized world.

With those truths—and with great respect

I am Dear Sir

London Newman Street
December 24, 1814

Yours with Sincerity,

Benjamin West

APPENDIX E

Κακία's Clothing

The literary description in *Memorabilia* 2.1.22 of Κακία wearing "clothing from which her youthful beauty could especially shine through" (ἐσθῆτα δὲ ἐξ ἧς ἂν μάλιστα ὥρα διαλάμποι) has its visual counterpart in the nearly contemporary depiction of clothing on three larger than life size female figures (known generally as "The Three Goddesses") from the east pediment of the Parthenon (*c.* 438-432 BCE).[44]

"The Three Goddesses" (east pediment, Parthenon; figures K, L, and M)

Various identifications have been suggested by scholars, but the one most widely held is that the three represent (from left to right) Hestia, Dione (in some mythological accounts, a wife of Zeus and mother of Aphrodite), and Aphrodite. Their posture varies in order to accommodate the slope of the triangularly-shaped pediment. The figure on the left is on the point of rising and tucks her right foot in to raise herself up, while the central figure cradles a companion reclining luxuriously in her lap. Their clothing clings to them, creating very intricate folds that cascade around their bodies in deep, swirling patterns while simultaneously modeling the underlying physical forms so that what conceals also reveals.

---

[44] Prodicus probably composed (and first performed) his "Choice of Heracles" between 425-420 BCE, while the *Memorabilia* was most likely completed sometime after 371 BCE. The date for the purported conversation between Aristippus and Socrates that takes place in *Memorabilia* 2 must be between *c.* 415-401 BCE. The artist responsible for designing (some?, most?, all?) the sculptural decoration of the Parthenon was Pheidias (*c.* 480-*c.* 430 BCE), though many different sculptors were employed in the actual carving.

Also on the Athenian Acropolis, but created a little later, is a relief from the parapet of the Temple of Athena Nike (*c.* 410 BCE) depicting Nike ("Victory") adjusting her sandal.[45] A manifestation of the goddess Athena in her role as bringer of victory, the figure of Nike in this relief is, perhaps, meant to be seen in the process of undoing the knot that will allow her sandal to slip off, thus permitting her to walk on the sacred ground of the sanctuary (all of the other relief panels of the Temple's parapet depict Nikes leading animals to sacrifice and setting up trophies). Like the "The Three Goddesses," this sculpture's diaphanous clothing also mirrors that of Prodicus' Κακία.

"Nike Adjusting Her Sandal" (parapet; Temple of Athena Nike)

---

[45] The relief is *c.* 3 ft. 6 in. (1.07 m) in height.

APPENDIX F

Dürer, *Der Hercules*

At the end of Xenophon's paraphrase of Prodicus' "Choice of Heracles" it is only implicitly suggested to the reader/listener that the young hero chose Ἀρετή over Κακία. Most artists follow Xenophon's lead, selecting a somewhat indefinite (and ambiguous) moment in time—either before, during, or just after the two have spoken to Heracles—to illustrate.[46]

With his engraving *Der Hercules* ("Hercules"; *c.* 1498), however, the German Renaissance artist Albrecht Dürer (1471-1528) decided not to illustrate Prodicus' allegorical tale in such a traditional manner.[47]

Within a late-medieval/early Renaissance contemporary setting—castle to the left, other buildings (a cathedral, keep, small town and bridge) on and above the banks of a meandering river to the right, and a copse in the middle—, Dürer depicts a striking scene of conflict: exactly in the center of the illustration before the copse is a simply dressed woman with a calm expression on her face that belies her current action: she wields a branch in her hands with which she is about to assault violently a second, seated female who has removed most of her clothing and is sitting on the left thigh of a satyr, the two of them in an intimate, "picnic-like" pose. This seated woman raises her left hand, which is holding onto a bit of her clothing (to shield herself/protect her face from the impending blow? to prevent herself from seeing what is shortly going to befall her?). Her expression is (naturally) one of shock and fear, her open mouth suggesting that she is in the act of crying out. Her satyr companion, on the other hand, has a look of consternation with (perhaps) a hint of anger. He rests his left hand on the naked woman's right shoulder, while his right hand is shown to be taking hold of the jawbone of an ass lying next to him on the ground (to counterattack? to defend himself?). A small

---

[46] The one exception I am aware of is that of Frans Francken II's *Mankind's Eternal Dilemma: The Choice Beween Virtue and Vice* (1633), a work that combines aspects of *Cebes' Tablet*, Prodicus' "Choice of Heracles," the Judgment of Paris, and Christian symbolic elements. In this painting, a mature Heracles stands with Athena at the center of the work, with three Christian virtues (Faith, Hope, and Charity) between them. The hero and his patron goddess are looking towards the figure of Paris, who is about to choose which goddess—Hera, Athena, and Aphrodite—was the fairest.

[47] The engraving does not officially have a title, though it may have been called "Hercules" in one of Dürer's diary entries. The classic art-historical analysis of Dürer's engraving, and the one that argues for it as an illustration of Prodicus' allegory, is that of Erwin Panofsky (*Hercules am Scheidewege* ["Studien der Bibliothek Warburg" 18, Leipzig, 1930], 161ff.; see also E. Panofsky, *The Life and Art of Albrecht Dürer* [London, 1955], 73-6). For an analysis of Dürer's engraving from an ethical perspective, see R. Geuss, *Outside Ethics* (Princeton, 2005), 78-96.

Dürer, *Der Hercules*

child (*putto*), who appears on the right, is grasping with its left hand a bird by its wing and is running "off-stage" while looking back at the scene with a slightly perturbed expression. A naked man with his back to us is holding a long stick in both hands in front of and slightly above his head before the attacking female. He is wearing a "rooster" helmet and seems to be crying out something ("Stop!"?).

If Erwin Panofsky is correct (and most art historians believe he is) in identifying the naked man wearing the "rooster" helmet as Heracles (Hercules), the female assailant as Ἀρετή ("Virtue") and the intended victim of the violent assault as Κακία ("Vice/Pleasure"), then Dürer's treatment of Prodicus' tale is quite radical. In fact, it may be the most innovative version of the allegory since Prodicus' original.

Dürer begins his retelling of the allegory by reconfiguring the nature and character of both Ἀρετή and Κακία. Let us begin with the latter. In Prodicus' telling, if Heracles chooses her, Κακία promises him a life of comfort and ease, one in which he may especially enjoy himself sexually with his beloved (2.1.24: τίσι δὲ παιδικοῖς ὁμιλῶν μάλιστ᾽ ἂν εὐφρανθείης). Ἀρετή, however, counters by describing how the sexual pleasures that Κακία promises are, in actuality, forced, unnatural, dissolute, and wasteful (2.1.30: τὰ δ᾽ ἀφροδίσια πρὸ τοῦ δεῖσθαι ἀναγκάζεις, πάντα μηχανωμένη καὶ γυναιξὶ τοῖς ἀνδράσι χρωμένη· οὕτω γὰρ παιδεύεις τοὺς σεαυτῆς φίλους, τῆς μὲν νυκτὸς ὑβρίζουσα, τῆς δ᾽ ἡμέρας τὸ χρησιμώτατον κατακοιμίζουσα.). As Prodicus' allegory was continuously retold through the centuries, the name given to the figure of Κακία was more often changed to that of *Voluptas* (Latin, "Pleasure"). And it is *Voluptas*, not Κακία, who confronts *Virtus* (Latin, "Virtue," "Goodness" = Ἀρετή) in most Renaissance and Baroque texts and artworks. So it is with Dürer's engraving.

More interestingly, in Dürer's *Der Hercules* actions have replaced words with regard to both spokeswomen. What I mean by this is not the simply obvious—in most visual works actions are, of course, more evident than words. Visual representations of this allegory, however, until the 17th and 18th centuries, were usually quite static. There is a sense in such works from this period that either Pleasure or Virtue is speaking or has just spoken, while Hercules is simply listening in silence. It is true that in 17th- and 18th-century illustrations slightly more action is (occasionally) depicted, but it is usually of an amatory quality (Pleasure, for example, is clinging to Hercules, or Virtue is pulling him away from Pleasure's embraces). Even compared to those later depictions, however, Dürer's engraving is more "action-packed." Indeed, there is little sense that Pleasure has *ever* spoken to Hercules (or that she will even need to!). Clearly, it is her actions (together with Dürer's use of symbols) that do the speaking for her, embodying her way of life and its temptations/rewards. Her erotic picnic rendezvous with a satyr (a powerful symbol of lust), her physical appearance (she has already removed her clothes), and the "child" who is running away—the *putto* is often a stand-in for/representation of Eros/Cupid, while Pleasure is often depicted in the guise of Aphrodite/Venus in Renaissance-Baroque artworks, and as such she is usually accompanied by one or more *putti* (her counterpart in these images illustrating Prodicus' allegory is Athena/Minerva as a stand-in for Ἀρετή/*Virtus*), all convey to the viewer what she promises her followers. Even the bird in the *putto*'s hand is usually understood as a symbol of erotic activity—though the fact that the child is here violently grasping it seems to mirror the treatment *Voluptas* is about to receive!

Even more innovative, perhaps, is Dürer's characterization of Ἀρετή/*Virtus*. In visual representations of Prodicus' fable during the Renaissance and Baroque periods, Hercules usually occupies the center of the image, flanked on either side by the two allegorical figures. In Dürer's engraving, Hercules has been displaced by *Virtus*. No longer a talker (in Prodicus' allegory her aggressive verbal counterattack to Κακία's promises to Heracles employed more than three times as many words as those used by her opponent), Dürer's *Virtus* is depicted as some sort of deranged fundamentalist, who calmly and quietly appears to be "collecting all her strength to smash Pleasure's face in."[48] In all of the many textual and visual representations of Prodicus' allegory, Dürer's portrayal of *Virtus* is unique. Indeed, its force is such that it appears to shatter the allegory's expected (but almost never explicitly revealed) conclusion: that Heracles/Hercules will ultimately choose to follow the life of Ἀρετή/*Virtus*.

But the greatest innovation is what Dürer has done with Hercules. No longer a static, sitting, brooding figure as he is in nearly all other representations of this scene in Renaissance and Baroque art (see, e.g., Batoni's image in **Appendix G**), this Hercules has made his choice "to intervene to prevent manifestly unfair practice, i.e., to *stop* armed Virtue from attacking the defenseless semi-recumbent Pleasure. His gesture is a spontaneous reaction of simple humanity in the face of immediate, self-evident brutality."[49]

Not only is this a morally just action on Hercules' part, it is an intensely liberating one as well. After nearly two millennia of being bound by Prodicus' allegory to an admittedly simplistic and utterly unnatural binary worldview where he is forced to choose the exclusive either-or possibilities for life set forth by Ἀρετή/*Virtus* on the one hand and Κακία/*Voluptas* on the other, Hercules is now free to select a

---

[48] R. Geuss, *Outside Ethics*, 81. It is a nice touch that Dürer chose to depict the formerly verbose Ἀρετή/*Virtus* as the only figure in the illustration whose mouth is completely closed and whose expression is devoid of any kind of emotional reaction. The expression of this Ἀρετή/*Virtus* is thus (unnervingly) a complete blank. Unlike Prodicus' passionate advocate for her way of life being the *only* one worth considering, this Ἀρετή/*Virtus* talks not at all and carries a large stick.

[49] R. Geuss, *Outside Ethics*, 80.

different course, one that may (or may not) partake of elements both allegorical figures have to offer.[50]

Dürer's innovative retelling thus injects a tale that had become rather ossified over time with some needed dramatic interest (along with a nice dash of pathos). By doing so, Dürer also brings the story of Heracles/Hercules back to its original mythological foundations, for after encountering Ἀρετή/*Virtus* and Κακία/*Voluptas* in his youth, the hero went out into the world and lived a life that clearly embraced—with much drama and incredible pathos—aspects of both allegorical figures' worldviews.

---

[50] David Ligare titles his painted version of Dürer's engraving *Hercules Protecting the Balance Between Pleasure and Virtue* (1993): http://www.davidligare.com/paintings.html

APPENDIX G

Batoni, *Ercole al Bivio* and *Study of Hercules*

Pompeo Girolamo Batoni (1708–1787) was one of the 18th century's most celebrated painters. Born in Lucca, Batoni established a famous and influential studio in Rome where he received commissions from popes, princes, and British aristocrats on the Grand Tour. Highly sought after for his theatrical yet incisive—and often flattering—portraits, Batoni was also prized by his clients for his learned and technically brilliant allegorical, religious, and mythological compositions.

Batoni painted several versions of Prodicus' "Choice of Heracles" (in Italian frequently called *Ercole al Bivio*, "Hercules at the Crossroads"). The one on the facing page, now in the Galleria d'Arte Moderna, Palazzo Pitti, Florence, is the first of these. It is signed and dated 1742.

Batoni's composition is structured along a diagonal moving from upper left to lower right. The body of a heavily draped female figure, Virtue in the guise of Athena/Minerva (note the helmet)[51], stands upright, her posture running strongly parallel with the left frame of the picture. She extends her left hand towards a seated young man, and with her right points over his head in the direction of a large circular temple perched on top of a distant mountain in the upper right of the frame (a symbol of the gods, whom Virtue refers to repeatedly in Xenophon's paraphrase of Prodicus' allegory in *Memorabilia* 2.1.28-33). The young man, Hercules, is naked save for a lionskin draped over his right thigh. His right hand rests on that thigh, while his left holds on to a club. He looks at neither female figure but stares in the direction of the lower left of the frame. The final figure, Pleasure in the guise of Aphrodite/Venus, is seated on the groud in a picnic-like pose, with her clothes having fallen away from the top of her body. Her skin, illuminated by the sun, appears intensely white. She delicately holds a single flower between the thumb and index finger of her right hand, while her left hand, which touches the ground, holds a theatrical mask—both flower and mask symbolically referring to the visual, olfactory, and audial pleasures of life that she promises the youth.[52] Lying next to her on the ground are additional symbols of a life filled with the different pleasures she provides her followers: an open book

---

[51] Virtue and Vice often became less purely allegorized in certain Renaissance and Baroque versions of the "Choice of Heracles" as the former took on the guise of Athena/Minerva while the later, who had recently often made the transition from Vice to Pleasure, assumed the figure of Aphrodite/Venus. This moved these pictures closer to the so-called "Judgment of Paris" artworks also popular at this time, in which the shepherd Paris (prince of Troy) has to choose which of three goddesses, Hera/Juno, Athena/Minerva, or Aphrodite/Venus, is most beautiful.

[52] See *Memorabilia* 2.1.24 (ἢ τί ἂν ἰδὼν ἢ ἀκούσας τερφθείης ἢ τίνων ὀσφραινόμενος ἢ ἁπτόμενος).

(literature, i.e., the life of the mind) and an oboe (music and relaxation, the pleasure of sound).[53] Her gaze seems to be clearly directed at Athena/Minerva, though also suggesting she will shortly turn to see what Hercules' reaction is to her rival's offer.

Batoni, *Ercole al Bivio* (1742)[54]

Like nearly all Renaissance and Baroque painted versions of this theme, Batoni's composition is far more traditional than Dürer's *Hercules*. That said, it still possesses certain interesting qualities that I find lacking in many paintings on this

---

[53] Literature/the life of the mind is a new wrinkle not present in Vice's enumeration of the benefits she confers on those who choose her. Its understood antithesis, however, the life of the body, i.e., of hard physical work, sweat and toil is something Vice promises her acolytes will never have to endure (cf. *Memorabilia* 2.1.25). For the pleasure of sound, see *Memorabilia* 2.1.24 (τί ἂν...ἀκούσας τερφθείης).

[54] The image reproduced here, courtesy of the Fondazione Federico Zeri at the University of Bologna, is a black and white photograph made of Batoni's painting between 1950-1970 and housed in the Foundation's archives. The photo measures 10 × 9 in. (25 × 20 cm). The original painting measures 37 × 29 in. (93.5 × 73.5 cm).

subject created by his predecessors and contemporaries. The most important, perhaps, is the dynamic interaction of figural "intimacy" with the powerful sense of Hercules' indecision. First, Batoni's figures are less schematized and much more closely grouped and interactive than many others on this theme. His Athena/Minerva looks down at Hercules, Aphrodite/Venus looks up at Athena/Minerva, while Hercules studiously avoids both of them—as well as the viewer him/herself! The figures' hands and legs cross over into each other's space (Hercules' right hand and leg actually touch Athena/Minerva's clothing, while Aphrodite's/Venus' outstretched hand holding a flower is mere inches from touching Hercules' left thigh and erotically placed directly in front of Hercules' groin, thus serving a twofold function: discreetly covering Hercules' "private parts" while pointing to them at the same time). In the middle of the painting, Hercules occupies a very constrictive space—he seems to be squeezed between a rock (literally) and two "hard places." In addition to his gaze, Hercules' body language, which appears somewhat contradictory, reinforces the point of extreme indecision he clearly is experiencing, for one leg seems to be resting, while the other appears poised to lift him from his seated position and, possibly, follow one of the two women. The study Batoni made of this figure in preparation of the painting (see image on the facing page), already embodies these features in terms of gaze and contradictory body language. Note, however, the change made from the figure study to that of the finished painting[55]: the hint of a smile on the former is no longer present in the latter, in which the young man's (mostly) calm gaze conveys a sense of indecision mixed with just a hint of fear. It seems, Batoni is suggesting, that the challenge of making such an apparently life-altering choice has focused his mind to such a degree that his facial expression has taken on a nearly suspended state of incipient anxiety.

At first glance, the note of ambiguity in Batoni's painting as to Hercules' final choice is nearly overwhelming: decisions like this *are* challenging, the painting seems to be saying. Batoni, however, is unwilling to leave the viewer (or his Hercules) in a perpetual state of uncertainty as to his final choice. How the artist does this is by employing iconographic clues that indicate clearly not only *who* the central figure is (Nemean lion skin, fabled club), but *what* choice he does make in the end, for (paradoxically, at least in terms of chronology), Hercules will not possess the Nemean lion skin until *after* he has chosen to follow Virtue.

---

[55] The following text accompanies Batoni's drawing on the Philadelphia Museum of Art's website (http://www.philamuseum.org/collections/permanent/72352.html): "Batoni selected a muscular model, young and beardless, to assume the exact pose of the seated Hercules in the painting. The study from life was presumably made at a relatively late date in the evolution of the composition because the pose of the model corresponds quite closely to that of Hercules in the painting, and it was Batoni's practice to finish his paintings with the model before him (see *Art in Rome* cat. 314). Edgar Peters Bowron, from *Art in Rome in the Eighteenth Century* (2000), cat. 315, pp. 473-474."

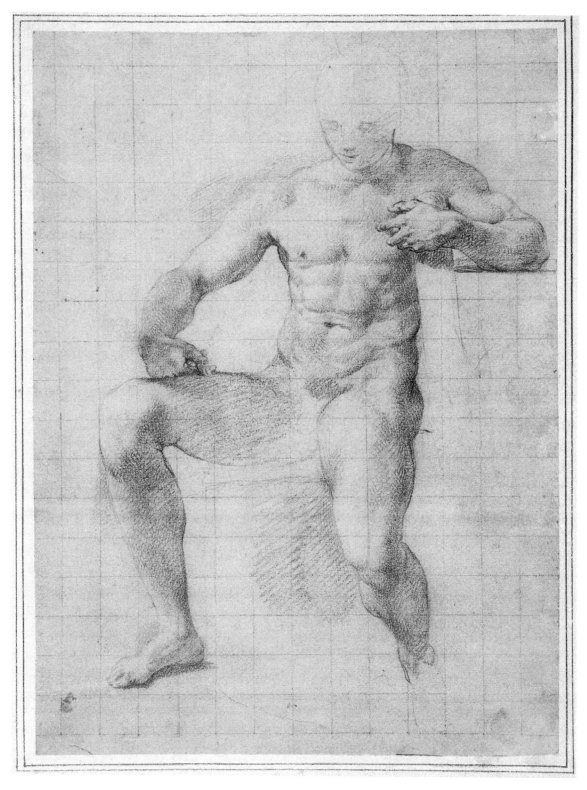

Batoni, *Study of Hercules* (1740-1742)

APPENDIX H

Dunkin, "The Judgment of Hercules"

Eighteenth-century British writers evinced an extraordinary amount of interest in Prodicus' "Choice of Heracles" and *Cebes' Tablet*. Much of this must have been due to the fact that these works were an essential component of the curriculum at private boarding schools (e.g., Winchester and Eton). Young men engaged these texts not only via bilingual Greek and Latin student editions (at least fourteen different ones were published between 1670-1771), but also through exercises that included composing their own versions of these works in English verse.[56]

It was within this pedagogical tradition that the Irish poet William Dunkin (1706/7-1765) was educated. Due to extraordinary circumstances, however, Dunkin did not attend an elite private school, but was raised by Trinity College, Dublin—his parents had died when he was young and his aunt left her property to the college on condition that it should provide for his education (Dunkin received his B.A., M.A., and D.D. [Doctor of Divinity] from Trinity College). In his twenties he began writing comic poetry that won him the friendship and patronage of Jonathan Swift. A linguistically gifted poet, Dunkin composed in both English and Latin (and, occasionally, in Ancient Greek, Irish, and French).

"The Judgment of Hercules" appears in the first volume of a two-volume set of Dunkin's poetry published posthumously (William Dunkin, *Select Poetical Works of the Late William Dunkin, D. D., in Two Volumes*, vol. 1 [London, 1769], 421-9). Since no earlier publication of this poem has come to light, and since Dunkin was active as a writer from the late 1720s until his death, its date of composition must have occured in the last four decades of his life.

Dunkin also wrote a poem in Latin on the same theme, *Judicium Herculis* ("The Judgment of Hercules"), which appears in the pages immediately before the English poem (410-20). The two works, however, are quite different, with the Latin version having an old-fashioned "earnest" tone (one so serious, at times, that it verges on parody), while the English poem possesses a sly, comic wit. Indeed, Dunkin's "The Judgment of Hercules" is an example of a translation that, while paying respect to the original text in form, in spirit it charts a new direction, especially with its conclusion, which imposes on its readers a radical reassessment of Prodicus' allegory similar to that effected by Dürer with his *Der Hercules*.

---

[56] E. R. Wasserman, "The Inherent Values of Eighteenth-Century Personification," *PMLA*, Vol. 65, No. 4 (1950), 438. A wonderful example of such student work is Robert Lowth's "Choice of Hercules" in Spenserian stanzas. Although a mostly conservative translation in its faithfulness to the Greek original, Lowth's poem demonstrates impressive technical expertise. It is available here: http://spenserians.cath.vt.edu/TextRecord.php?textsid=34157

"The Judgment of Hercules"

τῆς δ' Ἀρετῆς ἱδρῶτα Θεοὶ προπάροιθεν ἔθηκαν.

HESIOD

—— *Qui potiores*
Herculis aerumnas credat, saevosque labores,
et Venere et coenis, et plumis Sardanapali.[57]

Two nymphs of old contending strove
To gain the mighty son of Jove;
Virtue and Pleasure were their names;
Alcides[58] stood between the dames,
A blooming but unsettled youth,
Yet willing to be sway'd by truth,

---

[57] In the preface to his poem, Dunkin quotes Hesiod, *Works and Days* 289 (see **Appendix A**) and the Roman poet Juvenal, *Satire* 10.360-2 (which forms part of a list of what is desirable in life, and which begins with the famous phrase [356]: *mens sana in corpore sano*, "a healthy mind in a healthy body"). The Latin verses translate as: "(when praying, ask for a brave soul...) that thinks the troubles and hard labors of Hercules are better than Venus [i.e., sex] and banquets and the downy pillows of Sardanapalus." Sardanapalus was a semi-legendary king of Assyria depicted since the time of ancient Greece as an individual who passed his life in decadent self-indulgence and died in an orgy of destruction.

[58] Epithet of Heracles/Hercules. "Alcides" literally means "descendant of Alcaeus." The son of Perseus and Andromeda, Alcaeus was father of Amphitryon, a man who was married to Alcmene, the mother of Heracles. Heracles' father, however, was Zeus, who had visited Alcmene during Amphitryon's absence in the guise of Amphitryon.

191

The latter summons all her charms,
Scarce equall'd by celestial arms,
The taper waist, the swelling chest,
The languish not to be express'd,
The bloom of either cheek, which shews
The lilly mingled with the rose,
The rolling eye, whose humid fire
Darts sudden, uncontroul'd desire,
The hair, that wanton'd with the wind,
In ringlets o'er her neck reclin'd,
The coral lip, and arched brow,
That might engage a Cynick's vow[59],
The veins, sky-tinctur'd thro' the skin,
The smile, that dimpled on her chin,
The robes, that flow'd with careless air,
And half the snowy bosom bare;
When thus the weening nymph began
To captivate the godlike man.

Hail! happy youth, whose form divine
Bespeaks a Jove in every line,
O! born for universal sway,
And boundless love without allay,
Assert, assert thy native right,
In pleasures matchless, as in might.

The heav'nly beings, who possess
An endless round of happiness,
Securely lead their Halcyon days
In downy indolence and ease;
No care their gentle breast annoys,
No labour to malign their joys.

The happy few, whom Jove hath bless'd
With sense, superior to the rest,
To me their chief fruition owe,
And lead the lives of Gods below.
For me the Sun renews the spring,
The seasons smile, the warblers sing,
The ruder winds are hush'd asleep,
And azure ocean smooths the deep,

---

[59] Many adherents of ancient philosophical schools (e.g., the Cynics and the Stoics), took a vow of chastity.

The scaly people of the main[60],
Tho' mute, in sport confess my reign.

For me the shepherds tend the flow'rs,
And weave the crown, and arch the bow'rs[61],
For me the spicy Zephyrs blow,
And streams in tuneful murmurs flow;
The summer-rose displays its bloom,
And blossoms breathe a rich perfume:
For me, pursu'd through every clime,
The lusty autumn in his prime
Unlocks his store, delicious feast,
To gratify sight, smell, and taste.

The barren winter too performs
My rites, tho' discompos'd with storms,
And labours to support my crown,
Although the face of nature frown.
Lo! then the nymphs and swains[62] advance
To mingle in the mazy[63] dance,
The lyre awakes the soul to mirth,
And gives the softest passions birth;
Whilst love, and youth, and gay delight
Expel the horrors of the night:
No troubles interrupt the scene,
Or, if a doubt should intervene,
Lyaeus[64] stands with sprightly air
To wash away the dregs of care:
The various seasons thus agree,
In one perpetual jubilee,
To propagate my gifts divine,
My gifts, and all those gifts be thine,

---

[60] "the open ocean."

[61] bower: "a shady, leafy shelter or recess, as in a wood or garden."

[62] "a country youth"; "a male lover or admirer."

[63] "dizzy," "full of dizzy turns."

[64] Often identified with—and sometimes an epithet of—the god Dionysus/Bacchus, Lyaeus (Λυαῖος, "The one who sets [you] free [from care]"), the god of wine, fruitfulness, and vegetation, was often worshipped in orgiastic rites.

If thou —— she cast so sweet a look,
That all the growing hero shook;
Her form, her words his heart unstrung,
While wild confusion chain'd his tongue;
And yet his eager eyes intent
Had utter'd more than half consent.

    When Virtue with becoming grace,
But far less soft, alluring face,
Prepar'd her suit, a goodly queen,
With more majestic look and mien[65].
A living crown of ivy boughs,
And olive, mantling o'er her brows,
Adorn'd her head; her gentle hand
Sustain'd the scepter of command;
Her awful front was deeply sage,
The' effect of thought, and not of age;
Her eyes, that fed no loose desire,
Keen sparkled with celestial fire;
Expressive emblems grac'd her robe:
There might you see the pendent globe,
The Sun, the Moon, the starry pole,
And all the planets, as they roll.
There Heav'n was fill'd with strange alarms,
And angry Gods appear'd in arms:
The rebel sons of earth arise
Thrice 'tempting to usurp the skies,
And mountains huge on mountains pil'd;
The fire of Gods indignant smil'd,
And thrice his dreadful thunder hurl'd,
That sunk them to the nether world.
There lawless Lust was curb'd by reins,
And mad Ambition bit his chains,
While Justice high-enthron'd prevails
With temper'd sword and equal scales.[66]

---

[65] "A person's manner, bearing, or appearance, expressing personality or mood." Pronounced "meen".

The son of Ammon[67], as he viewed
The figures, undetermin'd stood:
A dawning ray of thought refin'd
Quick darted thro' his op'ning mind;
He look'd on Virtue o'er and oer,
The more he look'd, she charm'd the more;
When thus the Goddess silence broke,
The hero panting as she spoke.

'Tis Pleasure's task by specious shows
Of joys to nourish real woes;
Short are the transports, which she brings,
Her sweets but ill reward her stings:
Profusion madly runs before,
And blindly scatters all her store,
While poverty with racks and wheels
Tormenting presses on her heels:
Self-love and self-sufficient pride
With sloth are ever by her side,
Delusion holds her glass between
The senses and her gaudy queen,
And fancy fond[68] her art employs
To grasp at unessential joys,
But flounders in a vast abyss,
Where Gorgons glare and Hydras hiss.

Short and uncertain is the date
Of mortal men, and fix'd their fate;

---

[66] With Virtue's robe, Dunkin provides an ecphrastic description of the mythological battle of the Olympian gods with the Giants (the so-called Gigantomachy), here allegorized with the personified "Lust" and "Ambition" (stand-ins for "Pleasure") being defeated by "Justice" (i.e., "Virtue"). In the earliest extant Gk. account of the Gigantomachy (Apollodorus 1.6.1-2), Heracles himself assists the Olympian gods in the battle. In the Roman poet Ovid's account of the Gigantomachy (*Metamorphoses* 1.151-62), from which Dunkin borrowed certain expressions in this ecphrasis (e.g., "And mountains huge on mountains pil'd" = *Metamorphoses* 1.153) there is no Hercules.

[67] I.e., Hercules. The Greeks syncretically combined elements of Zeus with the Egyptian god Amun-Ra, and so Amon, when used as a classical reference, is equivalent to Zeus.

[68] "fancy fond" is a compressed expression meaning something like "fancy of which it is far too easy to become fond," with "fancy" having the sense of "a liking for something shallow or transient."

'Tis mine to add by worthy ways
In glory, what they want in days;
To file the passions from the rust
Of sordid sloth and brutal lust;
With industry to purchase wealth,
With temperance to strengthen health;
Instead of selfish views confin'd,
To plant the love of human kind,
To point the duties, which extend
To father, brother, kinsman, friend.

Above the reach of human pride
Upon a mountain I reside,
To which but few from earth aspire,
Whom Jove hath wing'd with purer fire;

For millions, who propose to climb,
Are frighted at the top sublime,
And, looking backward as they soar,
Fall lower than they were before.

That hero, who would reach the height
Must keep me steadily in sight;
Thro' dreary wilds his road he makes,
O'er pointed rocks and thorny brakes[69];
But, once the difficulty past,
A Paradise appears at last,
From whence he views with high disdain,
The pilgrims of the nether plain,
And thence, when summon'd by his fate,
Passes thro' bright Olympus' gate,
With joy reviews the paths he trod,
And from a mortal grows a God.

Alcides, hail'd the voice divine,
And, bowing, said, "my life be thine."
Thus was the son of Jove refin'd[70]
To chuse the beauties of the mind,

---

[69] "thicket," "place overgrown with bushes, brambles, or brushwood."

[70] "refin'd," i.e., "cleared of impurities," with "impurities" here having the metaphorical meaning of "doubts (in his mind as to which of the two women to follow)."

Virtue with pain entail'd to wed,
While Pleasure from his presence fled:
But, Phillis[71], had the hero seen
A nymph like thee in mind and mien,
The mien, where in conjunction sweet
The tender loves and graces meet;
The mind, adorn'd with ev'ry art,
That could engage the coldest heart:
Good-nature, join'd to solid sense,
And wit, that never gives offence;
A double conquest he had won[72],
Nor in the conquest hazard run,
Exalted Virtue without stain,
Transporting Pleasure without pain.

---

[71] Phillis (< Gk. Φυλλίς, "foliage"]) was employed in English literature as a generic proper name for an attractive, rustic maiden beginning in the 1630s. This use comes from the Roman poet Vergil, where it appears several times in his *Eclogues*. Another reference is the name's appearance in Horace's *Odes* of (1) a slave girl beloved by her master, Horace's friend (2.4), and (2) of a middle-aged woman who is a musician (and courtesan/prostitute?) invited to celebrate the birthday of Horace's patron, Maecenas, at Horace's Sabine farm (4.11).

[72] "he had won" = "he would have won."

GLOSSARY

(OF WORDS THAT OCCUR MORE THAN FIVE TIMES)

A

ἀγαθός, -ή, -όν, good

ἄγε, (imper. of ἄγω used as adv.) come, come now, come on, well

ἄγνοια, -ας, ἡ, ignorance

ἄγω, lead, strive

ἀκούω, hear (+ acc. or gen.)

ἀκρασία, ἡ, intemperance; lack of power or control over one's passions

ἀληθινός, -όν, true

ἀλλά, (conj.) but, yet

ἄλλος, -η, -ο, other, any other, another

ἄν, (modal adv.)

ἄν, (contraction of εἰ ἄν)

ἄνθρωπος, -ου, ὁ, human being

ἀρετή, -ῆς, ἡ, courage, manliness, virtue, (moral) excellence

αὐτός, -ή, -όν, he, she, it; himself, herself, itself; ὁ αὐτός, the same

αὐτοῦ = ἑαυτοῦ

ἀφικνέομαι, ἀφίξομαι, ἀφικόμην, arrive

B

βίος, ὁ, life

βούλομαι, wish, want (+ inf.)

Γ

γάρ, (conj.) for, since

γέ, (adv.) at least, certainly, indeed

γί(γ)νομαι, γενήσομαι, ἐγενόμην, become, be; (3rd sing. often =)
  it happens

γυνή, γυναικός, ἡ, woman

Δ

δέ, (conj.) but, yet, and

δεῖ, (impers. vb.) it is necessary, one should (+ acc. and inf.)

δεικνύω, show

δή, (particle) now, quite, particularly, certainly

διά, (prep. + gen.) through, on account of; (prep. + acc.) on account of, because of δίδωμι, δώσω, ἔδωκα, give

διό, (conj.; = δι' ὅ, "on account of which thing") wherefore, for which reason, therefore

Διός, see Ζεύς

δοκέω, seem, think

δόξα, -ης, ἡ, notion, opinion, good reputation, honor

δύναμις, -εως, ἡ, power, might, efficacy

E

ἐάν, (conj. =) εἰ ἄν

ἑαυτοῦ, -ῆς, -οῦ, himself, herself, itself; (pl.) themselves

ἐγώ, I

εἰ, (conj.) if

εἶδον, (not used in act. pres.; ὁράω being used instead) saw; (inf.) ἰδεῖν, to see

εἰμί, ἔσομαι, ἦν (imperf.), be

εἶπον, (2nd aor.; pres in use is φήμι, λέγω, ἀγορεύω) said, spoke; (inf.) εἰπεῖν, to say, to speak

εἰς, (prep. + acc.) into

εἰσπορεύω, lead in; (pass.) enter

εἶτα, (adv.) then

ἐκ/ἐξ, (prep. + gen.) out of

ἐκεῖνος, ἐκείνη, ἐκεῖνο, that, he, she, it; (pl.) those, they

ἐν, (prep. + dat.) in, among

ἕνεκα, (prep. + gen.) on account of, for the sake of, because of, for; as far as regards, as for; as far as depends on; as a result of; on behalf of

ἐπί, (prep. + gen.) in; in the case of; (+ dat.) on, upon, at; (+ acc.) to, toward

ἕτερος, -έρα, -ερον, other, one or the other of two; another; τό ἕτερον, further

ἔτι, (adv.) still, further, moreover

εὐδαίμων, -ον, happy

ἔχω, ἕξω or σχήσω, ἔσχον, have, possess

Z

ζάω/ζῶ, live

Ζεύς, Διός, ὁ, Zeus

H

ἤ, (conj.) or; ἤ...ἤ, either...or

ἤν (= ἐάν), if (ever)

Θ

Ι

ἵστημι, make X (acc.) stand; (perf. act., mid./pass.) stand

Κ

κακός, -ή, -όν, bad, evil; τὰ κακά, evils
κακῶς, (adv.) badly, poorly; wickedly
καλέω, call, name (often w/ double acc. constr., i.e., call X [acc.] Y [acc.]); (pass. part.) being called or named, so-called
καλός, -ή, -όν, good, beautiful, fair, noble
καλῶς, (adv.) beautifully, nobly

Λ

λαμβάνω, λήψομαι, ἔλαβον, take, receive; get, obtain
λέγω, say, speak (of); mean

Μ

μάλα, (adv.) very, very much, altogether; καὶ μάλα, (lit., very much indeed [w/ καὶ as adv.]) certainly, yes
μέγας, μεγάλη, μέγα, great, tall
μέν, (conj. followed by δέ) indeed, on the one hand
μετά, (prep. + gen.) with; (+ acc.) after
μή, (adv.) not; (as conj.) that not; (after vbs. of fearing) lest, that
μηδέ, (conj.) and not, nor yet, neither; μηδέ...μηδέ, neither...nor
μηδείς, μηδεμία, μηδέν, no one, nothing
μηνύω, reveal
μήτε, (particle) and not; (mostly doubled) neither...nor

Ν

Ξ

ξένος, -η, -ον, strange, foreign, unusual; ὁ ξένος, stranger, foreigner; guest-friend

Ο

ὁ, ἡ, τό, (article) the
ὅδε, ἥδε, τόδε, (dem. pron.) he, she, that one/thing
ὁδός, -οῦ, ἡ, way, path, road

οἶδα, (2nd perf. w/ pres. sense) know

ὁράω/ὁρῶ, ὄψομαι, εἶδον, see

ὅς, ἥ, ὅ, (rel. pron.) who, which, what

ὅσος, -η, -ον, as great as, as much as; (pl.) as many as

ὅταν, (conj. adv.) whenever (+ subju.)

ὅτι, (conj.) that, because

οὐ (οὐκ, οὐχ, οὐχί), (adv.) not

οὐδέ, (conj.) and not, nor yet; οὐδέ...οὐδέ, and not...nor

οὐδείς, οὐδεμία, οὐδέν, no one, nothing; no; οὐδέν, (acc. of respect used
    as adv.) not at all, in no way

οὐκοῦν, (adv.) then...don't...? (introducing a question that expects the
    answer "yes" and carries the thought forward from a previous assent; cf.
    οὔκουν, certainly not; so...not)

οὖν, (conj.) then, therefore

οὔτε, (conj.) and not; οὔτε...οὔτε, neither...nor

οὗτος, αὕτη, τοῦτο, (dem. pron.) this, he, she, it

οὕτω(ς), (adv.) so, thus, in this state, manner or condition

ὄχλος, -ου, ὁ, crowd

Π

παιδεία, ἡ, education, discipline

πάλιν, (adv.) back, again

πάνυ, (adv.) (w/ adjs.) very, very much, exceedingly; altogether, entirely

παρά, (prep. + gen.) from, from the side of; (+ dat.) beside, in the
    estimation of; (+ acc.) unto, opposite, beside, near, by, alongside

παραγί(γ)νομαι, παραγενήσομαι, παρεγενόμην, arrive, be near, be
    present at

πᾶς, πᾶσα, πᾶν, every, all

πάσχω, πείσομαι, ἔπαθον, suffer, experience

περί, (prep. + gen.) around, about; (+ acc.) w/ regard to

περίβολος, -ου, ὁ, enclosure

ποιέω, make, do

ποιητής, -οῦ, ὁ, poet

ποῖος, -οία, -οῖον, what sort or kind of ?, of what sort or kind?

πολύς, πολλή, πολύ, much, many; πολύ, (adv.) more; much

ποτέ, ever, once; (makes a directly preceding interr. indef.) who/what in the
    world

πότερος, -έρα, -ερον, which of the two? πότερον...ἤ, whether...or;
    πότερον, (as an interr. adv. introducing a dir. quest., it is not translated)

πρεσβύτης, -ου, ὁ, old man

πρός, (prep. + dat.) near; (+ acc.) to, toward; (+ gen. in swearing) by

πρότερος, -έρα, -ερον, former; πρότερον/τὸ πρότερον, (adv.) previously πρῶτος, -η, -ον, first; πρῶτον, (adv.) first, first of all

πύλη, -ης, ἡ, gate

πῶς, (adv.) how?

Ρ

Σ

σύ, (pron.) you

σῴζω/σώζω, save; (pass.) arrive safely (esp. w/ preps. πρός, εἰς, or ἐπί + acc.)

Τ

τέ, (conj.) and; τε καί / τε...καί, (both)...and

τις, τι, (indef. adj. and pron.) any one/thing, someone/something, (a) certain; τι (adv.) in any way, at all

τίς, τί, (interr. pron.) who? which? what?

τοίνυν, [τοι + νυν] (particle; in dialogue, to introduce an answer) well then

τοιοῦτος, -αύτη, -οῦτο, of that kind, of such character

τόπος, ὁ, place

τύχη, -ης, ἡ, fortune, luck

Υ

ὑπό, (prep. + gen.) under, by; (+ dat.) under; (+ acc.) toward, beneath

Φ

φαίνω, φανῶ, ἔφηνα, bring to light; (pass.) be seen, seem, appear

φημί, φήσω, ἔφην (imperf.), say

Χ

Ψ

Ψευδοπαιδεία, -ας, ἡ, False Education

Ω

Ὦ, ὦ, oh!, O!

ὧδε, (adv.) here

ὡς, (adv. and conj.) so, thus, as; (conj.) how (heading an exclamation); that; how (i.e., in what manner); (+ fut. part. expresses the alleged purp.); so that, because, on the grounds of being; (+ indic. past tense vb.) when

ὥσπερ, (adv.) just as (if), as if, as it were
ὥστε, (conj.) so that, consequently

OTHER GREEK AND LATIN READERS BY THE AUTHOR

ANCIENT GREEK

The Infancy Gospel of Thomas

The Infancy Gospel of Thomas (c. 150 CE) is an excellent text for students who have completed the first year of college-level Ancient Greek. Its length is short, its syntax is generally straightforward, and its narrative is inherently interesting, for it is the only account from the period of early Christianity that tells of the childhood of Jesus. This student edition includes grammatical, syntactical, literary, historical, and cultural notes. Complete vocabulary is provided for each section of the text, with special attention paid to the differences between Koine Greek and Classical Greek meanings and usage. Since The Infancy Gospel of Thomas possesses an unusually rich textual history, this edition also includes a selection of the most interesting variant readings.

Lucian, *On the Death of Peregrinus*

Lucian's *On the Death of Peregrinus* is an excellent text for students who have completed the first year of college-level Ancient Greek or its equivalent. Its length is relatively short, its syntax is generally straightforward, and its narrative is inherently interesting, for it recounts the life of a man who was so determined to establish a new religious cult to himself that he committed suicide at the Olympic Games in 165 CE by self-immolation. Lucian, an eyewitness to this event, depicts Peregrinus as a glory-obsessed impostor who began his career as an adulterer, pederast, and parricide before becoming a leader of the Christian Church, a Cynic philosopher, and an aspiring "divine guardian of the night." Also of interest to readers today is that Lucian's text contains some of the earliest and most fascinating comments made by a member of the Greco-Roman educated elite concerning Jesus and the Christians of the 2nd century CE. This edition includes grammatical, syntactical, literary, historical, and cultural notes. Vocabulary lists are provided for each section of the text, with a glossary of all words at the end.

Lucian, *True Stories*

Lucian's *True Stories*, an experimental work of "pre" post-modern fiction, is an excellent text for students who have completed the first year of college-level Ancient Greek or its equivalent. Its length is relatively modest, its syntax is generally straightforward, and its narrative – a sophisticated satire that blends elements of fantasy and science fiction – is both engaging and thought-provoking.

This edition includes extensive grammatical, syntactical, rhetorical, literary, historical, biographical, and cultural notes. Complete vocabulary is provided for each section of the text, with special attention paid to Lucian's comic verbal coinages. Since Lucian's *True Stories* abounds with references to and appropriations from nine centuries of Ancient Greek literature, this edition also includes a generous selection of comparative passages (including the entirety of Iambulus' "Journey to the Islands of the Sun") to assist the student in appreciating still more this cunningly crafted and densely allusive work.

Xenophon of Ephesus, *An Ephesian Tale*

Xenophon of Ephesus's "pulp-fiction" novel, *An Ephesian Tale*, is an excellent text for students who have completed the first year of college-level Ancient Greek or its equivalent. Its length is quite short, its syntax is straightforward, and its narrative – an adventure romance between two young ill-starred lovers (Habrocomes and Anthia) – is one of the most action-packed and enjoyable in all of Ancient Greek literature. This edition includes brief grammatical, syntactical, rhetorical, and cultural notes. Complete vocabulary is provided for each section of the text.

Aesop's Fables (a selection)

This book, containing 35 Aesopic fables/versions of fables, is designed for students who, at a minimum, are finishing, or who have just finished, the first year (or the high school equivalent) of college Ancient Greek. It is also for individuals who studied Ancient Greek years ago and would like to return to the language and its literature in as easy and engaging a manner as possible. In order to serve better the needs of such readers as these, numerous grammatical and syntactical notes, along with extensive vocabulary lists, have been provided.

A special feature of this text is the generous selection of different versions of the fables that have been created over time. Although many of these are retellings of the same fable in Ancient Greek (some of which are in verse), six come from La Fontaine's celebrated French versions as recently translated with great verve by Craig Hill. The vast majority of these different versions, however, are from the rich tradition of English translations/ adaptations made between the 17th and 20th centuries.

Another special feature is the inclusion of a substantial number of illustrations from the 18th to the 20th centuries that showcase the various approaches artists have employed in illuminating the fables.

206

Ancient Greek Cyclops Tales

This collection of Ancient Greek "Cyclopea," the companion volume to *Euripides: Cyclops*, contains the following works: Homer, *Odyssey* 9.105-566; Theocritus, *Idylls* 6 and 11; Callimachus, Epigram 46 Pf./G-P 3; Lucian, *Dialogues of the Sea-Gods* 1 and 2). In addition to providing an introduction to each of these texts, the commentaries include extensive grammatical, lexical, and metrical assistance, with notes focusing on the thematic and intertextual connections between these various works.

Euripides, *Cyclops*

This edition of Euripides' *Cyclops*, the earliest extant post-Homeric work of Ancient Greek "Cyclopea", is the companion volume to *Ancient Greek Cyclops Tales*. In addition to providing students with an introduction to Euripides' unusual dramatic work, the only surviving specimen of its genre, the satyr play, this commentary offers extensive grammatical and lexical assistance, with notes focusing on the drama's fifth-century Athenian cultural context as well as the thematic and intertextual connections with its source, *Odyssey* 9.105-566.

Ancient Greek Lyric Poetry (a selection)

[forthcoming]

LATIN

A Medieval Latin Miscellany (with Art Robson)

This Medieval Latin reader is aimed at intermediate undergraduate/ advanced high school Latin students. The texts included in this collection cover religious biography (excerpts from Jerome's *Life of Hilarion*), tall-tales (*Asinarius* and *Rapularius*), heroic journey (*Alexander the Great Meets Thalestris, Queen of the Amazons* and Letaldus of Micy's *The Fisherman Swallowed by a Whale*), fables (Odo of Cheriton) and jokes (Poggio Bracciolini). Introductions to each text, as well as assistance with vocabulary, grammar, and syntax are provided.

Three Medieval Latin Liturgical Dramas

This edition makes available to intermediate Latin students three dramatic works of Medieval Latin literature. The earliest of these, the eleventh-century *Tres Clerici* ("The Three Students"), recounts one of the miracles of that most popular of medieval saints, Nicholas. This drama's economical construction and refined use of a simple metrical unit exemplify how a playwright can convey much in few words. The other two plays included in this collection are the outstanding examples of Latin liturgical drama composed in the twelfth century. The *Danielis Ludus* ("The Play of Daniel"), written in the cathedral school of Beauvais, adapts material from the Bible to relate the meaning of a story from the ancient past – the Hebrew prophet Daniel's interactions with two foreign rulers, Belshazzar and Darius – to contemporary issues. This play's rhetorical sophistication, metrical variety, and musical invention are unsurpassed in the dramatic works from this period. Hildegard of Bingen's *Ordo Virtutum* ("The Play of the Virtues") has the distinction of being the only play in this group whose author is not anonymous. Hildegard left behind more than just a name, however, for her impressive literary, scientific, theological, and musical oeuvre rivals those of her more traditionally educated male peers in quality and surpasses them in diversity. In addition, Hildegard's female-centered play, whose verses are rich with symbolism, fuses together liturgical drama and theological allegory in an innovative manner that anticipates the new genre of morality plays written in the vernacular languages two centuries later. This edition provides significant assistance with vocabulary, grammar, and syntax, with special attention paid to Medieval Latin forms. There are also extensive literary and historical notes.

Gesta Francorum: An Eyewitness Account of the First Crusade

[forthcoming]

Made in the USA
Middletown, DE
10 May 2018